Inside the Teaching Machine

Inside the Teaching Machine

Rhetoric and the Globalization of
the U.S. Public Research University

CATHERINE CHAPUT

THE UNIVERSITY OF ALABAMA PRESS
Tuscaloosa

Typeface: Perpetua

∞

The paper on which this book is printed meets the minimum requirements of American
National Standard for Information Sciences-Permanence of Paper for Printed Library
Materials, ANSI Z39.48-1984.

Library of Congress Cataloging-in-Publication Data

Chaput, Catherine.
Inside the teaching machine : rhetoric and the globalization of the U.S. public research
university / Catherine Chaput.
p.   cm. — (Rhetoric, culture, and social critique)
Includes bibliographical references and index.
ISBN 978-0-8173-1609-9 (cloth : alk. paper) — ISBN 978-0-8173-8010-6 (electronic)
1. Education, Higher—Research—United States. 2. Education, Higher—Political
aspects—United States. 3. Education, Higher—Economic aspects—United States.
4. Globalization. I. Title.
LB2328.62.U6C48 2008
378′.050973—dc22

2007042106

Contents

PART III

Preface

We live and learn in an increasingly interconnected world, or so goes one commonplace of globalization. This interconnectivity not only ties individuals and their actions to people in faraway places—as popular films like *Babel* and *Crash* suggest—it also makes individuals and actions meaningful in new ways, often blurring the divisions among cultural, political, and economic experiences. Note, for instance, these recent snapshots of higher education in North America:

- University students in Quebec oppose a proposed tuition increase and argue instead for free education—popular sentiment indicates the futility of this movement.
- University students in Oaxaca protest what they believe to be the illegitimate election of their governor—news coverage comments that such civil unrest hurts tourism.
- The National American University adds a Mall of America campus—the advertisement focuses on its convenience to shopping and entertainment.

Straddled with a cultural imperative to amuse and an economic imperative to produce profit, a university inside a gigantic entertainment complex epitomizes a global economy that seeks opportunities for privatization and consumption at every turn. University protests, on the other hand, appear increasingly antiquated experiences in such a world. Canadian universities have generally adopted a student fee structure akin to that of U.S. public universities, leaving the Quebec protestors swimming against the tide. Students in the politically tumultuous state of Oaxaca similarly struggle as reporters redirect readers from student concerns to Mexico's number one industry—tourism. But if the protests in Quebec and Oaxaca seem anomalous, they are anomalies that refuse to go away. Instead of disappearing, these stubborn cultural and political conflicts become filtered through the sphere of economics, tempting many to proclaim the triumph of global capitalism. Against such cries, this book cites a different triumph, arguing that the intermingling of cultural, political, and economic processes like these stems from the worldwide hegemony of the U.S. public research university.

These examples of contemporary education suggest a tripartite relationship among the cultural, political, and economic realms: Quebec students demand free education for a functioning democratic culture; Oaxaca students attempt to oust the allegedly illegitimate political regime of its state; and Minnesota students take in business classes between their busy shopping schedules. These incidents also reveal the interconnectivity of individual, state, and corporate interests within the institutionalization of this university structure: individuals seek community within student bodies and identification through course content; governments look to universities for both the information and the personnel necessary to its geopolitical interests; and corporations partner with university faculty for much of their research and development. None of these interests unilaterally dominates higher education and none exists in isolation from the others. These educational snapshots expose not the extremes of North American education but its normal operations. Indeed, I understand the National American University's Mall of America campus to be the predictable extension of a system of public higher education that has long intertwined the cultural, political, and economic agendas of an evolving capitalist political economy. To emphasize, we are not witnessing the corporate takeover of higher education so much as the evolution of an institution constructed through a complex weave of cultural, political, and economic values—none independent of a constantly fluctuating capitalist system. This book, therefore, explores the U.S. public research university structure by investigating its rhetorical assembly rather than simply bemoaning the less-than-perfect institutional outcome resulting from its assemblage.

Primarily concerned with the rhetorical valuation of university education, I offer both a rhetorical history of the U.S. public research university and a rhetorical perspective on the political economy within which this university system works. Unlike other systems of higher education, the U.S. public research university structurally reproduces capitalism at the same time that it absorbs various challenges to the capitalist political economy, such as those in Quebec or Oaxaca. Other educational institutions existed before and alongside this system, but none was structured in explicit collaboration with the needs of the capitalist political economy, primarily because none grew up—as did the U.S. public research university—in lockstep with an evolving market economy. Further, because the specific title of the public research university emerged in the early 1970s as part of the Carnegie Foundation's taxonomy of higher education, the naming of the public research university developed concurrently with the global political economy. As a consequence of this relationship to capitalism and especially to its current global configuration, the U.S. public research university is the primary model of tertiary education worldwide. Not surprisingly, the U.S. model has become a mandatory component of many economic recovery programs initiated by the World Bank and the International Monetary Fund, effectively reconstructing higher education as a professionalizing apparatus that works on behalf of global capitalism's worldwide exigencies.

In order to investigate the U.S. public research university structure and its relationship to this global political economy, *Inside the Teaching Machine* includes three parts. Chapters 1 and 2, which make up part 1, historicize the U.S. public research university system and argue that it has always been a vital component of the capitalist political economy. Although the popular narrative of public higher education emphasizes civic preparation and upward mobility, these chapters demonstrate how supposedly egalitarian policies like the Land-Grant Act (Morrill Act) and the GI Bill serve the changing interests of capitalism. Such legislation forges and enables a university-produced professional class that functions both ideologically and structurally to facilitate transitions in the capitalist political economy. Part 2 explores the university system within contemporary globalization. Mapping economic and cultural globalization onto the university system, chapter 3 discusses how contemporary university professionalization contributes to new methods for producing surplus value. Chapter 4 examines how the U.S. public research university model circulates outside the United States, changing the global political economy in its wake. Focusing on a range of U.S. public research universities, I argue that the rhetoric and structure of mission statements move overseas through supranational organizations such as the Organization for Economic Cooperation and Development (OECD) and become implemented through policies attached to World Bank and International Monetary Fund (IMF) loans. Part 3, chapter 5, develops strategies for professionals who oppose the capitalist logic of this global university system. Informed by Marxists scholars like Louis Althusser and Antonio Gramsci, critical pedagogues such as Paulo Freire, Peter McLaren, and Paula Allman, as well as the U.S. Third World politics of Chela Sandoval, Gayatri Spivak, and Edward Said, this chapter proposes concrete options for engaging and redirecting globalization.

I begin, however, with an introduction to my methodology, which blends rhetorical studies with cultural studies and works through a unique interdisciplinary lens—a rhetorical hermeneutic of valuation. The introduction explores various critical theories in order to situate my method for understanding institutions like the U.S. public research university from an historical materialist perspective. This methodological lens maneuvers between the details of rhetorical hermeneutics and the metanarratives of historical materialism, bringing into focus a new picture of globalization and higher education.

Acknowledgments

Authors often use the acknowledgments to thank funding agencies and universities for buying release time and granting sabbaticals; I have only people to thank. I am deeply indebted to many colleagues, friends, and family, both inside and outside the university, and consider this far more valuable than institutional rewards.

Even as I use this book to take the university to task, I cannot imagine working anywhere else. No doubt this is because of the extraordinary people one finds there. My first colleagues as a student of rhetoric were forged at the University of Arizona. It was there that I met Danika Brown and M. J. Braun, the people I turn to when beginning any new project. They have patiently read multiple drafts, provided endless feedback, given me suggestions for further reading, and, most important, encouraged me, entertained me, and supported me as friends and colleagues. It was also at the University of Arizona that I met Ken McAllister, without whom I am sure this book would never have been published. Ken helped me throughout the process, offering advice, discussing ideas, and modeling the kind of academic, personal, and political work to which I aspire.

I owe much also to Thomas P. Miller and Suresh Raval, both of whom supported and challenged my thinking throughout the early stages of this project. My work was further shaped by the activist community in Tucson, especially those involved in the Sex, Race, and Globalization project, Students Against Sweatshops, and the Coalition to Organize Graduate Students. I thank especially Miranda Joseph, Arne Ekstrom, Curtis Ferree, and Kat McLellan.

It does not seem to matter what university one enters. Whether in the Southwest, the Deep South, or the Niagara Peninsula, I have met innumerable scholars committed to making the world a little better than they found it. I wish to thank Lori Amy, Steve Engel, Frank Arasanyin, Larry Burton, Karen Powers, Amy Wan, Angela Crow, Sonja Pérez, Rob Alexander, Jackie Rae, Mathew Martin, Greg Betts, Adam Dickinson, Tami Friedman, Jon Eben Field, and Shannon Pomerantz. Taking time out from their busy academic and activist schedules, these scholars read my work, listened to my ideas, and guided my thinking. I am also grateful to the staff of The University of Alabama Press, as well as to John Lucaites and James Arnt Aune for their close readings and helpful suggestions throughout the revision process.

There are also those who helped by coaxing me away from work. Tina, James, and Kaley Whittle met me for movies, days in the park, and leisurely dinners. Julie and Webb Willmott, who never tired of requesting my definition of rhetoric, accompanied me for margaritas every Thursday, fed me dinner every Sunday, and treated me to cigars more than once. Kellie Carter kept my dogs and me active with runs on the beach; Miriam Klein and Christian Hempelman offered many wonderful diversions over drinks, dinner, and karaoke; and Shaun Slattery celebrated the finished revision with me in Montreal. Katherine Mack, who shared a home with me during the final editing, deserves particular thanks for questioning my ideas, encouraging me to stretch, and provoking me to explore the world through different paths.

Finally, I know that university work is a privilege afforded me because of a family who has sustained me, both emotionally and financially. Most especially, I have my parents, Jean and Pauline Chaput, to thank, but, I also have my siblings to thank—Chris and Marcia Chaput; Mary Jo and Gregg Robinson; Ann and Tom Vrbanac; and John and Sandi Chaput. For me, the world is an immeasurably richer place because of time spent with you. None of that time would be complete, however, without the most creative communicators I know—Jessica, Michelle, and Joseph Chaput; Abigail Robinson; Matthew Vrbanac; and Megan and Michelle Claire Chaput. I thank you for sharing yourselves and your words with me, and I look forward to living in the world you will no doubt construct with your imagination, your intelligence, and your compassion.

Inside the Teaching Machine

Introduction

Historical Materialist Rhetoric and the Hermeneutics of Valuation

Capitalist production is not merely the production of commodities, it is, by its very essence, the production of surplus-value. . . . If we may take an example from outside the sphere of material production, a school-master is a productive worker when, in addition to belabouring the heads of his pupils, he works himself into the ground to enrich the owner of the school. That the latter has laid out his capital in a teaching factory, instead of a sausage factory, makes no difference to the relation.

—Karl Marx, *Capital*

It is not only that lines separate ethnic, gender, and class prejudice in the metropolitan countries from *indigenous* cooperation with neocolonialism outside, in the Third World proper. It is also that arguments from cultural-ism, multiculturalism, and ethnicity, however insular and heteromorph-ous they might seem from the great narratives of the techniques of global financial control, can work to obscure such separations in the interests of the production of a neocolonial discourse.

—Gayatri Spivak, *Outside in the Teaching Machine*

Raymond Williams defines *culture* as "one of the two or three most complicated words in the English language" (*Keywords* 87). Cultural studies disputes since this proclamation bare the truth of his statement, but another term, one that Williams does not define, seems to qualify as the other one or two most complicated words in our vocabulary. Among the oldest intellectual and practical arts, rhetoric consistently eludes definition. I emphasize this uncontainable understanding of rhetoric in order to reiterate what Williams's *Keywords* suggests: when we work from different definitions, we embrace different interests, values, and valuations (11). Rather than adhering to a strict disciplinary definition, I use rhetoric in this cultural studies fashion—focusing on rhetoric as an epistemic process within specific spaces that are always inflected by more than one set of productive apparatuses. Specifically, I explore how cultural, political, and economic imperatives contribute to a process that produces a hegemonic truth about higher education, naturalizes it within the U.S. public research university, and eventually distributes this model worldwide. To ask how this happens is to ask not just about politics, economics, or culture; it is also to inquire into the rhetorical processes that mediate political messages, move them through institutions, and produce a specific model of education.

According to this paradigm, institutions and the truths that support them are rhetorically constructed within and on behalf of the political economic imperatives of the sociohistorical moment in which they are situated. Donna Haraway's *Simians, Cyborgs, and Women,* for example, relies on such a belief as it challenges critical theorists to account for the embodiedness of knowledge—for the way that knowledge becomes materialized in and from bodies as diverse as they are complex. Yet it is precisely this kind of embodied knowledge—in particular, its ability to be quantified, categorized, stored, and contained—that has allowed university-produced work to support and sustain evolving forms of capitalist exploitation. Indeed, any Marxist scholar can recite the way universities have conquered and divided knowledge in order to create a professional class that oils the often rusty cogs of the capitalist machinery. This internal contradiction (the need to position oneself even as institutional structures inevitably usurp and redirect such positionalities) informs the fundamental question for oppositional thinkers in the university: How do we invent ways of locating ourselves within capitalist institutions at the same time that we attempt to invent anticapitalist knowledges and practices?

One way to maneuver through this complex subjectivity, I suggest, is to reappropriate our professional embodiedness and initiate what I will call a working-class professionalism. This conception radicalizes professionalism by linking it with its imagined Other—the working class—and by privileging connections between the professional and the working classes. Working-class professionalism unites a divided consciousness and allows for dialectical and material understandings of university work. In Haraway's terminology, such a class consists of the university's various "illegitimate offspring," intellectuals who are "exceedingly unfaithful to their origins" as they attempt to redirect traditional capitalist relations (151). Committed to this illicit redirection, *Inside the Teaching Machine* examines how the university functions on behalf of capitalist cultural and political economic foundations in order to better understand the apparent faithfulness of its subjects as well as to theorize potentially unfaithful positionalities. This investigation depends on an intellectual scaffold that welds cultural studies to rhetorical studies through a mutual investment in the production of counter-knowledges.

Cultural Studies, Critical Rhetoric, and the Revaluation of Professionalism

In the 1980s, critical scholarship zeroed in on cultural interpretation and the politics of everyday life, implicitly connecting rhetoric and cultural studies as it did. Thomas Rosteck made this relationship explicit in 1995 when he published "Cultural Studies and Rhetorical Studies" in the *Quarterly Journal of Speech*. In part, he says, the fundamental congruence between rhetoric and cultural studies stems from the fact that both fields are wedded to political action rather than mere philosophical inquiry. To clarify this interrelatedness, Rosteck entered the often heated debate about the appropriate scope of rhetoric—with Michael Leff's close textual analysis on one side and Michael Calvin McGee's material analysis on the other—and suggested that a rhetorical cultural studies perspective promotes dialogue between the concrete textual analysis of traditional rhetorical studies and the explorations of power so central to critical rhetoric. Rhetoric and cultural studies, he argued, function as twin fields that crumble the either/or positionality of less publicly minded, practice-oriented approaches to texts. For Rosteck, the merging of these fields resounds from the unavoidable fact that because "texts are concrete material instances of culture/ideology and that culture itself is the rhetorical mosaic writ large, then the criticism of texts deflects economic, political, and social factors into analysis" ("Form and Cultural Context in Rhetorical Criticism" 483–84).

Theorizing the intersection of rhetoric and cultural studies, to borrow from the title of Rosteck's edited collection, has engendered new kinds of work. Rhetorical studies of texts have been enhanced by attention to cultural studies analyses. Public monuments, memorials, cemeteries, and theme parks have all become the object of rhetorical cultural studies inquiries. Even debates about academic disciplines have been deepened through this dual analytics. Steven Mailloux, for instance, encourages using rhetorical hermeneutics in concert with transnational cultural studies to engage "debates over the future of higher education" ("Disciplinary Identities" 22). I takes seriously both Mailloux's call to merge cultural studies with a rhetorical hermeneutic and Rosteck's claim that textual production deflects the cultural, the political, and *the economic*. I emphasize this third constituent element of textual production because so many of the important projects emerging from the integration of rhetoric and cultural studies explore the cultural and the political but exclude the economic. When scholars do address the material, it often takes the form of concrete things, focusing primarily on the politics of cultural interpretation. The need for renewed attention on this triangulated relationship among the cultural, political, and economic, particularly its vexed economic component, becomes clear through a survey of the major divisions within critical rhetoric and cultural studies.

Reducing theoretical nuances with sweeping categorizations, I suggest three schools of thought within the overlapping fields of rhetoric and cultural studies. The first theory stems from Pierre Bourdieu's and Michel de Certeau's interest in everyday discourses and emphasizes popular culture, style, and class performance as the keys to understanding individual difference. In rhetorical studies, this camp focuses on cultural materialism, from ethnographic studies such as Ralph Cintron's *Angels' Town* to the material hermeneutics in Jack Selzer and Sharon Crowley's edited collection *Rhetorical Bodies*. In rhetoric, these approaches can be traced back to the groundbreaking work of Michael Calvin McGee, who suggested that we begin with concrete data and not philosophical presuppositions, enabling rhetorical critics to "*make* discourses from scraps and pieces of evidence" ("Text, Context, Fragmentation" 279). This form of critical rhetoric asks rhetoricians to explore a work "by considering three structural relationships, between an apparently finished discourse and its

sources, between an apparently finished discourse and its culture, and between an apparently finished discourse and its influence" (280). The task
of connecting rhetorics that appear finished and autonomous, but actually
form a larger rhetorical structure, requires that we investigate relationships among texts as well as motivations for obfuscating these relationships. Missing from this materially focused, critical rhetoric, however,
is an emphasis on the role of economic processes. This omission carries over into other critical rhetoric and cultural studies projects that offer contextualization of everyday rhetorical fragments as they piece together speculative interpretations that—although insightful—lack fully
theorized economic dimensions.

Inspired by theorists such as Michel Foucault and Antonio Gramsci,
a second school of thought maintains that multiple cultural differences,
rather than a single economic base, determine oppression and suggests
that radical democratization will counter injustice. Ernesto Laclau and
Chantal Mouffe are at the forefront of this movement in cultural studies
while Raymie E. McKerrow best represents its rhetorical manifestation.
McKerrow's foundational essay, "Critical Rhetoric: Theory and Praxis,"
coined the term "critical rhetoric" and beseeched rhetoricians to explore
"power within and among institutions, groups, and individuals" (448).
Calling for a critique of domination and of freedom, he explains that a
"recharacterization of the images changes the power relations and re-
creates a new 'normal' order" but that "once instantiated anew in social
relations, the critique continues" (450). This version of critical rhetoric
and its cultural studies antecedent illustrates how power functions everywhere and not just through identifiable institutions and capitalist machinations; it also reminds us that truth must be understood as contingent,
subject itself to further investigation. McKerrow's critical rhetoric invited the study of power, inspiring such work as Kent A. Ono and John
M. Sloop's investigation into gendered language as well as Marouf Hasian
and Fernando Delgado's exploration of racialized discourses. Yet these
studies begin by coupling critical rhetoric with other critical theory; indeed, the most frequent critique of McKerrow's project is a lack of clear
political commitment. Robert Hariman argues that to avoid slipping into
relativism, critical rhetoric "needs a stronger sense of how discourses can
be used in specific situations" (68); Norman Clark concurs that "if left

unchecked, radically relativistic critique can slip into ungrounded self-expression" (111); and Joseph P. Zompetti demands that critical rhetoric "has an ethical responsibility to take a position on the subject matter being criticized" (67). Each of these critical rhetoricians seeks complementary theories in order to achieve his critical ends, suggesting both the breadth of critical rhetoric and a profound limitation in that McKerrow's critical rhetoric does not appear able to stand on its own political footing.

Working from explicit anticapitalist foundations, traditional Marxist theory does not have this problem of political positionality. Adherents of this third school identify with Marx's explanation of class as a capitalist process resulting from the private ownership of the means of production and the subsequent exploitation of wage labor for the creation of surplus value. As a cultural critic informed by Marxism, Dana L. Cloud stands out among rhetoricians as representative of this school of thought. For traditional Marxists, postmodern cultural studies has done little more than blur the power relationships within capitalist structure; or, as Cloud more generously states, postmodern cultural studies offers several worthwhile cautions for ideological critique—cautions already available in the classical materialist traditions ("Affirmative Masquerade"). Calling the McGee tradition of critical rhetoric idealist in its belief that audiences construct textual meaning and potentially alter material conditions in nearly autonomous acts of consumption and labeling the McKerrow tradition relativist in its groundless cycle of critique, Cloud advocates historical materialism as a critical rhetorical method ("The Materiality of Discourse as Oxymoron"). While I acknowledge and even sympathize with those who would rather not sit through another harangue against contemporary cultural theory, I cannot help but support Cloud's assertion that we have neglected to discuss the role of economic production within these critical and material rhetorics. Her insistence on historical materialism as the solution seems promising not only because it provides a vehicle toward economic analyses but because it offers a means of understanding the relationships among cultural, political, and economic processes as they value, circulate, and revalue the textual. Historical materialism attempts to understand root causes and to demonstrate relationships between an entire system of actions, interactions, and exchanges. According to Cloud, "historical materialism appeals to truth claims in evaluating rhetorical discourse, but without embracing a notion of universal, objective truth" ("Affirmative Masquerade" 3). The superstructure is not an epiphenomenon of the economic base, yet because political and social institutions function to influence a particular kind of world, including a specific political economy, capitalism's ruling elite has a clear stake in how those institutions function. Historical materialism, with its attention to discursive boundaries, tracks these stakes.

Attention to economic relationships is central to my investigation, but so are many of the arguments made by the other two schools of critical rhetoric. My goal is to move within various left-of-center arguments, culling the most appropriate strategies for analyzing the university as an economically and discursively constructed institution. Most studies of higher education examine the university from just one of these frequently polarized perspectives. Either the university is economically determined—relying on Louis Althusser's notion of ideological state apparatuses—or the university is culturally determined—embracing Bourdieu's notion of symbolic capital. Alternatively, this study blends postcolonial and Marxist theories and connects them to rhetorical insights to show that the U.S. public research university responds to the historical exigencies of a multivalent and dynamic political economy. Together Marxist and postcolonial theories code and decode the values placed on class and race; workplace communities and nation-states; systemic oppression and local resistance; theory and practice; the academic and the experiential; and, ultimately, the material and the psychic. They explain how what appear to be reified economic and cultural products participate in a larger system of social relations that produce and exchange value, persuading individuals and nation-states into specific identity formations. The exchange of values, both symbolic and economic, requires these two cultural studies approaches. To these I moor the lens of critical rhetoric in order to remind readers that economic and cultural decisions reflect embodied knowledges and have political repercussions. Consequently, rhetoric has two distinct meanings and functions in this study. In one sense, rhetoric serves as the marker for public and political deliberations—arguments about the university and its purposes from politicians, practitioners, and

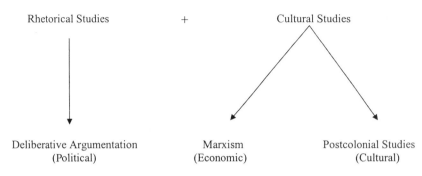

Figure 1: Rhetorical hermeneutics of valuation.

taxpayers. In a different sense, I see the process of constructing the cultural, political, and economic realities within the university as potentially enlightened by a rhetorical hermeneutics of valuation (see figure 1).

As a measurement of cultural, political, and economic work, value and the process of valuation crucially inform this rhetorical hermeneutic approach. According to educational theorist Paula Allman, the importance of the movement of value cannot be underestimated. The process of valuation strings together disparate areas of analysis and "mediates or binds the activities of the individuals engaged in these activities, and thus it brings them into social relations with one another" (75). The rhetorical process of identification exemplifies how our affiliations, made possible through the circulation of value, are simultaneously political, economic, and cultural. For instance, individuals often identify more readily with others of similar education. They share cultural experiences, but they also hold similar political and economic values embedded in those experiences. Though these cultural, political, and economic valuations have been separated into different disciplines, we do not experience them discretely. Rhetoricians interested in how language functions in relation to power, therefore, need to explore both economic and discursive valuation processes as well as the interpenetration of these valuations.

Unfortunately, Marxists often theorize value only within the economic sphere. In this strict economic sense, value represents the process by which one commodity can be equated and exchanged with other commodities—especially the money commodity. Surplus value, the ultimate goal of all capitalist activities, signifies the extra value produced from unpaid labor—laborers work longer or more intensely and thus add more value to the commodities they produce than the value paid to them in wages. Marx argues in *Capital,* for instance, that an educator produces surplus value "when, in addition to belabouring the heads of his pupils, he works himself into the ground to enrich the owner of the school" (644). In the global political economy, unlike earlier stages of capitalism, individuals create surplus value as frequently in the consumptive or cultural realm as in the productive or economic sphere, making economic valuation inseparable from political and economic valuations. To return to the example of education, the political and cultural identification one associates with a college education has economic value because educational demographics can be sold as a predictor of political and consumer behavior. This occurs, in part, because globalization relies on technologies that encourage unpaid consumer labor wherein individuals produce and help distribute surplus value through their consumptive practices. An individual who provides personal information in order to enter a Web site that assists in finding old college friends freely adds to a nearly invisible database. The value of this cultural activity (surfing the Web) cannot be measured apart from the economic value added to the databases and the potential ramifications resulting from those who purchase this information to secure political power.

To explore this overlap among the cultural, political, and economic terrains of the university is to acknowledge its professional class as the embodiment of cultural and economic valuations as well as a site of political struggle. The professional embodiment of cultural difference within the university exemplifies this complex relationship. In *Outside in the Teaching Machine,* Gayatri Spivak discusses the myriad implications of institutionalizing traditionally marginalized people, knowledges, and cultures within the research university. This institutionalization has been taking place since the early 1970s—the historical emergence of globalization—as a result of widespread student protests that erupted in conjunction with and on the heels of anti-imperialist movements. Thus, she argues, previously marginalized professionals who are now housed comfortably inside the university have both an outsider consciousness and an insider status. Amplifying the predicament of embodied knowledge, this double positionality makes professionals responsible to multiple communities and enables institutions to use both economic and cultural arguments to justify participation in the contemporary political sphere. This multicultural production tends to professionalize—and, therefore, locate, isolate, and neutralize—cultural texts that might otherwise problematize, if not directly challenge, the global political economy. Professionalizing culture makes cultural differences more visible but often at the expense of oppositional political possibilities. From the working-class professional perspective—one that acknowledges professional labor as work, attaches such work to class structures, claims alliance with adjunct labor and other insecure university workers, and highlights the split consciousness often covered over by the "professional" title—I examine how these emergent economic and discursive productions of value function rhetorically to perpetually reconstitute the university. Before proceeding, however, I want to briefly explain some of the most important aspects of this study, beginning with the role of economic inquiry in my rhetorical hermeneutic.

Beyond the Rhetoric of Economics: Constructing a New Economic Inquiry

By using the rhetorical hermeneutics of valuation I have described, I no doubt commit myself to working through several political economic questions. Such inquiries should not be confused with the rhetoric of economics debates. Deirdre N. McCloskey has contributed in important ways to such debates from within her own discipline of economics. Throughout her extensive oeuvre, she argues that economists use narrative and metaphor and are, therefore, rhetorical even while they rely on mathematical principles and scientific jargon. James Arnt Aune recently asserted that McCloskey's "rhetoric of economics has reached a conceptual dead end. By emphasizing the institutional context of economic arguments and by emphasizing rhetoric in the public, rather than academic, realm, perhaps the conversation can be advanced a bit" (*Selling* 182). His *Selling the Free Market* offers an excellent extension of this economic investigation to the public sphere and provides one way out of the political stalemate characterizing these debates. McCloskey's main limitations, from Aune's perspective, are that she focuses on academic communication and privileges a rational choice model of economics. I do not fault

McCloskey for focusing on the academic any more than I fault Aune for looking toward the literary, cultural, and political public spheres—each of these sites is the comfortable zone of their respective fields. Aune's second point has more saliency for me: however much McCloskey recognizes rhetoric as functioning within economics, she fails to explore the full implication of this realization. She does not entirely come to grips with how espousing different rhetorics belies fundamentally different valuation systems. A free market and rational choice model differs from an institutional and individual taste model more substantially than the metaphors used in each argument. Rational choice and individual taste represent two different ways of seeing/creating the world and not just two different ways of describing what already exists.

McCloskey does not make this step because for her rhetoric is a thing—persuasive language—that can be identified in opposition to factual matter. Her foundational text, *The Rhetoric of Economics,* illustrates this through a grid, the rhetorical tetrad, that aligns fact and logic with the discourse of science opposed to narrative and metaphor typical of nonscientific discourse (19). Such opposition notwithstanding, McCloskey encourages economists to understand themselves as rhetoricians, to acknowledge their use of metaphor, and to defend their choices. For instance, she and Arjo Klamer acknowledge the rational choice model as the master trope in economics and admit that this model functions to discipline scholars—if you do not use it, you are not taken seriously (14). According to them, we need to understand the differences in economic models not as political or ideological differences but as stylistic differences wherein rhetoric is conceived as ornamentation used for convincing an audience of a predetermined truth. They identify different economic theories as "being more or less similar yet having different notions of how to persuade," lamenting that such a suggestion "makes a monist angry" (15). But their claim unsettles me for other reasons. It bothers me because it trivializes both the differences in economic schools of thought and the role of rhetoric. This limited understanding of rhetoric allows Stanley Fish, in the same collection, to argue that philosophical questions are unimportant to nonphilosophers and that the rhetoric of economics revelation will not shatter "our confidence in the arguments we make" (29). Such a statement can only be true within a rather impoverished understanding of rhetoric that asks individuals to state and defend their positions but does not require that they listen to or engage the ideas of others. Fish and McCloskey share what Patricia Roberts-Miller calls an expressivist view of rhetoric—one that encourages individuals to express their views without providing a space to discuss the implications and underlying values of competing assessments (12–13). Using this static definition of rhetoric, McCloskey fails to note the lack of both ethical discussion and historical perspective in her analysis of rational choice metaphors.[1]

Offering a glimpse into the possibilities of a different rhetorical understanding, Robert L. Heilbroner agrees that the founding myth of economics is the market, but adds that "because we see the market as a 'mechanism' for the rational allocation of resources, we are able to speak about its workings without the encumbrances of guilt" (41). He claims that "the deepest problem of economics is not its failure to shake off an obsolete and damaging rhetoric, but its failure to recognize the inescapably ideological character of its thought" (42). He goes so far as to tell McCloskey to refocus from style onto substance. That McCloskey's rhetoric of economics lacks substance is a repeated critique in *The Consequences of Economic Rhetoric* collection. Philip Mirowski suggests that her "tendency has been to admit to the metaphor in a coy and indirect manner, hedged about with the qualification that it is merely a matter of words, and therefore of no consequence to the evaluations of the content and significance of the theory" ("Shall I Compare Thee" 136). Nancy Folbre and Heidi Hartmann believe "serious consideration of both the rhetoric and the ideology of economics can not only enhance awareness of hidden assumptions, but also help to make those assumptions more realistic" (198). These varied responses point to two critical insights: rhetorical analysis of economics acquires additional value when accompanied by ideological investigations and economic discourse is multiply determined by different contexts. These statements might appear commonsensical to rhetoricians, but they are nonetheless significant within the realm of economics, a space where rational choice, purportedly unencumbered by conflicting realities and uncertain futures, solidly prevails.

The overarching critique against McCloskey's rhetoric of economics is her reliance on this rational choice logic. Rather than simply claim rational choice as a flawed logic, I stress that rational choice economics (in the university as elsewhere) operates within several overlapping spheres. Rational choice is part of a larger rhetorical process and not merely a metaphor that explains preexisting realities. So conceived, the rhetoric of economics becomes a process of overlapping activities better exemplified by the so-called Washington Consensus, a phrase that circulates in the rhetoric of economic debates as frequently as it does in popular, political, and academic discussions about globalization. Coined by John Williamson, the "Washington Consensus" describes "the common core of wisdom embraced by all serious economists, whose implementation provides the minimum conditions that will give a country a chance to start down the road to the sort of prosperity enjoyed by OECD countries" (15). The notion of a Washington Consensus does not quarantine fiscal questions from the political and the cultural spheres of society. Instead, it offers supposed wisdom on such wide-ranging issues as corporate tax policies, trade liberalization, increased privatization, and deregulation. The Washington Consensus refuses to mark globalization as an inevitable economic teleology signaled by the fall of Western communism in the early 1990s; on the contrary, it acknowledges a site of power (Washington) and suggests collaborative support (consensus), admitting clear ties between economic globalization and both the political and cultural spheres. For me, this is a better rhetorical conception of economic inquiry than McCloskey's simply because it works through the interconnectivity of the cultural, political, and economic realms.

Using a rhetorical hermeneutic of valuation, one I call historical materialist rhetoric, I privilege the interplay among these three spheres. I define and use this rhetorical hermeneutic throughout this book but do not presume that its method should supersede others. I fully agree with Robert L. Scott, who argued, in concordance with his view of rhetoric as epistemic, that "any definition of rhetoric that is taken as once-and-for-all is apt to be gravely misleading" (95). No definition of rhetoric will be adequate to the range of questions academicians seek to explore. As rhetoric proliferates and takes on continually new objects of study, as different identities and activities take on public significance, as knowledge grows more interdisciplinary, and as paradigms shift, definitions of rhetoric emerge fitted to new purposes. The point is not to limit the role of rhetoric but to match its uses with the needs of a particular inquiry. I trace the valuations between and among these spheres, for instance, because I wish to explore how rhetoric can negotiate and secure institutional power in our contemporary landscape. To answer such a question, rhetoric must be allowed to extend beyond an individual address targeted to a particular audience on a specific occasion and encompass the more ambiguous activity of persuading masses of diverse people in disparate locations. In this way, the rhetorical hermeneutic of valuation aligns the rhetorical process with the constitutive, fractured, and equivocal realities of contemporary society.

Social theorists argue for various understandings of this contemporary landscape, all of which fundamentally differ from the classical conception of political relations as finite, stable, and transparent. Marshall McLuhan emphasizes the mediation of all reality; Michel Foucault argues that power is decentered; Frederic Jameson contends that reality and fiction have converged to form the logic of late capitalism; David Harvey theorizes the collapse of time and space within contemporary capitalism; and Michael Hardt and Antonio Negri suggest that empire functions as a multiplicity. Although the rhetorical turn is undoubtedly part of this theoretical shift in understanding the political, cultural, and social terrain of everyday life, rhetoricians have not adequately adapted their understanding of rhetoric to accommodate these new processes. Instead, rhetoricians interested in the political sphere tend to believe in the possibility of rational communication—exemplified in Jürgen Habermas's ideal speech act and underscored by McCloskey's economic theories. The rational, unified subject of rhetorical communication has not left our theories even as we admit the death of such a subject. We need, therefore, a theory of rhetoric that understands individuals not as rational subjects but as multiply constituted participants in institutions that distribute power and authority unevenly; we need, I believe, the rhetorical hermeneutics of valuation, an interdisciplinary theory that complicates, but does not abandon, the hope of rhetorical interpretation and deliberation as powerfully transformative processes.

The Rhetorical Hermeneutics of Valuation: Situating an Interdisciplinary Project

The rhetoric of historical materialism is an interdisciplinary approach to inquiry made possible by what others have called the "globalization" of rhetoric. The ongoing debates about the scope and function of rhetoric both enable this approach and call it into question. As I have already indicated, the rhetorical turn of the 1970s and the lessons of such theorists as Hans-Georg Gadamer, Thomas Kuhn, and Chaïm Perelman and Lucie Olbrechts-Tyteca exploded the boundaries of rhetorical studies and initiated interpretive practices of innumerable genres and discourses. Steven Mailloux labels this work rhetorical hermeneutics. Edward Schiappa characterizes it according to "the symbolic interactionist rationale," summarizing its theoretical foundations with the following syllogism: "All persuasive actions are rhetorical. / All symbol/language-use is persuasive. / Therefore: All symbol/language-use is rhetorical" (261). The upshot of these seemingly endless debates is that because all discourse can now be understood as containing rhetorical aspects, all discourse can be interrogated rhetorically. Postmodernists have made everything rhetorical, giving critical rhetoricians justification to move into spaces previously off limits. Yet these rhetoricians frequently use the same rhetorical maps—as we saw with the rhetoric of economics debates—for inquiries with fundamentally different structures than traditional public speech.

In fact, stretching rhetorical studies beyond speeches and public discourse has raised concern primarily because it oversteps hard-won disciplinary boundaries, functioning as Haraway's illegitimate offspring. For example, Dilip Parameshwar Gaonkar challenges what he believes to be the suspect practices of contemporary rhetorical hermeneutics in his "The Idea of Rhetoric in the Rhetoric of Science." Among his concerns are whether classical rhetorical theory is appropriate for interpreting diverse contemporary language practices and to what degree new rhetorical vocabularies are, in fact, rhetorical. As many have pointed out, this critique places practitioners of the so-called big rhetorics in a bit of a conundrum—using classical rhetorical vocabulary to explain contemporary phenomena is deemed insufficient while developing new vocabulary positions one's work outside the boundaries of rhetoric. Although critics sometimes respond defensively to Gaonkar, I believe his argument merits consideration. In the concluding remarks of his essay, he notes three different ways of understanding how rhetoric works in the rhetoric of science debates—as a form of dilution that simplifies and clarifies information, as a sweetener that makes information more palatable, opening space for deception, and as a placebo that stands in for an empty reality and therefore becomes substantive itself (77). This array of choices recalls another highly contested term: ideology. Discussions of ideology, like this discussion of rhetoric, tend to move in circles and arrive at impasses because they confuse things with processes, nouns with verbs. Rhetoric is and has always been productive, which means that rhetoric is both a process and the thing enacting that process. Gaonkar's three rhetorical functions posit some "thing" acting on or within something else even as his analogy implies a system in which these "things" operate. As we define the role of rhetoric, we need to do so with an eye to this systemic work. Simultaneously defining rhetoric as a product and a process is especially crucial to understanding its role within institutions, across diverse social terrains, and ultimately embodied within individual agents.

Primarily taking Gaonkar to task, Herbert W. Simons's review of *Rhetorical Hermeneutics* unintentionally stresses the importance of these systemic processes. In partial concession to Gaonkar, Simons agrees that "the rhetorical tradition cannot help very much when it comes to social change processes that engage multiple forms of social influence. Not just persuasion has been used in the globalization of the economy or in the McDonaldization of world culture, but also new information technologies, conformity pressures, entertainment, intimidation (and other forms of coercion), and lots of material inducements. But rhetoric, broadly considered, can help explain how people disadvantaged by social change processes are made to feel at home in their new conditions" (96). What stands out in this response is not the limitations of rhetoric but the need for multiple analytical lenses in order to clarify the polyvalent activities that converge to create the experience of different public spheres. For me, this is a call to enlarge rhetoric through interdisciplinary ties. Against the narrow proscription of rhetoric to political persuasion, the spectrum of concerns surrounding new objects of inquiry—whether the rhetoric of science or the rhetoric of the university—can be read as an invitation to interdisciplinary hermeneutics that interpret how institutions persuade individuals into actions and affections.

Cloud does an excellent job tracing one such rhetoric in her *Control and Consolation in American Culture and Politics*. Bridging rhetoric and cultural studies, she explains therapeutic discourse within political and cultural spheres as a product of the historical exigencies of late capitalism. Just as she studies the way the rhetoric of therapy prevents collective critique, I wish to explore the various rhetorical processes that sustain the U.S. public research university as it evolves along with changes in the capitalist political economy. In her study, rhetoric functions as a persuasive discourse that achieves its economic ends through various cultural and political mechanisms. My study analyzes shifts in persuasive discourses in order to sketch the historical materialist processes of rhetorical production. In this way, *Inside the Teaching Machine* is politically aligned with the historical materialist commitments of Cloud at the same time that it takes a cue from Michael Calvin McGee's understanding of rhetoric "as a medium, a bridge among human beings, the social equivalent of a verb in a sentence" ("A Materialist's Conception" 27). McGee and McKerrow's critical rhetoric explains the process whereby the circulation of language, vis-à-vis individuals, groups, and institutions, constructs the material landscape within which we operate; however, it does not offer an explanation of how this process works in tandem with our contemporary economic moment. This book provides one such explanation—in the critical rhetoric tradition but with an historical materialist commitment.

Some scholars argue that rhetoric already has its own interpretive frames, preempting the need for such interdisciplinarity. According to William Keith, for instance, rhetoric is defined by its commitment to the process of democracy. He believes that public address, social movements, and political communication are the traditional subjects of rhetoric and that rhetoricians have "the goal of producing better citizens" (100). However, the political discourse of our contemporary moment requires definitions of democracy and citizenship proposed since the rhetorical turn. Social theorists as different as Antonio Gramsci and Louis Althusser make it clear that democracy and citizenship take place not only within state apparatuses but also within heterogeneous civic organizations. Further lessons from the rhetorical turn suggest that the traditional public sphere does not lead easily nor directly to democracy. As early as 1962, Habermas's *Structural Transformation of the Public Sphere* identified the deterioration of the modern public sphere and the movement from a culture-debating society to a culture-consuming society. Against the desire to recapture this ideal space, I want to theorize the kinds of democracy and citizenship that take place in the cultural spaces of the university and how these spaces are inflected by the economic sphere that produces and distributes them as well as the political sphere that regulates such production. To answer questions like these, I must allow rhetoric to function interdisciplinarily, building a more complex hermeneutic framework as it does.

With shifts in both the contemporary public spheres and our understanding of how they work, rhetoricians are increasingly pursuing such nontraditional studies. Michael Leff indicates that rhetoricians "have appropriated a variety of objects for study, including scientific monographs, fiction, film, and material artifacts such as monuments and museums, that fall outside the ambit of public rhetoric as traditionally conceived" (85). Gregory Clark's *Rhetorical Landscapes in America* is one recent example. Relying primarily on Kenneth Burke but also including a breadth of American studies scholarship, Clark argues that experience with the landscape functions rhetorically to help individuals identify as Americans. Encounters with city life, highway travel, and national parks are public experiences because they help us understand ourselves as connected to a larger national public made up of people with similar experiences. Many, even among more traditional scholars, are moving beyond the standard rhetorical canon. For instance, George A. Kennedy's *Comparative Rhetoric* makes the rather scandalous claim that "rhetoric is biologically prior to speech and to conscious intentionality" (26). He argues that rhetoric can be understood as a form of energy for self-preservation. If one is empowered, rhetoric functions as conservation; if one is not empowered, rhetoric seeks advantage. What is useful about this definition is that it addresses the substance of rhetoric apart from semantics and avoids the trap of rational agency that Gaonkar critiques in the rhetoric of science. Whether comparative or interpretive, rhetorical projects that seek out new territories benefit from their interdisciplinary methodologies, even though such disciplinary miscegenation makes this work appear strange or illegitimate to traditionally professionalized eyes.

I sketch out these debates about the scope of rhetorical studies not to contribute to them directly but because they help position and explain my own study. *Inside the Teaching Machine* is highly interdisciplinary—I see myself as what Gaonkar rather disparagingly calls "the critic as sort of *bricoleur*" (32). I use cultural studies—focusing primarily on its Marxist and postcolonial theories—within what I believe to be a rhetorical study in the big rhetoric sense. I do not use classical rhetorical terminology, not because it lacks thick interpretive potential but because it is wedded to what Keith calls the animating myth of democracy and what M. J. Braun calls democracy-hope. This connection to democracy, regardless of which way it cuts, would not serve my goals, which are, in part, to question higher education's own democratic myth. Before taking up that task, however, I end this introduction with a more precise description of my interdisciplinary method, the rhetoric of historical materialism, and its relationship to the book's inquiry—interpreting and analyzing how cultural, political, and economic values circulate within the U.S. public research university and its globalization.

Historical Materialism Rhetoric and the Institutionalization of University Education

Just as this book is not a contribution to the rhetoric of economics debates, neither is it a study of rhetorical education. For such work, I would refer to the many historical monographs in the field, authored by scholars like James Berlin, John C. Brereton, and Thomas Miller. I would also read a recent collection titled *Rhetorical Education in America,* edited by Cheryl Glenn et al. My book studies the U.S. public research university as constituted through a rhetorical process that evolves with and adapts to different stages of capitalism. Rather than understanding rhetoric as a thing produced and contained within the university, I want to promote an understanding of the U.S. public research university as a flexible institution produced through particular rhetorical processes. Mine is neither a critique of the university as an apparatus of capitalism nor a critique of the privatization of higher education. For these, I would read Cary Nelson, Michael Bérubé, and Stanley Aronowitz. Finally, my study is not a history of political economy; for this I would read Philip Mirowski, Craufurd D. W. Goodwin, and other economic historians. This book has none of these specific foci, and yet it touches on each of these topics, offering a rhetorical analysis of the persuasive processes—historical and contemporary—that helped constitute the U.S. public research university so that it could effectively participate in the cultural, political, and economic work of a nation-state in flux.

My rhetoric of historical materialism joins three fields in order to study the circulation of values among the cultural, political, and economic spheres. Several fields have attempted to combine two or more of these interpretive spaces. In the political economy of communication, Peter Golding and Graham Murdoch are known for merging economic and cultural analyses: they say we should explore "the interplay between the symbolic and economic dimensions of public communications" (15). Even though such calls are intimately tied to the founding statements of early cultural studies projects, this political economic approach has been criticized by cultural studies scholars (like Terry Lovell) who believe it overdetermines economic production at the expense of creative consumption patterns. Policy studies—a field identified with thinkers like Herbert Gans and Tony Bennett—emphasizes the role of government regulation in the production and distribution of culture. Such scholars (including Angela McRobbie) often attack cultural studies analyses for failing to effect the concrete changes for which they advocate, suggesting that greater attention to policy will help facilitate concrete intervention. Each of these three fields—the political economy of communication, cultural studies, and policy studies—believes it contributes what McRobbie calls "the missing agenda" or gap between economic and symbolic understandings of culture, but none offers a comprehensive picture of the complex circulation of texts among the cultural, political, and economic spheres. Instead, all are necessary components in a larger picture of what one might call the rhetoricality of culture.

John Bender and David Wellbery suggest that rhetoricality explains "the nature of discursive action and exchange" (26). For them, rhetoricality creates the boundaries of a truth-regime, but not an ultimate truth. Rhetoricality eschews the rhetorical situation as a static placement in order to trace the fluctuating boundary created by and enclosing texts, guide one's sense of self as well as one's action in the world, and ultimately constitute the power of discourse. Bender and Wellbery explain that "discourses are no longer to be measured in terms of their adequacy to an objective standard"; instead, they should be "analyzed in terms of their strategic placement within a clash of competing forces themselves constituted in and through the very rhetorical dissimulation they employ" (27). They conclude that rhetoricality covers "the general condition of human experience and action"; "cannot be the object of a homogenous discipline . . . [because it] is irreducibly multidisciplinary"; and unlike rhetoric which concerns itself with property and propriety, rhetoricality "designates the thoroughgoing impropriety of language and action" (38–39). If we truly believe that reality is discursively constituted, we must examine fully the spaces of its constitution as well as the exchange and negotiation among these constituting spheres. Such analysis requires a mode of investigation capable of tracing the movement of texts. For me, this mode of inquiry is the rhetorical hermeneutic of valuation that I call the rhetoric of historical materialism.

This more expansive definition of rhetoric allows us to see the multiple ways that the production-consumption relationship operates within the overlapping, semi-autonomous, and circulating cultural, political, and economic spheres. Scholars of any one of these realms utilize their own methods of analysis, focus on different aspects of the circulation process, and employ discipline-specific terminology. Yet none addresses the fact that our world, if not our educational institutions, operates interdisciplinarily. None adequately addresses the fact that the cultural, the political, and the economic operate in concert to construct a dynamic discursive boundary of possibility that elicits a rhetorical effect. Nor does any acknowledge that this rhetorical effect surfaces as a new boundary defined by the circulation and interplay of these three spheres (see figure 2). Consequently, they miss the important fact that as value circulates among these constitutive spheres, the rhetorical boundary fluctuates and possibilities change. This book, on the other hand, seeks to define the rhetorical boundary developed from the cultural, political, and economic processes that have combined to create the contemporary U.S. public research university. Marking the limits of the university's institutionalization, this boundary outlines possibilities, empowers agency, provides meaning, and offers understanding about the appropriate knowledges, pedagogies, and public responsibilities of professional work contained by this institution. In short, this is the boundary that enables communication within and about the U.S. public research university.

Focusing on the institutionalization inherent in this rhetorical process recalls an array of critical theorists from Antonio Gramsci to Louis Althusser to Michel Foucault, all of whom were interested in the po-

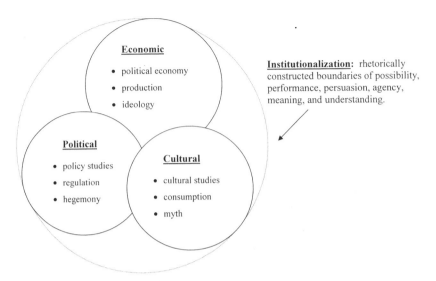

Economic

- political economy
- production
- ideology

Institutionalization: rhetorically constructed boundaries of possibility, performance, persuasion, agency, meaning, and understanding.

Political

- policy studies
- regulation
- hegemony

Cultural

- cultural studies
- consumption
- myth

Figure 2: Rhetoric of historical materialism.

litical and social work of institutions. But it also highlights the relationship between the rhetoric of historical materialism and the school of institutional economics (including such theorists as Thorstein Veblen, Philip Mirowski, and John R. Commons), which studies the role of institutions in shaping behavior and is premised on the belief that economic analyses cannot be separated from the political and social systems in which they are imbricated. According to this economic theory, institutions are human-made and open to revision even as they powerfully shape human behavior themselves. Institutional economics demands attention to the historical, the cultural, and the political in addition to the economic; thus it matches the needs of an historical materialist rhetoric. Noting the role rhetoric plays in shaping boundaries of acceptable discourse, David Sebberson encourages institutional economists to consider rhetorical theories in their investigations. Because these economists see institutions as "constantly subject to and undergoing change" (1025), he suggests that "rhetoric may, for instance, shed better light than behavioralism for coming to terms with 'institutional boundaries' and the motivations for action that at once shape and are shaped by those boundaries"

(1024). If McCloskey informs us that economic theory is rhetorical, Sebberson explains how rhetoric performs economic functions.

While these intersections with rhetoric may seem like uncharted territory to many institutional economists, institutional analysis has not been unexplored by rhetoricians. Most rhetorical analyses, however, tend to focus on the kinds of discourses produced within particular institutions—political rhetoric, protest rhetoric, religious rhetoric, and workplace rhetoric, for example—rather than coming to grips with how rhetoric constitutes discursive-producing institutions. George Cheney and Dana L. Cloud's discussion of organizational communication in the workplace emphasizes the need for more broad-based studies of institutions. They explicitly articulate a desire "to provoke further thought and discussion about a more complete conception of democracy—economic, political, and social—not only for organizational communication, but for the multidisciplinary studies of social institutions generally" (508). Institutional critique of this kind, I believe, is necessary to an understanding of rhetorical production and circulation as well as an understanding of the material conditions that simultaneously make possible and are sustained by such processes. I further believe we cannot approach broad understandings of the cultural, political, and economic relationships constituting institutions unless we commit ourselves to an historical materialist approach.

Two different takes on institutional critique illustrate how a commitment to historical materialism fundamentally alters the scope of our analyses. "Institutional Critique: A Rhetorical Methodology for Change," by James E. Porter et al., argues that rhetoricians in composition who seek university change should shift their critical focus from classrooms, departments, and disciplines onto the university as an institution. Traditionally, they argue, rhetoricians in composition try to alter university structures through disciplinary change; institutional critique, on the other hand, enables structural change. In short, they promote a kind of usability study of the university, claiming that universities "can be sensitized to users, to people, systematically from within and that this sensitizing can potentially change the way an entire industry perceives its relationship to the public" (611). Their elaborate visual representation of institutional critique places disciplines in lateral, reciprocal relationship to macro institutions like the university and claims that these are theoretical spaces while the classroom offers a practical space. For them, institutional critique operates between these two locations through locally focused critique and action (622). Marc Bousquet attacks this proposal for its managerial subjectivity, calling instead for explorations of the university through "a *labor* theory of agency and a rhetoric of solidarity, aimed at constituting, nurturing, and empowering collective action by persons in groups" (494). His stake is informed by the unique structure of most composition programs—the Writing Program Administrator (WPA) "manages" graduate students, adjuncts, and full-time, but often overworked and underpaid, composition instructors and is therefore "conditioned by contradictory class status" (497). As professionals whose job requires that they oversee the work of others, they tend to identify with the administration and sympathize with its need to deliver an educational experience within highly proscribed economic constraints even though these WPAs frequently experience the financial anxieties of other workers who live paycheck to paycheck with less and less job security. Like Bousquet, I privilege a labor theory of agency; however, I do not think that the managerial consciousness represents a phenomenon unique to WPA work. Professionals across the university are rhetorically encouraged into this space of divided consciousness and, therefore, I place my hope in the potential of working-class professionals.

Recall that Raymie McKerrow's critical rhetoric centers on the ability to change consciousness, and thus alter material reality, through the remapping of discursive fragments. Specifically, he argues that we "pull together those fragments whose intersection in real lives has meaning for social actors—meaning that confines them as either subjects empowered to become citizens or social actors with a potential to enact new relations of power. As such, the invented text functions to enable historicized subjects to alter the conditions of their lived experience" ("Critical Rhetoric and the Possibility of the Subject" 62). For Cloud, this method is likely redolent of both relativism and idealism, an accusation ready-made for my faith in a working-class professionalism. My defense against such charges, thin as it might be, is double: I am committed to a rhetoric of historical materialism that offers an institutional critique founded on the circulation of values among the cultural, political, and economic spheres, and this historical materialist hermeneutic acknowledges, through its promotion of working-class professionalism, that the professional ideal functions as an ideological euphemism for the classed nature of university work. My methodology is unfaithful, as Haraway might say, to both its origins in critical rhetoric and its alignment with traditional Marxism, using rhetoric as McGee's proverbial bridge connecting these schools of thought and perhaps paving the way for new kinds of rhetorical action necessary to our changing cultural and political economic terrains. Using a rhetorical hermeneutic approach helps me loosely map the perimeter of the university and explain how this university is encoded with meaning as well as how that meaning can be recoded for oppositional purposes.

I

I

Historicizing the U.S. Public Research University
Industrial Capitalism and the Professional Ideal

The socioeconomic category of "professional" emerged along with an expanding network of U.S. public research universities in the late nineteenth century. Together this national system of universities and its credentialed professionals solidified a largely dispersed middle class, helping to transform the United States from a nation of isolated rural communities into a sophisticated participant in the modern world. Various local universities existed within this network, trained a new professional-managerial class, and contributed significantly to the role of the United States in world politics. I explore this university system using the rhetorical hermeneutic of historical materialism by marking the valuation of the professional-managerial class within cultural, political, and economic spheres. Tracking the movement among the spheres simultaneously traces the rhetorical boundaries such valuations help construct and provides an opportunity to view the dialectic between this larger boundary and its local instantiations. With an eye toward history, this method attempts to understand how, as Gayatri Spivak says, "we are effects within a much larger text/tissue/weave of which the ends are not accessible to us" ("The Post-modern Condition" 25). The map I draw of the U.S. public research university should be seen as a small section of this pattern of social relations, one stitched in the late nineteenth century with the politics of nation-building, the economics of emergent capitalism, and the cultures of professionalism.

There are several excellent histories of the U.S. public research university.[1] This chapter does not attempt to be one of them. I do provide an interpretation structured through different historical materialist stages of capitalism. This history is intended to help frame the evolution of the university in relationship to changes in the social, political, and economic modes necessary to different moments in the political economy of capitalism. This model is fashioned off of Hayden White, an historian John Bender and David Wellbery endorse for his consciousness of narrative's rhetoricality. White claims, in his "Interpretation in History," that all history is "necessarily a mixture of adequately and inadequately explained events" (51). He further argues that all histories are ideologically informed and that there are as many historical accounts as there are ideological positions. Limited both by the oversights in my interpretation and the biases of my own positionality, I will not present a definitive picture of the U.S. public research university. Instead, I add new insight into old accounts by reorganizing historical narratives according to a rhetorical hermeneutic of valuation. Although I offer only one viable account among others, I hope to provide a corrective to the myriad nostalgic calls for a return to the democratic mission of higher education.[2]

Opposing uncritical nostalgia for the university's more democratic past, I argue that the notion of a previously democratic and noncorporate stage in the U.S. public research university never existed. Indeed, this university system has always functioned in collaboration with an evolving corporate system, and attempting a description of it in isolation from political economic processes is both culturally and politically naive. A more sound analysis of the system of U.S. public research universities explains the discursive and material boundaries historically constituted by different cultural, political, and economic valuations and exchanges. Colin Burke's *American Collegiate Populations* advocates such an inquiry. Specifically, Burke claims that one's analysis needs to account for the fact that "the emergence of the university depended upon alterations in the nature and orientation of students, a restructuring of the professions, and changes in the American economy" (7). These changes, he suggests, "did not mean an increase in either democracy or equality" (7). As Burke clearly articulates, the university grew out of changes in the social and political economic landscape. Any analysis of the university, then, is necessarily insufficient without attention to the rhetorical hermeneutic of valuation operating within and among different influential spheres. Following such logic, this chapter refocuses the source of historical analysis away from an exclusive emphasis on a cultural, political, or economic interpretation and onto an interpretation defined by the values produced, exchanged, and consumed as a consequence of various imbrications and interdependencies among these three realms. Shifting perspective onto this rhetoric of historical materialism brings into focus an outline of the rhetorical enclosure that these exchanges construct.

To do this, I turn to an explanation of the rhetoric of historical materialism as a hermeneutic and historiographic method connected to the fields of both rhetoric and political economy. Then I examine the U.S. public research university in relationship to the historical material exigencies of the market economy by focusing on the valuation and revaluation of "professional." This historical reading is organized according to the industrial, monopoly, and global stages of capitalism, which even as rough markers of the key movements in the university help maintain an emphasis on its historical dynamism. Because this historical account includes three major movements in the university's relationship to the U.S. political economy, it requires two full chapters. The remainder of this chapter deals with the relationship between the industrial stage of U.S. capitalism and the formation of the U.S. research university. The chapter ends with a brief examination of how English departments forged themselves in an effort to humanize and to nationalize this industrializing economy. Chapter 2 picks up this historical narrative with an analysis of how the monopoly and global stages of the capitalist political economy contributed to critical reforms in the U.S. public research university. Before I engage either this history or its implications for the global political economy, I briefly survey the history of political economic studies and explain why I use the rhetoric of historical materialism, rather than political economy, to grapple with cultural, political, and economic questions.

Historical Materialism: A Rhetorical Hermeneutic Approach to Political Economy

The term "economy," used up to the sixteenth century to denote the management of a household budget, merged with the term "political" in the late eighteenth century to signify "the art or practical science of managing the resources of a nation so as to increase its material prosperity" (*Oxford English Dictionary*). Soon afterward, "political economy" gave way to the shorthand, "economics," which continues to dominate even as various camps attempt to revive the original terminology. Most of those who prefer "political economy" to economics do so as a corrective to the narrow apolitical and asocial version of economics. According to economic and social historian A. W. Coats, "those who employ the term 'political economy' nowadays favor a broader conception of economics that explicitly recognizes the interrelationships between the economy, the polity, and society" (347). Dividing the term into three conceptions (liberal, nationalist, and Marxist), Coats adds that the use of "political economy" generally denotes a consciousness of power relations within economic discourse. The liberal view, one derived from Adam Smith, disconnects economics from politics through the notion of an all-powerful market force directing supply and demand. The nationalist position prioritizes power within the nation-state. From the Marxist perspective, economics remains most powerful. The prevalence of the liberal notion, which separates economics from both politics and culture while attributing power to the invisible hand of the market, does not seem to be challenged significantly by Marxist or nationalist attempts to forefront political economic power. On the contrary, these different attempts to rearticulate "political economy" lead to terminological confusion and provide one justification for avoiding the term in favor of historical materialism rhetoric.

Rather than entering into definitional arguments about "political economy," this study uses a rhetorical methodology—the rhetoric of historical materialism—to put forward what might be called a Marxist political economy of the U.S. public research university. Marxist political economists counter the liberal tendency to separate economics from other sociopolitical spheres and to displace power from institutions and individuals onto the illusive marketplace. They study the intersections of economics, politics, and culture situated within a specific spatio-temporal context and the meaning encoded onto value forms operating within a political economic enclosure. The problem with these studies, however, is that readers too often reduce their insights to arguments about the base-superstructure relationship. Given the circular and recursive nature of these social spheres, I doubt any resolution will result from questions about the ultimate origins and exact relationship of valuation and exchange. Avoiding these apparently endless debates, I focus instead on the rhetorical boundary constructed from exchanges about the U.S. public research university. I am convinced that the cultural, political, and economic realms operate through inextricable linkages, which can be traced by following the valuations and exchanges among these spheres. The resulting map indicates the rhetorically constructed boundary that, in turn, enforces rhetorical possibilities. In short, such a boundary both enables and confines rhetorical agency. Noting how this rhetorical boundary changes over time provides insight into institutional change as well as individual subjectivity.

Political economy as a field of study surfaced alongside discussions of rhetoric, as both were topics central to debates on moral philosophy. In the eighteenth century, for instance, scholars argued that political economy worked on behalf of the common good while rhetoric often worked against it. Not surprisingly, the study of political economy emerged as a discrete discipline of its own as universities, curricula, and professions underwent drastic changes. During this unstable formative period, those advocating the study of political economy legitimated the field by distinguishing it from professional work and by calling it a scientific branch of knowledge. Richard Whately's 1831 *Introductory Lectures on Political Economy*, primarily concerned with justifying political economic study, takes this approach. He argues that "it has been [his] first object, to combat the prevailing prejudices against the study" (vi). Among the most influential Enlightenment rhetoricians, Whately was also an endowed professor of political economy at Oxford University.[3] Declaring the importance of political economic study, he further contends that "while due encouragement shall still be afforded to those more strictly *professional* studies which conduce to the professional advancement in life of each individual, Political-Economy will, ere long, be enrolled in the list of those branches of knowledge which more peculiarly demand the attention of an endowed University" (x). Whately goes on to specify that because the political economy serves national interests, it belongs within the "endowed" university. Various professional studies, on the other hand, serve individual interests and are therefore less well positioned in a university equipped and funded for national well-being.

In the course of his argument Whately makes a double move that facilitates the project of defining disciplinary boundaries and including political economy as a specialized field of its own. First, he distinguishes between individual economic self-interest, characterized by the pursuit of a practical profession, and national economic self-interest marked by the scientific pursuit of political economic knowledge. Whately argues that while an individual may become arrogant or prideful because of excessive wealth, a wealthy nation undergoes "superiority in valor, or in mental cultivation" (51–52). Further, unlike a rich individual who often becomes lazy, a rich nation "is always an industrious nation; and almost always more industrious than a poor one" (56). In this framework, individuals are morally discouraged from aspiring toward wealth at the same time that nations are encouraged to prosper economically—universities serve the nation and not the individual. As part of this early disciplinary formation, Whately also separates the practical arts as the study of eloquence, beauty, and taste from science as the study of facts, numbers, and truth. He suggests that "a capacity of improvement seems to be characteristic of the Human Species, both as individuals, and as existing in a community" (101). Limiting individual improvement to the realm of the commonsensical and the aesthetic, he places national improvement in the realm of science. A person who exercises individual judgment may be said to use common sense, but national judgment requires the precision of science. In this way, Whately represents a hierarchy of knowledge such that science is primary and common sense secondary; accordingly, political economy supersedes rhetoric and the belles lettres. Ironically, Whately's efforts (among others) to solidify political economic study relied so heavily on the notion of science that it soon fossilized into the science of economics and operated in isolation from the ethical, moral, cultural, and political concerns that became more associated with rhetoric and the belles lettres tradition. After the eighteenth century, this separation normalized so that the study of economics, as an independent phenomenon devoid of significant cultural and political components, simply replaced the study of political economy.

The characterization of economics in moral terms, a hallmark of early political economic treatises, fell out of fashion as political economic inquiry formed into a scientific discipline commensurate with new directions in intellectual, social, and political life. The mid- to late nineteenth century witnessed sweeping historical changes: the rise of capitalism as a challenge to aristocracy, the shift from religious to secular beliefs, and the transition from philosophical to scientific thought. This changing historical moment placed demands on intellectuals to revalorize their disciplinary inquiry within these new sociopolitical parameters. Moral philosophy split off from political economy, in part, because without a unifying belief in religious and aristocratic values it became difficult to justify—as political economists like Whately so clearly did—that political economy served the social good (Skidelsky 40–42). After the shift to secularism, moral philosophy equivocated about ethics while economics created its own internal logic. The early connections between moral philosophy and political economy revolved around questions about the ethics of pricing or the justice of interest rates, but the new discipline of political economy sought a "scientific" explanation for its methods in the work of Adam Smith. Ignoring Smith's own concern with moral questions, nineteenth-century economists clung to his notion of an indirect and natural force regulating economic activity. Just as the laws of physics regulated the natural world, the laws of economics, they believed, regulated the monetary world. Within this schema, there was no need for either moralizing or regulating.

Comparative cultural historians George Marcus and Michael Fischer explain the emergence of Adam Smith as the "father" of modern political economy. They argue that political economy's broadly defined "subject declined during the nineteenth century as the popularity of the theory of the self-regulating market, derived from Adam Smith, grew" (79). According to Smith's *Wealth of Nations,* published in 1776, the market is regulated by its own internal logic, the "invisible hand," that naturally responds to the changes of local culture. Because the invisible hand alters the economy according to specific local needs, interference from state government is superfluous or even dangerously counterproductive. Smith's idea that the market self-regulates precludes interventionist politics of any kind. As a result of this market theory, claim Marcus and

Fischer, "the study of economics became isolated from the study of politics" (79). At the same time that knowledge became divided into compartmentalized disciplines and those disciplines became codified within professional and scientific discourses, Smith's theory of self-regulating markets further contributed to the isolation of economics from culture and politics. Emphases on the positivist methods of scientific inquiry, quantitative analysis, and divisions among intellectual fields as well as the logic of an independent market all played a part in the view that the inclusion of such things as culture and politics contaminated the natural workings of economics.

Borrowing from the discipline of physics, the followers of Adam Smith's market logic incorporated the law of conservative energy to defend economics as a scientific field. According to economic historian Philip Mirowski, the shift from political economy to economics occurred in the 1860s and 1870s when "attention moved away from broad and ill-defined growth and development issues to a much narrower set of concerns tethered to the notion of short-period equilibrium price" (*Against Mechanism* 26). Supply and demand equilibrium, or the law of conservation, functions as the scientific explanation for Smith's invisible hand metaphor, suggesting that capitalism adjusts according to the rules of a closed system. Minimum wage, for instance, is regulated by the cost of living. Owners pay workers the same amount it costs workers to purchase market products. If wages go down, the market will adjust by lowering the cost of products. In this liberal political economic theory, the market laws ensure that all value transfers exchange at equivalent rates. As the perfect exchange of equivalents, economics has no need for political and cultural policymaking. Ultimately, the physics metaphor allows theorists to construct the economy "as a self-contained and separable subset of social life" and to understand "'capitalism' as a natural entity [that] is implied to be timeless: it has always existed and will always continue to exist" (159). Such a conception of capitalism is antithetical to all but liberal political economic theory. Other political economists understand capitalism as historical: it emerged at a particular historical juncture, is evolving, and will eventually transform. The key distinction between these versions of political economy boils down to the role of history in animating the material and rhetorical possibilities of a given society. Indeed, the aspects that liberal political economists ignore in Smith are precisely those moments that he encourages historicizing rather than naturalizing the political economy.

Adam Smith, the adopted father of liberal capitalism, was not a scientist, a naturalist, or a strict disciplinarian. Early in his *Wealth of Nations,* he argues that the division of labor stems from "the propensity to truck, barter, and exchange one thing for another" (19). Rather than emerging from scientific evolution or human nature, this propensity develops through "the faculties of reason and speech" (19). Unlike future interpretations of his work, Smith clearly states that capitalism is not natural but historically constructed through rhetoric—reason and speech. Smith's *Lectures on Rhetoric and Belles Lettres* offers significant insight into the role of history within both rhetoric and political economy. This work is divided into two parts: the first is the study of linguistics and the second the study of composition. Of the twenty lectures on composition, fully half are dedicated to the writing of history while the other lectures touch on epideictic, deliberative, and judicial rhetorics as well as poetry. If such significant attention to writing history seems odd, recall that the belles lettres include history, poetry, and literary criticism or judgments of taste. Rather than placing rhetoric as the subjugated field within literary criticism, Smith links rhetoric to history and gives it significant attention. In his lectures, he argues that the narration of history "makes a considerable part in every oration" and that "it requires no small art to narrate properly those facts which are necessary for the groundwork of the oration" (89). After Smith's lectures were discovered many theorists explored his contribution to communication, but like J. Michael Hogan I believe that the "neglect of Smith's treatment of historiography has been a particularly significant oversight" (76).[4] Smith's lectures on historical writing indicate how historiography helps establish rhetorical frameworks that affect personal and institutional possibilities. In other words, historiography acts as the linchpin connecting rhetoric to political economic inquiry.

Smith argues that the narration of history adheres to objectivity in its recitation of both external and internal facts, but his emphasis on sympathy belies history's persuasiveness as well as its rhetoricality. External facts include those that occur in the material world while internal facts transpire within the minds of both historical actors and spectators. It is this second kind of fact that allows history writers to help readers identify and sympathize with historical actors. According to Hogan, Smith "assigned to history writing the function of helping to establish and to certify the general principles of morality in human conduct" (87). Rather than simply stating an external fact, the historian should explain the internal facts that compelled an historical figure to act as he or she did. In this way, the reader will come to understand certain actions as morally justified and through history "one thus derived rules which not only brought uniformity and stability to one's judgments of others, but also regulated one's own sentiments and conduct" (89). So conceived, history affects consciousness and regulates material activity. It is here that history writing performs a rhetorical function—it constructs the boundaries of legitimate action through sympathetic identification. Long before Hayden White's groundbreaking *Metahistory,* Smith describes history as narrative, as rhetorical, and ultimately as ideological.

Further relevant to me is Smith's interest in the cause-and-effect relationship within historical composition. He asserts that there are two forms of writing history: you can directly describe an event with vivid detail or you can explain the effects an event causes. The indirect method of describing effects is "by far the best," says Smith (*Lectures* 67). He believes that "when we mean to affect the reader deeply we must have recourse to the indirect method of description, relating the effects the transaction produced on both actors and spectators" (86–87). Attention to the effects of events resonates with my focus on rhetoricality. Rhetoricality is interested in truth-effects constructed from specific discursive choices because such effects form the boundaries of possible action in the world. Interested in institutional and individual agency, the rhetoric of historical materialism deals with the reality-effects constructed from monetary and sign economies operating within and between the cultural, political, and economic realms. Marx's commodity fetish, the foundation for his critique of the capitalist political economy, can be interpreted as one such analysis of truth-effects. According to the opening chapter of *Capital,* commodities in a capitalist society take on the social relations of the people involved in their exchange while such individuals often treat each other merely as things (165). Marx views social and productive relations as real-life effects of the capitalist mode of production. At its foundations, Marx's critique of the capitalist system is interested in the cultural, political, and economic consequences of historical structures. Questioning the validity of these consequences, Marx nevertheless acknowledges that they define our reality. They appear as the "natural" realities of society until further inquiry suggests that movement outside this cultural and political economic framework might produce different effects.

This attention to the effects—both material and ideological—on historical agents provides an unlikely connection between Adam Smith and Karl Marx and a justification for using the rhetoric of historical materialism. For me, historical materialism begins with Marx's exploration of the relationship between alienation and political economy in *The Economic and Philosophic Manuscripts of 1844,* in which he repeatedly cites Adam Smith and other classical political economists. Marx aligns himself with these theorists in pinpointing the division of labor as the source of wealth, but diverges from their notion that the pursuit of individual self-interest will result in both individual and national well-being. On the contrary, he believes that the pursuit of private wealth creates radically uneven material and psychic effects on individuals throughout society, causing feelings of alienation from oneself, others, and the products of our labor. This connection between materiality and consciousness is pursued in *The German Ideology* and *The Communist Manifesto* as well as in his preface to *A Contribution to the Critique of Political Economy.* Marx abbreviates these material relationships, stating in his preface that "the mode of production of material life conditions the general process of social, political and intellectual life" (20–21). This shorthand emphasizes the material and ideological effects of capitalism, indicating a causal relationship between the economic and the political and cultural realms. From a slightly different perspective, I want to stress the cause-and-effect relationship between the exchanges among these three spheres and the boundaries of containment they help constitute. Material and ideological facts interact and inform one other, but neither determines the other; instead, both the material and ideological determine and are determined by the historically constructed rhetorical boundaries of any given spatio-temporal moment.

Such a focus on historically constituted cultural, political, and economic experiences is not lost on Marx. Indeed, he uses a materialist dialectic to analyze the complex interdependency between the totality of legitimate possibilities and local institutions. He explores bourgeois-proletariat relations through an examination of "capital, landed property, and wage-labour" in conjunction with "the State, foreign trade, [and the] world market" (*A Contribution* 19). This methodology allows Marx to historicize the relationship between the local (capital, land, wage labor) and the global (the state, foreign trade, world market) as representative of the kinds of exchanges between human beings that characterize capitalism. In our contemporary vocabulary, we might say that Marx is interested in the way that the political economy subjugates an individual—transforms him or her into a particular kind of subject who occupies a specific role in society. Or we might say that Marx is interested in how individuals are hailed into particular positionalities and encouraged to respond to the world from those places. In Marx's words, an examination of the political economy helps us understand that "the conditions of labour which create exchange-value are *social categories* of labour or categories of *social labour,* social however not in the general sense but in the particular sense, denoting a specific type of society" (31–32). Whether looking at these relationships from a Foucauldian, an Althusserian, or a Marxian perspective, the significant point is that this notion of political economy concerns itself with how a particular society is constructed and, in turn, how that society constructs certain kinds of individuals.

Similarly interested in the relationship between materiality and consciousness as it contributes to individual and social identities but without the terminological baggage associated with "political economy," my definition of historical materialism rests on how the parameters of rhetorical possibilities materialize through the intersections of culture, politics, and economics. Examining the production, exchange, and consumption of values through the crossroads of these three social spheres allows me to emphasize individual agency while I draw a map of the rhetorical frame, which both enables and delimits these actions. To be clear, I am not limiting my view to a crude economism nor to a deterministic sense of materialism. As I have already mentioned, this notion of the base-superstructure hierarchy has been thoroughly critiqued within the cultural studies field by authors such as Antonio Gramsci, Raymond Williams (*Marxism and Literature*), and Stuart Hall ("The Rediscovery of 'Ideology'"), to name just a few. Because these authors wished to restore individual and collective agency within social theories, they necessarily highlighted the way that a certain branch of Marxism petrified a previously fluid and porous notion of the interdependency—but not determinacy—between one's economic position and one's cultural knowledge. Far from dismissing these contributions, I take such critiques and the sociality of historical materialism quite seriously. Informed by these theories, I eschew political economy as inevitably reduced to liberal economics and focus on the historical processes of institutional formation within an evolving capitalist system.

Working within a Marxist tradition and adjusting to various cultural studies critiques of that tradition, I will use an historical materialist method of rhetorical analysis to explore how various and differing ideologies become embedded within the university-based professional ideal at different historical moments. In the history that follows, I trace professionalism through three distinct, though overlapping and sometimes contemporaneous, periods of the capitalist political economy in order to denaturalize the link between higher education and democracy and to question the pervasive nostalgia for a more pristine democratic university. In each of the three periods—industrial, monopoly, and global—I focus my examination of professionalism and of the university on various articulations among the cultural, political, and economic spheres. Examining the language that academicians, politicians, corporate leaders, and the popular press use to discuss the early formation of the U.S. public research university, I argue that during the period of industrial capitalism the emphasis on a culture of individual achievement characterized by the national marketing of credentialed expertise is most critical. Chapter 2 asserts that during the stage of monopoly capitalism this emphasis shifts onto a politics of national power in world competition and in the global stage the weight of importance moves onto the economic sphere as the globalization of finance capital becomes critical to both university and community enterprises. Although I contend that one sphere takes on greater importance in each period, the interplay among culture, politics, and economics is significant to the development, value, and possibilities of professionalism in all periods. In all stages, the exchange of values among the different spheres rhetorically produces the university as an institution with its own logic of access, standards, and policies.

Industrialism, Professionalism, and the Emergence of the U.S. Public Research University: 1862–1918

I begin this periodization with the date, in the midst of the Civil War, on which President Lincoln signed the Land-Grant Act (1862). Although not synonymous with the U.S. public research university, land-grant colleges and universities significantly contributed to the emergence of a national system of public higher education. I close this period with the date of the U.S. entry into World War I (1917). World War I signified the official end of U.S. isolationism and provided the first major opportunity for the United States to appear as a world political force.[5] The historical materialist period enclosed by these dates consists of a culture of individual competition, local or regional political participation, and an economics of nascent corporate-industrial capitalism. The U.S. public research university emerged and drew its legitimacy from this historical materialist moment by providing a new class of professionals necessary to its functioning. Not only was professionalization responsible for tremendous historical changes, but it also emerged as a powerful product of these historically reconstituted rhetorical boundaries. Social historian Thomas Bender explains this cause-and-effect relationship, stating that "the product of these changes was a system of professionalized, academic scholarship that brought a very high proportion of learned discourse under the aegis of the university and gave power to a wide range of professions on the basis of authority conferred by a university connection" (31). For Bender, the organization of professions within the university resulted from the transition of late nineteenth-century urbanization. Face-to-face contact and small, local organizations had previously constructed and transmitted knowledge, but such a structure was no longer tenable within large, dense, and heterogeneous city populations. The research university solved this problem by supplying a new space from which to create and disseminate knowledge.

Although I do not disagree with the importance of this connection between urbanization and an emerging university system, I find both urbanization and a new public university system symptomatic of a much larger restructuring in the U.S. market economy. The explosion of city populations necessary to the new industrial mode of production was one of the most glaring results of this shifting economy, but it was not its source. Because the industrialization of the agricultural frontier, which displaced many small farmers, precipitates the growth of cities, it seems illogical to understand the city as the cause of industrialization. Marx, alternatively, argues that a new form of production, shifting agency from individuals onto machines, marks industrialization as a distinct stage of the market economy (*Capital* 494). This form of manufacture takes place in factories primarily located in cities. Marx suggests that rather than the cause of corporate industrialism, cities functioned as the critical nexus for this new mode of production. Along with cities, industrialization necessitated a new professional class to manage the workers filtering into the expanding urban boundaries. Filling this need, the emergence of the U.S. public university system helped shape disparate groups of individuals, previously isolated from one another because of a primarily home- and farm-based economy, into a new class of managers who could identify with one another culturally, politically, and economically.

The Future of Intellectuals and the Rise of the New Class by intellectual historian Alvin Gouldner identifies class formation by two characteristics. First, a group of people must occupy a new and unique position in relation to capital; second, they must begin to acquire distinct language behavior (5). This new university-educated population, what Barbara Ehrenreich and John Ehrenreich call the professional-managerial class, did represent a new relationship to capital. The professional-managerial class worked on behalf of the bourgeoisie by managing the working classes even though their professional interests were not immediately served by the ruling class. Distinct from both the ruling and the working classes, they functioned to reproduce an ideological justification for the capitalist relations of production and to maintain smooth production processes (Ehrenreich and Ehrenreich 9). Both of these functions were taught in the growing public university system. As the site where individuals learned specialized skills and cultural values like democracy and meritocracy, the university became the formal source for sanctioning this new professional class. Housed within the university, professionals readily adopted new and particularized language strategies—the second of Gouldner's criteria for signifying a new class formation. New disciplinary structures, departments, professional organizations, and specialized academic journals all provided the necessary infrastructure to sustain and delimit these new language formations. Historically new public universities produced a variety of specialized disciplinary knowledges, but they also produced and disseminated general cultural knowledge. One of the most enduring aspects of such knowledge was the idea of individual freedom linked to individual social mobility.

Individualizing Democracy within the Middle Class:
The Culture of Professionalism

Prior to the late nineteenth-century emergence of the U.S. public re-search university, the United States claimed its democratic integrity and rugged individualism primarily through its relationship to an expand-ing western frontier. Both imaginative and historical texts depicting the West emphasized the ubiquitous opportunities for homesteading free fertile lands. Such homesteading was supposed to ensure the comforts of a middle-class lifestyle. According to this frontier myth, U.S. democ-racy developed from individuals who struggled against an expanding na-tional boundary, forging what Frederick Jackson Turner famously called a "uniquely American" space (29). The industrialization of this frontier, however, transformed its labor structure from one dependent on land ownership to one dependent on professional university credentials. After this change, a democratic claim similar to that embedded in frontier lit-erature can be found in documents depicting the formation of the U.S. public research university. Indeed, Clyde W. Barrow's *Universities and the Capitalist State* suggests that the mythical "path to individual social mo-bility was thus shifted from the frontier to higher education during the late nineteenth and early twentieth centuries" (32).[6] Perhaps not co-incidentally, this university system first developed and thrived in the Western states—at that time, any state further inland than the Eastern coastal states.[7] Claudia Goldin and Lawrence F. Katz, for instance, lo-cate the formative space of public higher education within the turn-of-the-twentieth-century Midwest and West. They argue that Eastern states were reluctant to fund public higher education because they often had at least one strong private university. Without this private collegiate tradi-tion, Midwestern and Western states funded public colleges and universi-ties at a significantly higher level (58–59). The public research university system grew first and strongest in the Midwest and West, helping solidify an emerging U.S. nationalism.

One way to explain the strength of public higher education in the Midwest and West is through the university's appropriation of a democratic and individualized rhetoric already well established within the nation's developing frontier. Public higher education promoted itself, the corporate structure, and especially professionalization through the rhetorical suggestion that economic success was simply the result of hard work, intelligence, ambition, and talent.[8] Given the importance of both the frontier and these new universities in expanding our national boundary, exploiting its natural resources, and providing evidence of U.S. triumphalism, this shift of democratic potential from the frontier onto a national university system should not be surprising. The democratic myth associated with the expanding frontier simply rearticulated itself within universities emerging or expanding in every Midwestern and Western state. The promise of free land and economic mobility that drew thousands of people westward was replaced with the promise of a nearly free education and the same economic mobility. Because the equality inherent in free or nearly free helps counterbalance the inequality inherent in the drive to move up the class ladder, this frontier rhetoric was able to placate "the tensions between cultural democracy and economic progress as dual justifications for state-sponsored postsecondary education" (Chaput, "Democracy" 312). Taking its ethos from the highly publicized success of homesteading and other pioneering acts, these arguments played a significant role in the creation and growth of the U.S. public research university system.

The appropriation of this frontier helped supply the notions of individual freedom, democracy, and competition that became foundational to the U.S. research university. The key changes within U.S. higher education—taking place, according to Arthur Cohen, between 1870 and 1910 and including the formation of the public research university—developed along with a changing myth of American democracy (103). During this time the four-year collegiate experience became revaluated from an elite right of passage into an American myth of social mobility. Precipitating this revaluation was a discursive strategy whereby institutions "continually put forth ideals of equality and egalitarianism, emphasizing that anyone with academic qualifications could attend" (123). As part of this egalitarian myth, universities created mechanisms for fairly and accurately measuring faculty and student achievement. Besides categorizing individual achievement, these technologies individualized faculty and students within a larger prescribed matrix. For instance, the practice of ranking faculty from assistant through full professor dates from the end of the nineteenth century (131). Within this system, an appropriately ranked faculty member knew his professional peers and knew what he needed to do to ascend the professional hierarchy and rise above those peers. A meritocratic mechanism, faculty ranking reinforces individual competition as the test of intellectual and professional worth. Universities doled out democracy one rank at a time. This was true for professional faculty as well as students who were aspiring professionals.

Universities were legitimated as the gatekeepers of social, economic, and political progress connected to the democratic ideal while grades, transcripts, and other assessment mechanisms packaged this product in clear numbers and neat lists typical of the modernist drive for categorization. Instead of written comments assessing a student's progress, "grade marks that purported to indicate the depth of student learning in particular areas were introduced" (Cohen 148). After being assessed through individual course grades, students were further evaluated by the institution of objective transcript policies. During this historically transformative period, "students' grade point averages appeared on their transcripts along with the concentration of courses (the major) that they had followed" (149). Through this new grading system, individual students could be valued according to a clearly recognizable numerical scheme. The student with the right courses and the higher grade-point average was indisputably the better student; to achieve this position, one had to outperform his or her fellow students. These classifying and standardizing techniques pitted individuals against one another for the top rank and consequently the best career opportunities at the same time they effaced individual, subjective judgments from the assessment process. The structures for assuring democratic academic assessment were inseparable from the idea of competition as reasonable, open, and progressive.

Because this historical materialist moment focused on a culture of individualism, the notion of universities as democratic sites also became synonymous with the idea of individual achievement, personal success, and one's ability to move up the social ladder. Universities began offering individualized courses of study dependent on one's professional aspirations as opposed to a universalized curriculum characteristic of elite Eastern colleges. Students freely entered the university of their choice, chose their courses, and attained specialized credentials just as workers freely entered into job agreements. The desire to compete within a changing market was a free choice arrived at through rhetorical incentives as opposed to overt political or police coercion. University education, in this sense, reflected one's ability to cultivate a better life, adopt cultural values, and acquire a certain lifestyle rather than participation in a larger national or corporate-industrial scheme, even though students and faculty both played crucial roles in these areas. The accessibility of public universities to the middle classes easily reinforced a national ideology of equal opportunity through a discourse that constructed public universities in opposition to the elite and often erudite education of private Eastern colleges.

To say that universities were sites of democratic practices open to the public offers a rhetorical perspective capable of containing the boundaries of possibility within appropriate life choices. The new university professionalism might have offered democracy, but it did so by compelling people to live and work within the parameters necessitated by the market. Professionalism provided cohesive values that redirected individuals toward new lifestyle and occupational goals. As this new market economy increasingly supplied store-bought commodities, class became more and more signified by style—consumer products as well as speech, comportment, and stock cultural references. The acquisition of specific language norms and the ability to recognize key cultural texts, as my later analysis of English department curricula explores in greater detail, signified one's professional credentialization. Thus, the culture of individualism was codified into uniform signs so that only predictable styles properly signified individualism. Burton J. Bledstein reinforces this notion of a homogenous individual style by stating that as early as "the 1860s it was evident to an observer that ambitious middle-class persons were seeking a professional basis for an institutional order, a basis in universal and predictable rules to provide a formal context for the competitive spirit of individual egos" (31). The beginning of the nineteenth century saw the myth of open fertile land waiting for ambitious homesteaders pervade U.S. culture; the century closed with many of those homesteaders believing that university education was the means to individual success and socioeconomic mobility.

Against the pretensions of elite education, the university developed culturally, politically, and economically as a specifically middle-class space in the dual senses of creating a middle class and pooling its clientele from the middle classes. Public higher education individualized isolated educational participants as much as it galvanized an unstructured middle class into a collective and individualized social unit. Public education in general and public higher education in particular was the cultural domain distinct to the middle class. As a mark of class cultural formation, it is no wonder that higher education was significantly more characteristic of middle-class than of working-class students. Higher education was priced outside the reach of most workers and inconvenient to the work cycle of most farmers. Rather than opening its doors to ever wider classes of students, higher education was not only culturally foreign to broad segments of the population but simply too costly. The modernization of universities as sites of research in addition to places for the dissemination of knowledge drove the price of an education upward at precisely the moment when it supposedly became a democratizing venture open to the masses. In specific terms, Burke concludes that "the average cost of going to college, tuition, fees and room and board, rose from 33 percent of a skilled manual laborer's income in 1800 to approximately 60 percent in 1860" (50). Ironically labeled "democratic," U.S. public research universities were viewed as the means to secure a middle-class lifestyle only among individuals who were already economically more or less part of a dispersed middle class. Too expensive for the working classes, universities placed the middle classes into their necessary positions within the industrial economy.

While it is clear that professionalism emerges as the cultural glue that helped create a cohesive middle class, it is important to note that it does so with the promise of rising out of that class bracket. For this reason, higher education, as the seminal institution producing both the professional and the professional ideal, suggested that the middle class could acquire elite status without the labor associated with frontier pioneer-ism. Bledstein stresses that "professionalism was a culture which embod-ied a more radical idea of democracy than even the Jacksonian had dared to dream" (87). Characteristic of the first half of the nineteenth century, Jacksonian democracy appealed to the common person, the independent farmer or laborer. This democratic ideal was contained within the idea of self-sufficiency and a lifetime of continuous labor. The democracy of-fered by a university education, on the other hand, held out the promise of transcending sustenance and cultivating a better, more leisurely life-style. Rather than maintaining one's middle-class position, the univer-sity, as an outgrowth of the college and rhetorically linked to that elite history, promised to move the middle class closer to the ways of thinking shared by the wealthy. As farmland became less available to those seek-ing middle-class positionality, a university degree and an ability to com-pete with others in the industrial marketplace became the litmus test of middle-class identity.

The need for middle-class individuals to vie for a place at the best uni-versity, for the best grade-point average, and for the best professional position outside the university is symbolically modeled by universities competing among themselves for students, research dollars, and fac-ulty. Rhetorically persuasive claims drew students into universities and helped create neat parameters for university work. This brand of democ-racy, says Hugh Davis Graham and Nancy Diamond's *Rise of American Re-search Universities,* not only produced students who competed with each other for professional success. It also "produced, through no conscious design, a combination of structural arrangements and professional in-centives that encouraged competition in the academic market" (18). The culture of individualism that allowed "students to shop for majors and to declare or change their choice," they argue, "gave American undergradu-ates a consumer voice that helped shape patterns of institutional growth" (21). By controlling their own schedules, students were able to pursue other noncurricular activities. These extracurricular activities became crucial in attracting future students and forced higher education to seri-ously invest in noncurricular aspects of university life. Universities began to support athletic programs, sororities, and fraternities, creating what Clark Kerr would later call the "multiversity." These extracurricular activities, all of which function through some form of competition, formed the basis of later identification with other middle-class professionals. Whether you belonged to the right fraternity, whether your sports team succeeded, and whether your school newspaper won awards could all be recalled to help reposition cultural ranking later in life. This culture of competition—within the middle class as well as among universities—served a rhetorical function necessary to the larger industrial economy inasmuch as it helped individuals identify competition with freedom, democracy, equality, and social mobility.

Cultural valuations of the professional ideal as well as its exchange among individual students and institutions played a key role in shaping the national system of universities. If a university failed to provide what students desired, it became less competitive in the drive to attract students and fell off the national radar. Likewise, if a student was unable to make the appropriate grades or conform to the predesigned coursework for a major, that student could not acquire the university's legitimating credentials and thus could not be legitimately middle class. While this cultural belonging no doubt impacted individual decisions with regard to the pursuit of university education, shifting national goals equally influenced these individual decisions. Individual choices and the subsequent forms into which universities developed were clearly shaped by national interests and the economic research imperatives associated with a drive toward competing in the increasingly industrialized world. Indeed, particular U.S. research universities, almost without fail, developed as individual variations of a national mold based on industrial research. Analysis of this national imperative toward a market-defined university system, to which I now turn, highlights the relationship between research universities and the political landscape.

Merging Local Interests with National Imperatives:
The Politics of Professionalism

At the same time that it allowed for variation at the local level, federal intervention into higher education served the political needs of a developing nation-state. The strong industrial economy at the turn of the century necessitated the increased coherence, if not centralization, of national systems. Contrary to the political commonplace that the U.S.

remained strictly isolationist during the years leading up to World War I, the United States had not only expanded West as far as possible, it had also developed significant experience in overseas interventions including imperialist intrusions into Caribbean, Asian-Pacific, and African nations.[9] Yet individuals as well as states were leery of centralized government authority. This was particularly true of Midwestern, Western, and Southern states, which often understood themselves in struggle against national legislation they believed favored Eastern corporations.[10] In this political climate, any attempt to construct a national system of higher education had to pay close attention to the needs and interests of local populations. Rhetorically, this meant that public universities had to construct education in such a way that diverse state and local populations could identify themselves within the professionalizing goals of the institution.

The most significant political strategy used while developing a system of U.S. public research universities, in this sense, was the negotiation of national research needs with local agrarian and modernizing interests.[11] And this was perhaps done best through the creation of land-grant universities that professionalized the agricultural and mechanical arts— areas of practical concern for multiple local populations. Though only a subset of emerging public universities, the development of land-grant universities offers additional insight into the democratic ethos associated with the public university system. The passage of the ostensibly democratizing Land-Grant Act in 1862 had much to do with national interests in agricultural research and training. The Land-Grant Act, or the Morrill Act as it became known, granted land to each U.S. state. The state could then sell that land and use the revenues to establish universities "for the benefit of agriculture and the mechanic arts" (James 9).[12] Although framed in relatively benign rhetoric, this act helped create the U.S. public research university as a dominant force within Midwestern and Western states and thus worked to transform the agrarian frontier into an industrial component of an expanding nation.[13] Not unlike large grants of land and money given to the railroad corporations or other commercial endeavors meant to support a national infrastructure, these land-grant colleges and universities bolstered local economies while simultaneously serving national interests.

Yet the democratic notion that land-grant institutions increased access to higher education remains a vivid part of our national memory while the fact that these institutions were valuable to the creation of national strength has faded into the indiscernible background fabric of this historical text. The 1962 centennial celebrations of the Land-Grant Act clarify this point. As part of a national anniversary celebration, Harvard professor W. K. Jordon declared the land-grant mission "responsible for the democratization of education and for the establishment of a healthy diversity in our whole structure of higher education" (*After 100 Years* 13).[14] Nostalgic reflections on the egalitarian value of public higher education and the land-grant mission in particular need to be tempered by a more complicated history of the political and economic needs of the nation. Certainly this university system increased individual participation in higher education, but it did so by solidifying a previously disparate middle class at least partially as a means to expand national scientific research into technology, agriculture, and business. Intentional or not, the widespread access to higher education, characterizing many of these democratic claims, was both limited to a specific class and necessary to national political strength. Given the culturally constructed metonymic link between higher education and democracy, the valuation of land-grant universities as great equalizing ventures overrides the fact that these universities were funded to provide low-cost research and development sites that would help advance the United States in its struggle for international political legitimacy. The valuation and exchange of university signification between the cultural and political spheres, however, makes a more complex understanding possible.

Opposed to the classical education characteristic of private Eastern schools, land-grant universities favored a curriculum that emphasized a uniquely American identity as well as the need for scientific exploration. Advanced study of technology and science went hand in hand with American literary and cultural individualism. Coy F. Cross's historical biography of Justin Morrill, author of the Land-Grant Act, states that "faith in progress, fueled by the social, scientific, technological, and cultural advances of the early nineteenth century, caused Americans to see the traditional college curricula as 'hopelessly antiquated'" (78). Furthering this national scientific agenda without appearing to impinge upon local and individual values, universities created courses emphasizing the spirit of

American individualism. For instance, study of American literature and culture—a practice first institutionalized within public universities—helped forge a connection between local and national identities that ultimately garnered local support for national political programs. American literary romantics, who flourished during the first half of the nineteenth century, provided a body of work depicting a new national history, culture, and sensibility that emphasized the value of individualism. This new American literature, as I will explore further at the end of this chapter, was housed in the English department where it was interpreted through the dual tropes of individualism and humanism that became paired with the national drive for scientific research. Such an educational design affirmed individual contributions at the same time that it promoted scientific and technological progress. Public research universities declared the importance of local populations, cultures, and literatures in various humanities courses, while other courses enhanced local technical, scientific, and agrarian traditions in the name of an increasingly powerful nation-state. Collectively, these curricula fueled the notion of American exceptionalism and justified U.S. policy both nationally and internationally.

While universities were certainly seen as beneficial to local populations, a significant part of their justification came from the national desire to compete on the world stage. For instance, many advocates of the Morrill Act argued for greater investment in agricultural technology specifically because smaller European countries were producing larger crops than were American farmers (Cross 80–81). Viewed from this angle, the Morrill Act was not as much motivated by localized democratic intentions as it was motivated by a need to increase the wealth of the nation and its elite citizenry.[15] Consistent with these origins, federal legislation continued to support universities during this early industrial period in ways that simultaneously matched national and local interests. The "Hatch Act in 1887 gave federal aid to support state agricultural experiment stations" and other developmental research while the Second Morrill Act of 1890 was designed to promote instruction in accordance with this new research (Meiners 30). Universities and "colleges were required to meet specific standards in order to be eligible for the federal money" (31). Enforced standards like the kind and number of graduate programs as well as the availability of modern laboratory space in addition to emphases on technological and scientific development ensured that government investments would pay off as university professionals made discoveries of national importance. In short, "state funding on a per capita or per student basis was measly until the late 19th century, when scientific findings became important in agriculture, mining, oil exploration, manufacturing, and construction" (Goldin and Katz 51). At the crossroads of modernity, the United States created its commercially directed version of the research university in order to support the burgeoning scientific fields necessary to industrial capitalism. No doubt this funding created space for individuals who previously would not have attended a university. But it must also be noted that the emergence of new public universities, the explosion of student enrollment, and the widening scope of university curricula all critically contributed to national scientific investigations. These educational innovations established universities as the research, development, and personnel departments of corporate America.

The fluid relationship between the local and the national was, of course, mutually reinforcing. Just as the nation-state emphasized individualism through university participation, departments and individual academics stressed the national importance of their work. The connection between individual self-interest and national politics in higher education, in fact, often relied on the same rhetoric used to expand the Western frontier. Such language glorified individualism at the same time that it justified individual projects as revelatory of a national calling, manifest destiny, or a secularized prophecy of American greatness. Bledstein, for instance, points out that change within university lectures resulted from a desire to "become responsive to particular and local needs," but he also states that these local needs were loosely defined within a national political project (81). Because universities were local instantiations of national trends, the concept of "professionalism could hitch its calling to the star of manifest destiny. Scientists found themselves appealing to the national conscience—or helping to form it—by chiding the government and the populace for its lack of support for research, and by comparing the backwardness (vis-à-vis specialization) of the United States with the more congenial situation in England and on the Continent" (Gerstl and Jacobs 6). As we have seen, federal funding for individualized programs, improved university standards, and professional departments reinforced a culture of individualism. Fueled by that cultural ideology, scholars, politicians, and businesspeople used the notion of a unified national interest—a manifest destiny—in competition against other national interests to garner more money and better programs fitted to their own self-interest. Politicians did so in the classical American jeremiad fashion that followed a tripartite formula: our nation is predestined for economic, political, cultural, and intellectual greatness; by not professionalizing universities, we are ignoring our special calling; and having seen the error of our ways, we will repent by professionalizing and funding universities as a step toward our innate greatness.

Legislators and others actively promoting the formation of a public university system defined the university space as critical to both local economic development and national political dexterity. A public university, claimed an early letter written by state legislator George Forquer to his Illinois constituency, "would be the means of rapidly converting some one of our villages into a populous and wealthy city, thereby adding greatly to the value of property, and to the wealth of a country" (41). According to this and other documentation, the formation of a university was often integral to the building of cities and a strong infrastructure of wealthy cities was said to lead naturally to a strong and wealthy country. Moreover, early political economic discourse tended to moralize national wealth-making within a secularized notion of the good. In the United States, this moralizing grew along with a secularized Puritan rhetoric that defined American progress as God's will (Aune, *Selling the Free Market;* Bercovitch, "The Ends of American Puritan Rhetoric"). For instance, J. B. Turner's pamphlet *Industrial Universities for the People* argues that a federally sponsored state university system would allow the United States to "not only beat England, but beat the world in yachts, and locks, and reapers, but in all else that contributes to the well being and true glory of man" (75). Turner clearly viewed widespread university education, always locally situated and responsive to regional needs, as the institution that would transform the country into an international commercial and political leader. Signifying American progress and innovation as the "true glory" of humankind, an overwhelmingly Christian nation identified universities with the protestant ethic of hard work and rationalized prosperity as the outward manifestation of God's plan.

Arguments favoring federal funding for higher education emphasized that universities would help the nation compete agriculturally as well as technologically in the international marketplace. Such arguments simultaneously appealed to a culture of individualism, a politics of nation-building, and an economics of industrialization. One example of this kind of argument can be found in a statement by Massachusetts judge Marshall P. Wilder before the Berkshire Agricultural Society: "For want of knowledge, millions of dollars are now, annually lost by the commonwealth, by the misapplication of capital and labor in industry. On these points we want a system of experiments directed by scientific knowledge. Are they not important to our farmers? Neither the agricultural papers, periodicals or societies, or any other agents now in operation, are deemed sufficient. . . . We plead that the means and advantages of a professional education should be placed within the reach of our farmers" (quoted in J. B. Turner 98). Wilder defined professional education as the only sufficient mechanism for agricultural success. Although pleading on behalf of individual suffering farmers, he also invokes the great losses for the nation. The "commonwealth" underscores state sovereignty as well as national collectivity in the same way that "scientific knowledge" aids family-owned farms as well as the gross national product. Universities were the clear solution to what Wilder perceived as the scattered and unsystematized techniques for disseminating knowledge prevalent during the early part of the nineteenth century. Rhetorically, this solution worked because it offered a system that valued individual competition and success at the same time that it provided standardized practices, technologies, and business knowledge necessary to the more efficient use of money, labor, and resources.

Even with these clearly nationalized rhetorics, it could be argued that public universities understood themselves as responsive only to state and local interests and that national benefits were merely a fortunate, but secondary, consequence. Indeed, the organizational structure of the U.S. public university system reinforced such a view through a limited and fragmented national authority that reserved education policy for state and local governing bodies. Within this loosely organized structure, institutions "developed academic and service programs tailored to meet the community needs of donors and patrons rather than national standards and public service established by central ministry officials" (Graham and Diamond 23). The founding of the Association of American Universities in 1900, however, suggests at least some consciousness of the collectivity of these institutions. The local community and its population belonged to a larger national network whose interests were inseparable from theirs. The acquisition of land from coast to coast, a transcontinental railroad system, national unification after the Civil War, entry into World War I, and the development of a national university system all characterize this historical moment as one of profound nationalization—so much so that no local community or state could fully conceive itself in isolation from the larger nation-state. Whatever educational freedom existed within individual states was reined in to a degree by the rhetorical parameters of a nationalized notion of professionalism.

National political interests certainly helped define universities, but they did so in clear collaboration with the needs of industrial capitalism. Indeed, the key characteristic of the nation-state during this historical moment was the economic imperative of an increasingly industrialized economy. Without strong industrialization, there would be little international trade, a weak military with few provisions, and no realistic hope of competing in the high-stakes game of world politics. Industrial economic growth, however, required the formation of standardized business knowledges as well as standardized work practices. Therefore, the new university curricula addressed ways to manage fluctuating market prices, to develop new transportation technologies, and even how to organize wage labor in large mills and textile factories. Like the local and the national, the economic and the political are inseparable. An examination of how corporate players became integral to the formation of the U.S. research university will help clarify the university's role in relationship to its industrial economic needs.

Classified, Divided, and Standardized Knowledges:
The Economics of Professionalism

Because corporate capitalism had such a stake in the shape and the future of industrial research, many successful capitalists donated funds to particular universities or established national organizations on behalf of higher education in general. For instance, John D. Rockefeller established the General Education Board (GEB) in 1903 and the Rockefeller Foundation in 1913. The GEB proposed to "reduce higher education to something like an orderly and comprehensive system, to discourage unnecessary duplication and waste, and to encourage economy and efficiency" (Meiners 35). Research became centralized in universities while regional colleges were phased out as either redundant or unable to maintain the expensive research standards necessary for professional accreditation. Under the guise of order and efficiency, these supposedly philanthropic organizations supported the newly developed public research universities, privileging research that was economically profitable to corporations. Faith in the potential profitability of university research certainly played a role in this restructuring of higher education, but it did so through classified, divided, and standardized knowledges that supposedly helped the individual and the nation as much as they did corporate America.

Standardized lending policies and supposedly neutral assessment organizations often prevented less scientific universities from gaining state licensing or accreditation. Many small schools were attacked as unnecessary or inefficient by the 1909 Carnegie Commission report, named the "Flexner Report" after its author, Abraham Flexner. Working for the Carnegie Foundation for the Advancement of Teaching (CFAT), this commission was concerned that the scientific knowledge produced in research universities be effectively disseminated into practice.[16] In deciding whether state schools could be admitted into its pension program, therefore, CFAT first determined whether the various institutions in a given state "were really cooperating parts of a consistent system of state education or whether they were competing parts" (*Fourth Annual Report* 86).[17] Unless small teaching institutions became absorbed by larger research universities or taught techniques developed by those universities, such schools often did not receive corporate or state funding. While "small liberal arts colleges, independent professional schools, and sectarian institutions were at a competitive disadvantage" for these funds, new public research universities, many of which were land-grant institutions, were at an advantage because they were already commissioned to do the kind of industrial and agricultural research desired by corporations (Goldin and Katz 49). The federal government encouraged scientific and technical research, but corporate philanthropies helped make that research possible through imposed standards. Rhetorically invested in democratizing individual lives and strengthening the nation's political position worldwide, these goals cannot be separated from industrial goals of furthering commercially profitable research.

There was a clear understanding among late nineteenth-century educators that universities needed to accommodate the interests of corporations to achieve local and national economic growth. It was generally believed that the education characteristic of traditional Eastern colleges focused on impractical esoteric knowledge. Such an education offered cultural value, but it was often seen as politically and economically impractical to the needs of a modern nation. Historian David Noble aptly summarizes this view, claiming that the elite schools produced "'laborious thinkers,' while what industry required was 'thinking laborers'" (*America by Design* 21). Unlike early political economic theory espoused by Oxford theoreticians like Whately, academicians in U.S. public research universities saw practical business skills as worthy of disciplinary status. This difference marks not just academic shifts but also shifts in the rhetorically constructed boundaries of possibility. Corporations needed workers who understood industrial processes as well as various scientific methods for managing businesses. Business schools and scientific research developed along with the emerging public university system in order to serve this need. Like other units, they were organized, standardized, and departmentalized in partial response to a rising corporate interest in the future development of the nation.

The formation of business administration schools provides a good example of how universities standardized professional knowledge in accordance with the needs of a growing industrial economy. The University of Pennsylvania created the first school of business education in 1881 with other such schools springing up regularly through the first decade of the twentieth century. Alain Touraine, in his *Academic System in American Society,* argues that these commercially oriented studies were easily admitted into more traditional university curricula: "Classical studies were supplemented by commercial and industrial ones without the former being considered noble and the latter menial. [During the turn of the twentieth century] business administration schools were established. The first, the Wharton School of Finance and Commerce, was established by the

University of Pennsylvania in 1881; similar schools were created in 1898 by Berkeley and Chicago, in 1900 by Dartmouth and New York University, and finally by Harvard in 1908" (29).[18] As part of the developing research university system, these business schools suggest that public universities were fairly quick to respond to the new industrial labor market. John Urry documents that "the number of 'administrative employees' within American industry increased four and a half times between 1899 and 1929, from 7.7 percent to 18.0 percent of total employment" (92). University programs emerged just as this trend was beginning to take off, filling a clear need for workers trained in business administration. These business schools, as well as other academic units, created their own professional organizations charged with monitoring academic work and helping create professional standards compatible with market needs. In the latter half of the nineteenth century, seven professional organizations emerged in the business fields, eight in the humanities, ten in the medical fields, and eleven in the pure sciences (Bledstein 85–86; Cohen 131). Standardization of professionals inside and outside the university—a quality-enhancement mechanism fitted to the rapidly industrializing economy—became the norm. Industrial work benefited from a professional pool of similarly trained individuals and universities benefited from efficient administration of increasingly extensive university activities.

In characteristic reciprocity, disciplinary knowledge facilitated professional organization at the same time that those professional societies systematized various areas of study into discrete disciplines, each with its own technologies for standardization. Bledstein argues that "by screening students upon entrance, formalizing courses of study, publishing textbooks, standardizing examinations and awarding degrees, higher educators convinced the public that objective principles rather than subjective partisanship determined competence in American life" (124). Like the culture of individual competition, the enforcement of these standards, in large part, came from the economic imperatives of the corporate world. Unstandardized or random credentialization would require time-consuming and costly on-the-job training, which ran counter to the fast-paced needs of industrial capitalism. Not uncoincidentally, Abraham Flexner critiqued public universities as too unfocused and dangerously absent of standards in his first monograph on higher education published in 1908, titled *The American College*. This lack of organization caused administrative problems that he suggested could "be solved by sub-dividing the over-grown college into several bodies" (231) and providing discrete units "with a scientifically determined point of departure" (237). Certainly universities were not required to adhere to these standards. But funding from corporate foundations did depend on such adherence, simultaneously serving the rhetorical function of persuading universities of the benefits derived from uniformity and creating a community of professionals who could identify with a standard course sequence and professional problem-solving methods.

The 1908 Flexner plan offering pension funds to public universities meeting Carnegie standards provides only one example of corporate influence, but there were countless others. The CFAT, the Carnegie Corporation, and the Rockefeller Foundation all restricted their grant-making activities to institutions that met specific standards. University philanthropy, as the titles of these organizations suggest, was an activity spearheaded by businesses and business interests. The standards mandated by corporate philanthropists included such things as library holdings, faculty salaries, university endowment, entrance criteria, laboratory facilities, professorial credentials, and degree requirements. The essentially corporate nature of this standardization was not entirely lost on the public at large. Henry Pritchett, in a 1905 *Atlantic Monthly* article titled "Shall the University Become a Business Corporation?" explicitly noted that universities were modeling themselves after businesses and that strict CFAT policies followed a corporate model of education.[19] Although Pritchett claimed that universities differed structurally from businesses and would not accommodate well to a strict business structure, his analysis detected university corporatization and predicted that those ties would only strengthen unless rigidly opposed. Legislators and judges like James Morrill, George Forquer, and Marshall P. Wilder as well as academics like Abraham Flexner deliberated about the future of the university within political and business communities, but Pritchett's essay places this economic discussion squarely within educated, middle-class discourse, making it part of a much broader public discussion. While the middle class remained suspicious of corporations, Pritchett's concerns about the university may have seemed misplaced in a system supposedly guided by noncorporate organizations such as various national professional associations, regional accreditation bodies, and philanthropic foundations—none of these sources directly represents the business community and yet each is inescapably joined to economic interests. These indirect avenues of participation nonetheless helped universities quietly structure themselves as businesses in cooperation with industry trends.

Corporations undoubtedly acquired a growing influence over the administrations of U.S. public research universities during the late nineteenth century as the composition of regents boards changed to incorporate capitalist interests. During this transformational period, lawyers (many of whom also sat on corporate boards) slowly displaced clergymen as the leading professional group on university governing boards and the national interests of industrial capitalism replaced the interests of local merchants. Barrow points out that "in the two decades from 1901 to 1920, almost 45 percent of all university board members classified as either lawyers or businessmen were attached, either as an officer or a director, to at least one company affiliated with a northeastern financial group" (40). By the 1920s, that figure rose to 62 percent. At one level, this simply signifies the centralization of finance capital in the most industrialized region of the nation, connecting various companies in a variety of businesses back to financial sources in the Northeast. At another level, because of the clear affiliation between university board members and these financial groups, it also signifies the infusion of corporate culture within university decision-making bodies. Steeped within this corporatization, university research, pedagogical, and curricular goals soon adopted the economic imperative, rather than the educational process, as a bottom line.

Although economic interests appeared to be cornering the academic market through their indirect standardization of university curricula, not all economists endorsed these changes within higher education. Thorstein Veblen, associated with the institutional school of economics and well-known for his work on commodity consumption, sharply critiqued the composition of universities whose boards of trustees were made up primarily of businessmen.[20] Veblen's analysis of the university system, *The Higher Learning in America: A Memorandum on the Conduct of Universities by Business Men,* was published in 1918. The 1916 preface, however, tells us that it had been "more than a dozen years since the following observations on American academic life were first assembled in written form" (v). In other words, this critique is based on information just as relevant in 1904 (the year of its observation) as in 1918 (the year of its publication) and is therefore representative of at least the latter half of the industrial period in education. Veblen's primary argument suggests that governing boards prioritized vocational training over the process of learning. Consequently, education became concerned with a matter-of-fact, mechanistic, and dispassionate standardized curriculum. University administration typical of early twentieth-century research schools, he claims, proceeded "on grounds of businesslike expediency" (63). Taking an extreme anticorporate position, Veblen argued that these boards were completely superfluous to higher education. According to him, the only function governing boards served was "mettling with academic matters they do not understand" (66). Indeed, he argues that "the sole ground of their retention appears to be an unreflecting deferential concession to the usages of corporate organization and control" (66). Administrative boards dominated by individuals tied to major corporations not only forged practical connections between higher education and corporate-industrial capitalism, they also helped merge corporate culture with university culture. What corporations justified and naturalized, universities justified and naturalized; what corporations resisted (erudition) was marginalized within these universities, illuminating the rhetorically constructed boundaries of legitimate professional speech, behavior, and performance. Corporations forged inroads within the university—made primarily of financial assistance procured through the rhetoric of utility, practicality, and efficiency—that led themselves directly to the central governing boards.

Corporate involvement in higher education helped expand and organize research into its contemporary form at the same time that such involvement limited the scope of that research. Veblen worried about corporate control over university boards because it would "unavoidably incline to apportion the funds assigned for current expenses in such a way as to favor those 'practical' or quasi-practical lines of instruction and academic propaganda that are presumed to heighten the business acumen of the students or to yield immediate returns" (81). In the sociopolitical mi-

lieu in which universities found themselves, professional business training or practical business sense was the paramount signifier of general intelligence. "Business success," he states, "is by common consent, and quite
uncritically, taken to be conclusive evidence of wisdom even in matters
that have no relation to business affairs" (69). Education beyond the professional and technical needs of business is virtually useless. Certainly,
there was some room for scholarship that did not have a practical end, but
it was viewed as peripheral to the university's practical mission—a focus
easily reinforced by a middle-class culture already suspicious of elite pretensions and the supposedly impractical nature of classical education.

Veblen predicted a path in which corporate participation would lead
inevitably toward a system of higher education rife with corporate thinking and research. He forecast that "the principles of competitive business
will permeate the administration in all directions; in the personnel of the
academic staff, in the control and intercourse of teachers and students, in
the schedule of instruction, in the disposition of the material equipment,
in the public exhibits and ceremonial of the university, as well as in its pecuniary concerns" (98). This, he suggested, will result "in an administrative system of bureaux or departments, a hierarchical gradation of the
members of the staff, and a rigorous parcelment and standardization of
the instruction offered" (98). Though this picture seems bleak, it is not far
removed from what contemporary scholars warn is the dilemma faced by
an increasingly privatized university. University administrations are more
centralized, bigger, and better financed than ever before; a hierarchy of
staff from adjunct to tenure-track and from assistant to full professor
regulates the professoriate; instruction is frequently uniform throughout
state and even national systems and such standardization seems to be increasing along with the rise in prepackaged electronic courseware like
the now merged Blackboard and Web CT. Notwithstanding Veblen's remarkable foresight, however, the university did not arrived at this historical juncture without further organizational changes to the public research university as it responded to subsequent shifts in U.S. capitalism.
Before I turn to that analysis, I will end this chapter with a closer examination of how the industrial political economy was concretely mani-
fested in English department curricula. This examination will demonstrate that American literature, simultaneously reinforcing a culture of

individualism and a unified nation-state, provided one of the strongest defenses against critics of national conformity and commercially oriented research.

Localizing Industrial Capitalism: The Case of English Department Curricula

So far, my outline of the industrializing capitalist marketplace and its implications for the formation of the U.S. public research university has been painted with broad brushstrokes, tracking professionalism and its valuation within specific spheres in order to trace the boundaries of academic legitimacy constituted through this signifying process. While such a history is insufficient by itself, it is indispensable to an understanding of how localized texts fit into a larger global grid. It is only through constant movement between the local and the global that a more complete sociohistorical picture comes into focus—a picture with detail as well as a larger, albeit more vague, structural framework. I attempt to fill in such a picture by taking a closer look at the specifics of English departments and their curricula.

The study of English, as opposed to the classical languages, was one of the new and unique characteristics of the national curricula forged by the public university system. Public research universities were among the first to teach American literature, distinguish literature from rhetoric, and introduce the now foundational personal essay assignment (Berlin, *Rhetorics, Poetics, and Cultures;* Brereton; Connors, *Composition-Rhetoric*). As the place where students are introduced to imaginative literatures, the English department occupies a central role in the ideological reproduction of individual professionalism and national identity. Training in evaluating literature and composing written texts mediate the political and economic tensions that arise in the public sphere by teaching professionals to take leisurely detours into the artistic discourse of books and to use writing for appropriate political, economic, and personal goals. The English department, therefore, provides a rich site for examining how the imperatives of an industrial framework—forged through a multiplicity of professional valuation processes—became localized within the specific practices of university departments.

My analysis of early English department curricula is taken from two texts: *English in American Universities,* an edited collection of essays from twenty English professors representing twenty different universities, and *Essays for College English,* a college reader designed for Midwestern agricultural schools. *English in American Universities* provides a diverse range of insider opinions about English department curriculum in these new institutions while *Essays for College English* offers a random example of a late nineteenth-century textbook. Together the two books offer a broad sense of what professors thought about the increasingly standardized university curriculum as well as what students were required to read and write at this time. I argue that both of these texts introduced and framed the work of English departments through practices confined by the rhetorical boundaries of university education situated within industrial capitalism. They use language to reinforce a culture of individualism, often based on myths of the frontier experience; they reinforce the importance of building local communities as part of national strength; and they contribute to an economy based on the classification, division, and standardization of knowledge necessary to commercial success. These three aspects of the late nineteenth- and early twentieth-century social reality work in concert to help forge an entirely new kind of English department—one that produces professionalized individuals necessary to the industrialization of U.S. capitalism. In short, these two texts reveal the new value-form central to the cultural, political, and economic transitions of the industrial period.

William Morton Payne begins his 1895 introduction to *English in American Universities* by noting a critical shift in higher education. He tells us that instruction in English literature has, "for some years past, been in a transitional stage" and that this collection brings together many different professional voices in order to discuss those changes (7). Yet the twenty essays in the collection represent more than the individual beliefs of university professors. Each essay also represents the kind of institution for which the professor works: elite Eastern colleges, new state-supported universities of the West, and new institutions primarily supported by private philanthropy (22–23). Among these different universities, Payne says, "the new ideas and the novel methods reported come rather from the West than the East" (23). Reflecting the general cultural conviction of the late nineteenth century, he attributes the innovation of state-supported universities to the frontier spirit inhabiting the student population. According to Payne's argument, the uniqueness of the student body at public universities stems from "the environment of the pioneer settlement, which has not yet forgotten or outlived the hard struggle for subsistence" (24). This individual struggle for survival that he sees as still vividly part of Western identity helps reinvent higher education within Midwestern and Western universities. Resonating with the widespread cultural emphasis on frontier individualism, Payne's argument recalls pioneers forging their own democratic traditions and implies that the U.S. public research university, especially in the Midwest and West, modernized national higher education as part of this democratic mission.

The theme of individualism, in fact, permeates his whole collection. Payne argues that as English curricula began to focus on the local, the immediate, and the individual, teachers began to reorganize their pedagogies around the principle of "proceeding from the near and the familiar to the strange and the remote" (8). Because the new economy depended on professionals who understood themselves as critical intermediaries in the production process, universities had to invent a curriculum that maintained political and economic structures at the same time that they valued the unique positionality of their new student body. In this new curriculum, says the introduction, knowledge "must be discovered for each individual separately" (9). Payne does caution, however, that to allow individualism to have "the last word would be to abandon altogether the position that educational theory is bound to maintain" (11). Thus, individuals need to be guided early on by the "older and wiser" (11). In this local-national political schema, students were required to arrive at specific literary interpretations, but they were also allowed to use their disparate individual experiences as a method for achieving those conclusions.

In addition to respecting individual students and their differences, universities, as we have seen, also individualized departments according to their specific academic function. This departmentalization is apparent from Payne's efforts to legitimize the study of literature as a purely aesthetic pursuit distinct from the study of philology, rhetoric, and grammar. Defining the study of literature as a discrete departmental pursuit, he relegates both rhetoric and grammar to primary and secondary schools.

He then uses university reports to demonstrate the "well-marked differentiation of literature from linguistics" (25). With grammar and rhetoric displaced to earlier educational levels and linguistics fully distinct from literature, the profession of English is free to pursue its specialized area of expertise. Payne does not denigrate these other educational pursuits but simply asks that they not "be permitted to masquerade as the study of literature" (26). Demarcating their professional space for the study of English literature, Payne follows the general economic trend toward classification, division, and specialization. The division of knowledge, like the division of labor, expedites the production process. In one case, we produce and distribute commodities more quickly; in the other, we produce and distribute knowledge more quickly. Both were needed, it was thought, to ease the United States into international competition.

Not surprisingly, Payne's introduction ends with a proposal to create English literature as a distinct department of its own. In the proposal he specifies exactly what should fit into a department of English literature and provides a list of professorial qualifications. According to Payne, a department of English literature should include professors who are knowledgeable in the history of literary criticism, the wide canon of ancient and modern literatures, aesthetic literary sense, and teaching others to approach literature in the same way (27). It is clear from this list that while pedagogies can be individualized according to student demographics, the ultimate goal of an English department is to ensure that all students maintain uniform literary interpretations. Departments achieve uniformity by teaching students specific historical facts, the canon of "great" literature, and the appropriate tastes derived from these exposures. Students may be encouraged to be distinct individuals, but they are also encouraged to see their individuality as part of a complex, predetermined whole. The aesthetic veneer of literature, in this sense, makes conforming to national values, ideals, and principles more palatable. Appropriating a culture of individualism in order to support a national research agenda, Payne's ideal department allows for local, individualized methods of teaching a nationalized literary curriculum.

One particular suggestion Payne offers on behalf of individualizing pedagogies is the complete elimination of English readers. Such texts, Payne contends, lack good literature and rely too heavily on ineffective, rote, and repetitive exercises. Payne's argument, however passionate, seems more applicable to an older generation of textbooks than to the turn-of-the-century textbooks. According to Robert J. Connors's *Composition-Rhetoric: Backgrounds, Theory, and Pedagogy,* textbooks with repetitive exercises were popular during the first half of the nineteenth century. During that time, institutions and students of higher education were on the rise while qualified college professors remained scarce. Consequently, he argues, textbooks that mimicked secondary-level pedagogies such as recitation of repeated examples emerged as a stand-in for university professors (77). By 1890, however, a new composition reader was born—one remarkably similar to contemporary readers (87–88). This type of reader, organized as a collection of essays addressing focused topics, remained in demand because it played a crucial double role in the education process. It taught ideas, grammar, and good writing, but this new reader also taught values, morals, and good taste vis-à-vis the careful selection of model essays addressing wide-ranging social and political issues.

Composed of aesthetically powerful essays, readers such as the edited collection *Essays for College English* provided students with an array of texts meant to inspire similarly great composition as well as to elicit consistent values from the students who read them. One advantage of these readers was that the essays could be easily selected, removed, or rearranged in order to appeal to specific audiences. Intended primarily for students in the Midwest, this 1915 reader, for instance, was designed "to supply a collection especially suited to students of Agricultural Colleges" (Bowman et al. v).[21] While agricultural colleges were distinct from public universities, they often had common goals and objectives. And, as we have seen, agricultural colleges were frequently absorbed by the larger university. In this way, it is quite likely that the reader was used at land-grant or other public universities in the Midwest. Regardless of its specific use, this reader provides an excellent example of how Payne's idea of good literature mediated the historical materialist agenda of industrialization among a diverse and staunchly independent population. Readers like this one help construct students as middle-class subjects with the tastes, manners, and morals that appropriately signify their professional station in life. As Conners indicated, they teach the ideas and principles of good writing along with valuable life lessons tailored to an audience of university students on the cusp of radical shifts in the cultural, political, and economic realities of U.S. citizenship.

The editors of this reader, for instance, aspired to professionalize agricultural work and provide its managerial class with appropriate values. James Cloyd Bowman and his coeditors believed that the graduates of these colleges "who return to practical farming achieve at once, if they are equal to it, a position of prominence and influence in the whole life of their respective communities. It is of the greatest importance, therefore, that these students acquire a definite professional outlook characterized by perspective and breadth" (v). Characteristic of the industrial political economy, this passage places an emphasis on meritocracy by suggesting that all those who "are equal to it" will achieve immediate "prominence and influence." Assuming that college graduates will naturally return to their family farms reinforces the importance of local communities. But the national goals circumscribe the local and the individual. National values, infused within this collection of American essays, fuel American pride and give students the cultural cache to maneuver within the economic and political exigencies of their immediate contexts. The addition of "perspective and breadth" to student experience represents a subtle imposition of this national agenda. Students achieved this breadth and perspective by studying great American authors. The reader includes such well-known Americans as Woodrow Wilson, Theodore Roosevelt, Frederick Jackson Turner, and Ralph Waldo Emerson. Political and intellectual leaders, these authors were meant to introduce students to issues of national importance as well as to model stylistically sound writing (xi). Only after a student "has mastered" the writing of these authors, says the introduction, "will he find that he is able to express his own thoughts clearly and compactly" (xii). While the reader explicitly valorizes the individual, an individual's experiential knowledge is always grafted onto the predefined national experience through prescribed readings, belief systems, and values.

The four subdivisions of the text clearly illustrate the degree of complicity between the teaching of a fledgling American literary tradition and the historical materialism of industrialization. Specific to the needs of the agrarian frontier, these four section titles are: the problems of country life, science, education, and problems of life in general. The first and last sections deal with local and national experiences, respectively. The first section asks students to "consider what values ought to be achieved in individual and social life in the country" (vi). The last section, on the other hand, discusses the "influence that the open country has had in developing American characteristics" (vii). Read together, these two sections appear to value the particular experiences of students at the same time that they discipline the students into national civic and moral positionalities. In both sections, the object of study focuses on the lives of students who live and work in the "open country." Such an emphasis affirms the importance of their working lives and replays the frontier myth of an empty, virgin land waiting to be conquered. No longer isolated homesteaders, miners, and trappers, these farmers have become professionalized to the extent that they must recognize their work as crucial to national progress rather than simply individual sustenance. In fact, students are told by the essay "Traffic" that the ideal farmer makes "life good for all men as for yourselves" (425). The moral overtones of this text seem to ease this farming population into an emerging corporate-industrial economy. By highlighting the moral value and national importance of farming, these sections valorize the newly professionalized class of farmers not as individuals aspiring toward wealth in a burgeoning industrial economy but as citizens whose work helps others and the nation as much as themselves.

Presented in this altruistic manner, the reader explicitly claims to turn its students into leaders of their farming communities, set apart from their fellow farmers both by their superior class sensibilities and their scientific agricultural knowledge. In her insightful essay "The Bourgeois Subject and the Demise of Rhetorical Education," Sharon Crowley argues that essays like these teach more than good composition. They are necessary for what she calls a "pedagogy of taste" or the policing of the cultural sphere. According to Crowley, "a pedagogy of taste helps students to internalize a set of rules that mark their inclusion in bourgeois subjectivity at the same time as it sets them off from members of other classes" (43). An ability to recall these essays, their authors, and their basic arguments will allow "students to discriminate between the tastes of the educated and the uneducated classes" (36). After returning to their local farming communities, these students will ascend the political and economic hierarchy based, in part, on their ability to exhibit proper cultural taste, display cultural capital in the books on their shelves, and speak with cognizance of American history, geography, art, and science. Culture, as we have seen, is tightly interwoven within the economic and political spheres in its ability to construct appropriate paths for individual agency. Indeed, the more technical or scientific essays in this collection could not easily persuade students if they were not placed within these aesthetic and moralizing essays.

Couched in and perhaps overshadowed by these morally valorizing sections, the middle two sections position scientific progress as the natural complement to individual and social improvement. The second section advocates "scientific knowledge in order that man may conquer his environment," and the third section combines "education in the applied science of Agriculture" with "education in human letters" (vii). Although the introduction claims that the texts collected in the reader are "representative essays" chosen as models of good writing, the fact that the essays in these sections clearly promote scientific methods without disturbing the ideal of the agrarian countryside reinforces the inevitable, progressive, and assimilationist rhetoric of industrialization (xi). Two consecutive essays clarify this point. "The Way to Better Farming" argues that the business of farming will only succeed if, in addition to incorporating new technologies, farmers also exercise "certain social qualities of inestimable value to the community life" (99). As leaders of their communities, these university-educated farmers have a responsibility to guide others in practical farming techniques. "The Farmer and Finance" argues for the need to create specialized financial institutes for farmers so that they may have the necessary capital to engage fully in "scientific farming" (111). These essays do not present economic development in terms of class mobility and economic success but as the means for furthering the values of the farming communities. Rather than jeopardizing the dual frontier ideologies of individualism and democratic social formations, scientific progress—as defined by this sequence of essays—furthers those deeply embedded community goals. By focusing on the intrinsic social and moral value of the farmer, these essays reinforce the student's own identification and normalize that positionality by providing students with a sketch of the "successful" farmer. Consequently, this reader appropriates the familial, community, and cultural construction of the farmer within a newly developed professionalism and delimits the possibilities of that position.

Through many different curricular models like these the public research university system reflected, reproduced, and re-created the dynamic processes underpinning U.S. industrial capitalism. The fluidity of this capitalist system has repeatedly forced new shifts in the cultural, political, and economic spheres, preventing any one aspect of this constituting process from assuming central authority. Because culture, politics, and economics all work together through universities, governments, and businesses, participants in any of these spheres are responsible for the value-form this structure takes as well as the consequences it yields. Actively contributing to this fluctuating historical materialist scene, universities can never be accused of passively absorbing a corporate agenda. The U.S. public research university is not the victim of a corporate takeover but a vibrant participant in a complex social-corporate-state relationship. Working through discrete locations in vastly different ways, university practices constitute boundaries of possibility to which, in turn, it must conform or change. This chapter has sketched the history of that relationship during the emergence of the U.S. public research university to demonstrate that the corporatized university is not a new phenomenon but one deeply entrenched in the formation of this university system. What many academics—especially those in the humanities—currently fear as the sudden privatization of the university is simply the most current manifestation of a system that began with the formation of the U.S. public research university and continued to grow as that system transformed through the monopoly era and into the age of global capitalism. Historicizing current university structures in this way will force those of us interested in a less corporatized educational structure to develop more sophisticated strategies for institutional change, strategies such as those I propose in chapter 5.

2

Monopoly Capitalism, Globalization, and University Transformation

A Plea against Nostalgia

The formation of the U.S. public research university, I have argued, was not simply a democratizing venture. Neither was it merely a strategy to economically outdistance England and other European nation-states, as perhaps my account of the industrial era might too easily suggest. The establishment of public higher education created institutions for an entirely different class of students, helped industrialize the nation, and distinguished the United States from its European competitor nations. But this was not all it did. Because the public university system has always collaborated with the triangulated historical materialist structure in which it has been situated, universities also entered into major corporate contracts, conducted research for the federal government, and reproduced a capitalist culture stylized around consumerism long before the so-called corporatization of the university. The implications of these complex relationships proliferated at the same time that the political and economic foundations on which they were built became obfuscated by a culturally focused democratic rhetoric. Criticisms as well as accolades nostalgic for the democratic project of public higher education have consistently refocused public discussion of the university around calls for cultural inclusion and accessibility at precisely those moments when the university was adapting to the exigencies of a new stage of corporate capitalism. Not only are these pleas not new, they demonstrate the power of cultural identification—myth, ideology, and narrative—to trump political and economic realities. This chapter will show how this nostalgic rhetoric reinvented the past and enabled major curricular, financial, and institutional shifts to restructure the university system without much discussion about the political and economic ramifications of those changes.

Gayatri Spivak's analysis of how the rhetoric of "We the People" functions within the U.S. political landscape helps illustrate my point about the important political economic work performed by this nostalgia. In "The Making of Americans, the Teaching of English, and the Future of Cultural Studies," Spivak borrows from Bruce Ackerman's constitutional analysis, *We the People,* to argue that the Constitution of the United States and its invocation of "We the People" operate dualistically. During the vast majority of everyday life, the collective agency of a unified national identity—legally concretized in phrases like "We the People"—does not have a significant political role and frequently reflects acquiescence more than national deliberation. But during exceptional historical moments, leaders resuscitate "We the People" to mobilize consent and mandate political change. This is especially obvious during times of revolution, war, and sociopolitical or economic upheaval. Spivak takes this argument to heart and suggests that "involvements of the We the People in the law are also managements of crisis" (781). While most political acts maintain the status quo and need no large public endorsement, the politics of crisis management require popular warrant—a revival of "We the People"— to provide a political base for actions that often disrupt everyday activities. Using this discourse regularly might leave the nation bankrupt of any powerful rallying call, but infrequent revivals of such rhetoric reinforce national cohesiveness and help propel change. This rhetorical reserve, filled with phrases like "We the People," allows various individuals and institutions access to a ready-made justification for unprecedented or unusual political economic policies. Importantly, the collective, and often noble, purpose announced by such rhetoric functions to muffle division, struggle, and contestation over these new policies.

Using a similar rhetorical process, the public university system readjusts fairly smoothly during moments of political economic transition by nostalgically reclaiming the democratic mission of higher education. This democratic mission, lying dormant in the residues of our national consciousness, reemerges as a rationale for reorganizing the university system during critical moments such as the transition from one political economic epoch into another. Transformations within public higher education traditionally have been forwarded and have received popular enthusiasm through close association with the goal of spreading democracy, both internally and externally. Of course, a host of other values articulate with the notion of democracy—reason, rights, progress, reform, equality, and competition, to name only a few. These values connect themselves to democracy through a long chain of signification, but the master trope that ensures the widespread valorization of higher education remains its democratic foundations. Although democratic claims have saturated educational debates since the industrial era's pioneering Land-Grant Act and the formation of both black universities and women's colleges, this mission reappeared with particular strength during the monopoly era to support the Servicemen's Readjustment Act, the creation of community colleges, and the university protest movements of the late 1960s. It repeated itself again, in a slightly different way, during the global era with the "Johnny Can't Write" furor of the late 1970s, the canon wars of the 1980s, and the multicultural debates of the 1990s. As these examples suggest, the idea of equal access ensured under the democratic rubrics of public education primarily surfaces to critique the limitations of current structures, support innovations, and modify the university system.

Taking up Spivak's challenge to interrogate the cultural politics of such reoccurring language, this chapter traces the rhetoric of democracy embedded within the trope of professionalism as it is used to move the university into new stages of capitalism. Cultural work, as I have indicated, exists in a complex relationship to both the political and the economic spheres. For this reason, an exploration of the democratic ethos of professionalism will offer a richer understanding of how the U.S. market economy struggled to maintain international hegemony during the monopoly era and will also add texture to our understanding of globalization as the neocolonial structure emerging after European imperialism. Because of the university's ability to dip into its unique rhetorical reserve, its politico-economic role has often been overshadowed by its democratic heritage, creating a boundary of legitimacy most of us take for granted:

the university works to improve the lives of democratic citizens locally, nationally, and now globally.

Expanding such one-dimensional history, this chapter sketches a fuller picture of how the monopoly and global stages of capitalism functioned in relationship to an evolving public university system. I argue that cultural, political, and economic changes initiated by new stages of capitalism were met with widespread acceptance because various individuals and organizations employed a powerfully nostalgic democratic rhetoric to mobilize the public on behalf of or against certain university structures. The chapter ends with a short analysis of how nostalgia for a more democratic university-based professionalism serves to mask the way the economic and political operations of the university manifest within the larger structure generated from the rhetorical valuation and exchange among its three constituting realms. I turn now to my analysis of the university within the monopoly era. Popularly known as a moment of great democratization within higher education, the public university system rooted in monopoly capitalism comes into better focus once it is viewed through an historical materialist lens. Using such optics, I complicate the idea of an expanding democratic institution by contextualizing educational change within a culture that reproduces and contains professional knowledge, a politics of heightened nationalism, and an economy based on the rise of corporate conglomerates.

Reifying the Link between the Nation-State and the University: Monopoly Capitalism and Professional Reproduction, 1918–1973

Although the U.S. public research university took off during the monopoly stage of capitalism, the foundations for this university system's soaring influence were laid during its formation in the era of industrial capitalism. Even scholars like Hugh Davis Graham and Nancy Diamond who argue assuredly that the rise of American universities into positions of worldwide leadership was not achieved until after World War II also acknowledge that "most of the elements that were essential to catapulting the top American universities into positions of global leadership after 1945 were present well prior to the Manhattan Project" (12). Rather than being understood as an historically new system, the university created during the monopoly era must be contextualized as a variation on an already well-established structure. As the landscape changed, individuals, corporations, and the government relied on the university to change as well. Such needs were more often than not expressed as criticisms of the university structure, curricula, and organization. This section examines a range of critiques—derived primarily from progressive and radical educators enmeshed in these debates—through an historical materialist hermeneutic in order to reveal the numerous relations between a culture of professional containment, a politics of national imperialism, and an economics of corporate accumulation.[1]

Particularly indicative of these multiple and intertwined university relationships are the dual tropes of professionalism and democracy, equally conforming to the social and historical needs of the period enclosed by the end of World War I (1918) and the withdrawal of U.S. troops from Vietnam (1973). This historical periodization picks up where the story of industrial capitalism left off and continues until the early 1970s, the moment so often cited as the beginning of globalization. A broad interpretation of the monopoly era, this marking acknowledges the gradual emergence and gradual phasing out of this or any other historical period. The emergent and residual markers characteristic of any moment have to be attached to concrete signs and their different signification. The democratic ideology associated with professionalism, as one such signifier, is fluid and chameleon-like in its ability to subtly adapt to the changing needs of its sociohistorical moment. While the industrial period worked to forge and to systematize the idea of a professional class, the monopoly stage worked to reproduce this class within university borders in order to ensure a level of influence and determination over that class. But to more fully grasp this professional containment, we need to understand monopoly capitalism better.

The relationship of the monopoly era to the unfolding of capitalism has precipitated much discussion and spanned different historical moments. Among the most critical accounts of monopoly capitalism, Vladimir Lenin's *Imperialism: The Highest Stage of Capitalism* cites the proliferation of monopolies just prior to World War I as critical to what he names the imperialist stage.[2] He further argues that while the early twentieth century may not have witnessed an increase in the number of corporations in industry, key mergers did initiate an enormous growth in the U.S. corporation's ability to exercise power. In 1909, U.S. corporations made up about 25 percent of all industrial enterprises nationwide, but they employed over 75 percent of all workers and produced almost 80 percent of the total national product (Lenin 22). While individuals and private firms accounted for a statistically significant number of industrial enterprises, those endeavors were so miniature in scale and utilized such a small percentage of the workforce that their interests often took a backseat to corporate needs. Put simply, corporations maintained political and economic leverage by virtue of their size. The significance of these expanded corporations and the specific way in which they participated in capitalism did not, however, correspond to the term "monopoly capitalism" until Paul Baran and Paul Sweezy's 1966 *Monopoly Capital.* This groundbreaking study was the first to define monopoly capitalism as a distinctly new stage with its own specific logic.

According to Baran and Sweezy, this new stage of capitalism differed from industrialism because competition among large monopolies replaced competition between individual industrial capitalists.[3] This new form of competition allowed monopolies to increase their rate of profit by introducing new sectors—including new consumer markets, new government programs, and new military-industrial expenditures—into the capitalist mode of production. These new sectors were intended to provide new consumers as well as new investment outlets in order to absorb surplus profits that otherwise would have caused economic stagnation and thus a fall in the rate of corporate profit. Some of those investments—especially military expenditures—produced nonconsumptive goods that would need to be repeatedly reproduced without demanding additional expenditures from an already debt-laden consumer populace. Huge amounts of money could be put into products such as defense or space programs that did not depend on public demand nor on the public's ability to purchase goods. The emerging political economy of monopoly capitalism simultaneously created new markets for the surplus of products (available for the first time as a consequence of rapid industrialization) and created new investment opportunities for the surpluses of corporate profits. Without corporate monopolies where large pools of money and resources were brought together, these new sectors could not have been created and without these new sectors the large surplus of capital—both fixed and liquid—might have led to an enormous financial recession. While Baran and Sweezy primarily studied the overarching logic of this capitalist stage, other seminal texts such as Harry Braverman's *Monopoly Capital and Labor* and Andrew Friedman's *Industry and Labour* analyzed the specifics of the new management practices characteristic of monopoly capitalism.

Besides increasing the purview of capitalism by creating new markets for production, monopoly capitalism also created a highly bureaucratized and supposedly efficient site of production. Braverman and Friedman both analyzed how scientific management, as it was practiced in the United States, changed the national labor structure. The application of a prescribed scientific method to the management of workplace movements in order to create the greatest time and output efficiency significantly expanded administrative duties and isolated workers according to discrete, repetitive tasks. This change in management enlarged the percentage of administrative workers among the professional class. Monopoly capitalism was responsible for a huge increase in administrative workers, claims Braverman. For instance, although clerical workers accounted for only 3 percent of the U.S. workforce at the turn of the twentieth century, they accounted for 13 percent of that total in 1961 and 18 percent in 1971 (Braverman 204). I do not mean to imply that these changes occurred overnight or that they occurred without significant resistance from workers. Initially, in fact, administrative employees were only able to exercise scientific management by providing workers with a sense of workplace self-determinacy and greater pay (103–4). Along with an increased salary, management had to give "workers the illusion of making decisions by choosing among fixed and limited alternatives designed by a management which deliberately leaves insignificant matters open to choice" (27). Later, as the new scientific method became normalized workplace practices, such incentives became less necessary and eventually disappeared.

The changing productive and consumptive spheres of monopoly capitalism provided the impetus for studies on how to expand markets, create new military-industrial technologies, and determine workplace psychology: the university quickly responded to this new stimulus by extending academic research into each of these areas. The need to forge

and sustain corporate progressivism was among the most significant research needs for corporate management. During the era of monopoly
capitalism, corporate philosophy emphasized cooperation over individualism and was significantly supported by Theodore Roosevelt's Progressive Party. The progressive movement attempted to regulate class antagonisms by legislating safe labor conditions and fair access to public
resources, but it in no way challenged the legitimacy of corporate power.
Building on the popular theme of frontier individualism, progressives
claimed that "a well-working society combined the virility of the frontier with the workings of the modern corporation" (Spring, *The Rise of the
Corporate State* 13). Instead of abandoning the historical ethos of American
individualism, these reformists revised this ideology to include the individual who sacrifices himself for the greater good of the community, the
corporation, and the nation. As an institution critical to individual, regional, and national identity, higher education reflected this new definition of individualism, which stressed cooperation and self-sacrifice,
suggesting that corporate progressivism played a significant role in redefining public higher education. Because corporate progressivism relied on
cooperation among specialized groups, its platform emphasized the need
for a diversified curriculum that offered vocational training and practical business skills at all levels of public education including the university.
It was precisely these ideals that other scholars critiqued when arguing
against the vocationalization of university education and against the constraints placed on independent research.

The conversation between radical thinkers who focused primarily on
the economic sphere and the more politically legitimate progressive educational theorists who redesigned the culture of higher education exemplifies the central debate over education at this time. On the one hand,
"radicals during the early part of the century claimed that schooling prepared the individual [only] to accept the control of business and industry"; on the other hand, "progressive leaders saw themselves creating
an educational system which would prepare the individual to accept a
system of cooperation and control by a meritocracy" (Spring, *Rise of the
Corporate State* 150). Radicals protested the intimate ties between universities and corporations while progressives argued that a differentiated
curriculum should be standardized and monitored to ensure its overall

social good. Radicals viewed universities as inseparable tentacles of the capitalist system and dismissed progressive claims of a democratic meritocracy. Regardless of where one falls in this educational debate, the fact remains that during this historical moment formal education tended to be in the hands of businessmen, political leaders, and professional educators who were instrumental in the development of corporate capitalism and its attendant ideologies. This is significant not because it is a new development but because their conversations are the rhetorical foundations on which higher education builds and rebuilds itself.

If, as Baran and Sweezy claim, a new stage of monopoly capitalism emerged in the early twentieth century, then the cultural, political, and economic makeup of the political economic terrain must have also changed. These various revisions can be traced through the cultural, political, and economic spheres of their constitution in order to construct a larger picture of monopoly capitalism's structural framework. Monopoly capitalism required, for instance, a new kind of professional to manage not only an altered work environment but also a new social structure. Baran and Sweezy register this change when they characterize professionals of the industrial era as "individualists *par excellence,* while [the new professional] is the leading species of genus 'organization man'" (29). Identified with one's company, discipline, or profession, an "organization man" is loyal not to just himself but to the organization to which he belongs and through which he identifies himself. Thus, one way to examine how the larger structural changes of monopoly capitalism affected the U.S. public research university is through an investigation into the university's transition from a culture of individualism to a culture of differentiated cooperation.

Acculturating Cooperation and Defining the Boundaries of Professionalism

By the monopoly stage of capitalism, the frontier ideology of an independent farmer as the cornerstone of democracy began to give way to the myth of individuals who cooperate in a newly corporatized American landscape. As giant corporations absorbed the independent farmer, there was an attendant change in ideology from individualism to differentiated cooperation. This culture of differentiated cooperation requires individuals to understand themselves as participating in and reaping the rewards of a democratic educational sphere even when they are divided among tiers that correlate to the reproduction of a rigidly classed society. Although cooperating, these individuals also compete with one another for occupational rank, social position, and economic reward. Because of the key role that competition plays within this cooperative system, the democratic ideals of hard work and individual achievement remain active at the same time that this new ideology of cooperation helps ensure that those previously independent farmers and other professionals transition into a new role as one component within a complex network of relationships.

Consequently, one of the crucial functions of higher education during this period was to reformulate the idea of professionalism from one of competitive individualism to one of cooperation, with competition determining one's position inside an increasingly intertwined and interdependent structure. Progressive educators worked to denaturalize the link between educational democracy and individualism in order to focus university curricula on cooperation and advanced research. Although they continued to argue for specialization, standardization, and clarity in higher education, educators also stressed the need for a program of study that benefited the national as well as the individual good. Published in 1936, Robert Hutchins's *Higher Learning in America* illustrates this position, arguing that the incorporation of individualized professional training along with advanced research confuses the university mission by overemphasizing the individual at the expense of the larger whole. Because he finds professions complicit with individual achievement rather than social good, Hutchins and other progressives wished to reform the professions to make them less individually focused. He points out that "at present we do not know why the university should have professional schools or what they should be like. We do not even know what the professions are. Professional education consists either of going through the motions we have inherited or of making gestures of varying degrees of wildness that we hope may be more effectual" (2). The problem with professional training, as Hutchins saw it, was that it was too individualized, unsystematic, and inconsistent to serve the collective good. Critiquing the belief that educational democracy necessarily equates to serving individualized practical skills, Hutchins believed that democracy was best served by creating coherent but differentiated social structures that required individuals to collaborate for the good of the whole society. He adamantly opposed professional schools that too often worked on behalf of students wishing to acquire job training particularized to disparate individual, local, and regional needs, and argued that these units be contained within the larger research university structure. Reorganizing professionalism as a system of social cooperation would benefit the whole nation rather than only specific sections of that nation, contended progressives like Hutchins.

This call for re-formation helped replace the culture of individualism with a culture of cooperation by thoroughly outlining the problems resulting from the individualizing notion of democracy. "The democratic view that the state may determine the amount of money to be spent on education and may regulate education and educators by law," argued Hutchins, "has nothing to do with the wholly undemocratic notion that citizens may tell educators how to conduct education" (21). Hutchins cites the myth of individualized democracy as central to the confusion surrounding higher education. He believed that such an idea supports a system in which "a student may stay in public education as long as he likes, may study what he likes, and may claim any degree whose alphabetical arrangement appeals to him. According to this notion, education should be immediately responsive to public opinion" (13). In this inverted democracy, he protested, every citizen can tell a university or a professor what should be done in higher education because every citizen entertains the belief that he or she is an expert. Reliance on the common person to run the university creates what Hutchins and other progressives called "an anti-intellectual university" (27). Aligning himself with a traditional notion of intellectualism as the painstaking pursuit of theoretical knowledge, he worried that "both the needs of the universities and the sentiments of the public conspire to degrade the universities into vocational schools" (31). Rather than autonomous leadership, the role of the individual in a reformed professional structure is to take his—or, less often, her—place in the larger social collective. An expansive democratic nation like the United States necessitates, according to this logic, that citizens work different jobs within a structured marketplace instead of as independent or regional experts. The independent American spirit must learn to position itself in relationship to others and within the highly organized mechanisms of society.

Repeating Richard Whately's early distinction between the truly scientific and merely vocational, Hutchins argues that without reorganization, universities will remain both poorly prepared to teach the "tricks of the trade" necessary for vocational training and unable to pursue the study of theoretical knowledge. The industrial era university, he believed, was ultimately inhibited by the dilemma of professionalism. Structured as specialized and individualized enterprises, professionalism separated research from other organizations and prevented them from engaging, interacting, or utilizing that research. The professional system further contained disciplinary research within the confines of a specific institution through a cycle whereby a professor trained his successor, allowing professional work to remain isolated and particularized according the most pressing hometown agendas. Hutchins argues, in fact, that "it is hardly an exaggeration to say that university departments exist to train people to teach in university departments" (36). His critique of this isolation appears more than defensible, but it is important to note that Hutchins's proposal would also inhibit independent research by making it cooperative in a particular sense, and thus accountable to, other specific social entities—most notably, the federal government and corporate America. As a consequence, research would be held in check by the powerful networks that make up the monopoly stage of capitalism, possibly limiting inquiry to areas of profitability.

Although professional culture did reform in order to take on more collective, nationally focused goals, it tended to become even more contained within discrete and differentiated occupational and university boundaries. This can be attributed to the fact that professional reform responded both to new market opportunities, made possible by industrialization and urbanization, and to the decline of community-based warrants on the boundaries of professionalism. Part of the early formation of professionalism, as we have seen, was the intellectual transition from local communities sanctioning knowledge to university certification of knowledge. Local interests initially remained central to these new university standards, but that connection wore thin during the monopoly stage as government and corporate sponsorship assumed increasing control over university standards. Rather than expanding the availability of advanced knowledge, the progressive transition into cooperation gave university leaders further control over the institutional marketplace and refocused knowledge around the collective goals defined by universities, corporations, and the government. This new collective knowledge was exchanged with more frequency among professional peers but primarily remained out of reach to the average citizen. What knowledge did become available was, of course, already processed through the academic network: credentialed experts informed the lay workers who informed the masses. In this way, Laurence Veysey argues, "knowledge was definitely conceived as trickling down, perhaps eventually watering the masses of the population beneath" (123). Contrary to the ideals of progressive reform, this revised professional structure only tightened its grip on knowledge production and relegated the public to a position of reception rather than participation.

Published in 1930, progressive thinker Abraham Flexner's second major study, *Universities, American, English, German,* democratizes this trickle-down theory. In this text, Flexner clarifies that while universities are democratic spaces open to any hardworking individual wishing to move up the social ladder, they are also accountable to national and corporate standards. Universities, therefore, should not be open to all who apply. Because "the number of students who seek to enter college is far in excess of the number that can be admitted," Flexner argues, entrance standards need to be more rigorous and more universally enforced (52). Strict entrance requirements for public research universities served the gatekeeping function necessary to preserve rigor at the highest echelon at the same time democracy guaranteed that every qualified student with interest and funds be able to enter. Democracy meant that students with lower scores and less money be accommodated at academic rungs below the research university level. Although student enrollment in higher education did increase during this period, the trickle-down system protected the sanctity of research universities as it filtered students who could not demonstrate sufficient academic qualifications into newly emerging community colleges, two-year colleges, and vocational colleges.[4] The displacement of these students from the larger public research universities reserved such universities for advanced research and for those students whose future work positioned them to deal with this research. This hierarchical structure allowed for continued isolation of university professional work from the interests of vast numbers of students, faculty members, and social organizations. The creation of a multitiered system of higher education was crucial to the educational market as it appealed to a wide cross-section of individual desire for postsecondary education and secured public endorsement for educational expenditures. Perhaps even more important, this diversification of higher education reinforced differentiated cooperation by firmly fixing the university as the premier site for research and creating other nonresearch spaces that contribute to the practical needs of professional job training rather than research.

Diversification, argued Hutchins and other progressives, would expand the applicability of university research beyond the interest of individual professionals and particular regional concerns. The early university had relied on isolated disciplinary professionalism; the monopoly era demanded that professionals reflect the needs of their profession as well as the needs of the nation-state and the international marketplace. One way to make the professions more responsive to market forces was to oppose the individualized structure that developed out of the industrial era. During the formative years of the university system, disciplinary professions emerged with their own conceptual basis, methodology, and object of study. Each became a distinct epistemic community wherein disciplinary peers, not the general public, functioned as the legitimate evaluators of intellectual work. Capitalizing on the key problematic of independent professions pursuing individual interests in isolation from corporate, social, or other disciplinary interests, progressive reformers were able to reconstruct the professional structure of higher education by emphasizing a culture of differentiated cooperation that worked on behalf of society without giving the public a full voice in the process. Professionalism changed to better correlate with the needs of a changing marketplace. Unfortunately, because the capitalist political economy subjugates all interests to the primary goal of producing profit, the university's democratic culture—whether expressed as individualism or cooperation—repeatedly asserts itself as addressing social issues while the discursive parameters for knowledge production and agency within the university system necessitates that social problems be articulated as opportunities for profit-making. The newly reformed cooperative system, in other words, was no more socially responsive than the earlier individualized structure.

The ideology of isolated individualism so abhorrent to scholars of this new era served its purpose in the industrial era. Under financial pressures and struggling for economic stability from year to year, late nineteenth-century universities attempted to increase revenues by enlarging the student population. One way to attract more students was to expand course offerings to accommodate the needs of a diverse public. Such diversification, as we have seen, set the stage for a new culture of individualism within the university system. The limits of this differentiated cooperation became clear at the end of the monopolistic period when university students protested the cultural content of higher education, demanding that the campus environment and the curriculum be opened up to issues of particular concern to women, blacks, Chicanos, and American Indians. Student protests challenged the professional ideal, but they did so through collective arguments that resonated with a firmly entrenched culture of cooperation. If this cultural emphasis accounted for their successes, then perhaps the economic and national interests of monopoly capitalism account for their failures. As universities made an ideological shift toward a culture of differentiated cooperation, they also refocused academic research, tightened entrance standards, and looked for supplemental income from federal and state budgets. Consequently, professionalism had to take national interests into account and thereby strengthened the link between nationalism and higher education.

Adapting Professional Cooperation to the National Political Agenda

Prior to the monopoly era, universities often maintained strong connections to their state constituencies as evidenced by the large percentage of state funding to those universities. In many places, the public research university was viewed as a permanent economic responsibility of the state budget. Indeed, "west of the Mississippi, where public institutions dominated, the states provided nearly half of all higher education funds from the 1920s to 1940s" (Cohen 163). As universities began to house the specialized knowledge necessary for continued national success, however, the federal government more closely aligned itself with the public research university. This articulation between the nation-state and the public research university was by no means insignificant. University-government cooperation produced the atomic bomb that effectively ended World War II; it also produced language and cultural research critical to economic and political struggles in the Asian political economic theater. Even though universities loosened their connections to the local community and the individual state, they never ceased to explore issues of social import through professional organizations. These organizations simply refocused from state interests to an ideal of national exceptionalism based on a culture of differentiated cooperation and forged by political victories as well as economic successes.

As the belief that the United States exemplifies the moral, cultural, political, and economic perfectibility of a true democracy, exceptionalism functions as one form in which the repeated discourse of U.S. democracy takes shape.[5] Dating from the Puritan migration to the New World, the rhetoric of exceptionalism appears and periodically repeats itself in order to justify new political policies, maintain social structures, and rally individuals around the belief that the United States is destined to be the world's unchallenged leader. Deborah L. Madsen, an American studies scholar, claims that "the power and longevity of exceptionalism as a key element in American cultural identity" can be traced through its widespread appeal and its repeated eruptions into national consciousness (146). Connecting exceptionalism to American identity suggests that each individual citizen—no matter one's occupation or political-economic position—participates in and deserves credit for the nation's high principles, economic growth, and vibrant democracy. Exceptionalism serves the ideological function of defining national memory, hedging off criticism, and justifying transitional policies that shape our sense of individual and collective selves. Closely related to the industrial period's primary reliance on the jeremiad, the monopolistic era preferred the rhetoric of exceptionalism, which tends to omit any reference to falling behind and simply pushes forward with the notion that we are fulfilling a predestined greatness.

Although a notion of exceptionalism has existed since at least the seventeenth century, it was not until the 1940s, when the United States solidified its position as a world political leader, that this concept became attached to the U.S. public research university. Not surprisingly, then, most scholars agree with Graham and Diamond's assertion that "the rise of American universities to a position of world prominence was not achieved until after World War II" (9). Because of back-to-back military victories and corporate mergers that created a substantial economic concentration, the United States emerged from World War II as the world's most politically influential debt-free nation. As a result of these corporate mergers, military victories, and the lack of official colonial satellites, the United States had a greater surplus of wealth and workers than England and other industrialized European nations. Thus, the federal government was uniquely positioned among its competitor nations to invest money in research that would help secure its geopolitical position. The U.S. government had proven itself as a leader but needed to maintain that status as it became embroiled in political and military disputes worldwide. Economically, politically, and ideologically, the 1940s provided the perfect opportunity for the U.S. government to pour federal dollars into research universities for the benefit of national scientific and technological studies as well as cultural and military research related to international policies.

As a result of political and economic convergence, the monopoly era witnessed a plethora of public legislation on higher education, including both well-publicized and well-hidden government funding of the bifurcated, though cooperative, projects of student professionalization and advanced research. As one of many organizations created at this time, the National Science Foundation (NSF) formed in 1950 with the goal of funding university research grants as well as graduate and postgraduate fellowships. Established with relatively little financial support, its annual budget exploded from $3.5 million to $75 million in the five-year period from 1952 to 1958. Federal research dollars in the sciences, including the NSF and other projects, continued to expand until these funds pinnacled in 1964 with a $1.25 billion national budget (Cohen 260). Overall, federal funding of academic research reached a peak between 1967 and 1968, toward the end of the monopoly period (Graham and Diamond 88). In addition to funding research, the federal government also created new opportunities for students to enter higher education, to professionalize themselves, and prepare for new occupations. In 1944, for instance, the federal government passed the Serviceman's Readjustment Act—often called the GI Bill—to aid returning veterans in the pursuit of higher education. With this influx of new and often less well-prepared students seeking higher education, the government supported alternative programs that matched the occupational interests of these students. In fact, the first President's Commission on Higher Education Report, issued in 1947, encouraged educational participation at the tertiary level by claiming that at least half of the nation's high school graduates could gain occupational skills through college or university attendance.[6] Students wished to acquire professional skills that would help them with their future careers while the federal government wanted an organ for international and military research. Both of these desires were fulfilled within the new university structure vis-à-vis a division of labor that organized and separated different educational tasks into cooperating components of an expanded national university system.

Because the federal government, corporations, and academicians all wanted universities free to explore a national research agenda, many scholars of higher education argued for the separation of vocational training from these universities even while maintaining such training as part of an enlarged system of higher education. In a noticeably different tone from his earlier arguments and on par with Hutchins, Abraham Flexner now advocated for a university system that was somehow aware of, but also above, the minutiae of everyday local activities. Flexner believed that the modern university, unlike its earlier predecessors, "must at times give society, not what society wants, but what it needs" (5). Within this elitist logic, university knowledge no longer needed to address the immediate social needs of particular communities. The impetus for sociohistoric or economic change was neither the individual person nor the individual corporation. On the contrary, the university must work to give "society" what it needs. The U.S. public research university, according to Flexner's argument, should provide the scientific underpinnings of the nation-state as it competed for worldwide political leadership. Good universities, he maintained, forged "contacts with the actual world and at the same time continue[d] to be irresponsible" to them (15). Flexner continued by stating that such universities should have "no premature or trivial vocational studies [that] confuse the pursuit of a liberal education" (64). Although

Flexner and other progressives tried to counter the trend of including practical knowledge within the public universities, such studies persisted because they were important to the national well-being. One essential value of vocational studies, it turned out, was their ability to absorb a dangerously enlarged workforce population without disturbing the progress of advanced university research.

The nation—argued Flexner and other like-minded policymakers—was ultimately best served by avoiding a recession and the possible social unrest that might occur if a flood of workers entered a job market unable to accommodate them. With a rapid rise in the working population and a decrease in traditional industrial jobs, political and corporate leaders were desperately looking for ways to avoid economic crisis. The federal government passed child labor laws during the 1930s that alleviated some of this surplus, but education was also critical to the swelling workforce. Higher education rapidly expanded in the 1920s and 1930s to include community colleges and two-year schools, which often redirected surplus labor away from the job market. With community colleges serving as an overflow mechanism, research institutions diversified and increased in scale even as they raised access standards. Cohen documents that "in the West and the Midwest, where public institutions were already strong, the institutions expanded by building branch campuses, converting specialized colleges to all-purpose institutions, and opening community colleges" (186–87). Of the 600 new public institutions founded at this time, fully 500 of them were community colleges. While two-year institutions provided affordable education for working-class students, the goal that such education would provide a stepping-stone to four-year institutions was often held back by their vocational focus. Vocational studies contained working-class students by isolating them from both the professional job market and an increasingly significant national research agenda (B. Clark; Karabel). In short, the stratified market of higher education and its diversification of professional work formed itself according to monopolist interests that needed to place surplus workers into higher education but did not need those numbers diluting the content of research at top universities.

Individual states also facilitated national research projects by reconstructing state systems to incorporate the newly diversified educational model and separating student-focused professional studies from the work of research itself. Political and business leaders developed state-level versions of monopoly policies for higher education, making sure to include diverse students at inconsequential levels of higher education while strategically consolidating research and professional training within flagship universities. Stratification in the university structure eased a surplus workforce by containing its overflow within branch campuses and community colleges at the same time that it maintained the intellectual integrity of the research university. Collectively, federal policy, state cooperation, and economic necessity facilitated the coordination and implementation of interinstitutional hierarchies such as the three-tiered system adopted by California or the large consolidation and subsequent hierarchical structure adopted by the State University of New York system. These state organizations, characterized by cooperation among universities and a division of mission meant to prevent research universities from acquiring too much of the vocational studies burden, were quickly repeated in other states nationwide, eventually leading to the influential Carnegie classification system. In order to highlight the many different opportunities available within university education and encourage students to take advantage of new nonresearch alternatives, the Carnegie Commission developed an institutional taxonomy of higher education in 1971 and published its first report in 1973. The Carnegie classification helped prevent vocational and professional studies from muddying the waters of university research by simply identifying the specialized work of each component. Individuals involved in nonresearch units during this period were happily identified with the exceptional quality of the U.S. public research university system and had no reason to encroach onto the territory reserved for research units. Thus, diversification within the university maintained the hegemony of research at the same time that it strategically distanced nonresearch work within a structured hierarchy. With vocational studies booming in community colleges and professional studies sequestered within their own units, the research component of universities became increasingly available as a vehicle for the political and economic needs of the nation-state.

Social science research, in particular, flourished as it provided insight into cultural formations and political strategies specific to various nation-states. Government- and corporate-sponsored area studies centers and international studies programs helped bring U.S. capitalism into new markets across the globe.[7] Because of their in-depth knowledge of the diverse social, political, and psychological structures within and among nation-states, area studies helped market U.S. capitalism within various parts of the globe by adapting its logic to the unique cultural fabric of each different country. With the explicit goal of developing economic or political cooperation between the United States and non-Western locations, area studies projects often accompanied large-scale investments in the infrastructure necessary to bring international markets the resources located in nonindustrialized countries. These government-funded intercultural projects were designed to help non-Westerners recognize changes within the industrial infrastructure as necessary to economic and political independence. Unlike language studies, area studies tended to focus on nation-states. While communist and potentially communist countries, such as the Soviet Union, the Slavic countries, China, and North Korea, were studied for defense purposes, the majority of research focused on economically reformable countries in the "Pacific Rim"—Japan, South Korea, South Vietnam, Taiwan, Indonesia, Hong Kong, Malaysia, Singapore, and the Philippines (Cumings 160–61). Thus, the university's role in promoting international capitalism rapidly expanded during the monopoly era specifically because of the theoretical and practical attention given to the cultural, political, and economic configurations of individual nation-states that occurred inside the doors of U.S. research universities.

Max Millikan and Walt Rostow's "Notes on Foreign Economic Policy," prepared in 1954 as a report to CIA director Allen Dulles, concretizes this link between academic knowledge and the historical expansion of U.S. capitalism. Simultaneously lobbying to expand U.S. knowledge overseas and to fund centers of scientific and social scientific research, Millikan and Rostow argued that "the role of *technical journals* in transferring technique should not be underrated: anything that can overcome the inability of underdeveloped countries to purchase such journals in large volume deserves strong support" (48–49). The funding of academic research as well as the dissemination of its conclusions is crucial, they say, because "scientists today, given time and money, can produce almost anything that society requests" (50). In the CIA's view, university researchers produce what the government wants and their academic journals are the crucial mechanism needed to similarly persuade others. The funding they were looking for was not difficult to find. It came from the usual sources: the federal government and corporate foundations. According to Bruce Cumings's short history, funding for "the major American centers of area and international studies research came precisely from the state/intelligence/foundation nexus that critics said it did" (173). Such a nexus, along with significant individual donations and endowments, historically has been the primary source of funding to higher education regardless of the institution, the program, or the specific project. The contemporary public university system would not be what it is today without substantial government, corporate, and military support. Certainly individual scholars had agency and maneuverability within these structures, but economic practicality demanded most fields follow the path established by national and corporate funds.

Cognizant of these financial connections, Cumings and others criticize the university's role in national politics at this time because they believe it limited the scope of academic research. However, Jacob Neusner and Noam Neusner, a father-and-son partnership, look back to the university during the cold war and call it "the golden age of intellect on campus" (20). They see the first ten years after World War II as a critical time during which the university was reformed as an institution to combat communist doctrine and to advance technology in this fight. Unfortunately, they argue, because this goal was accomplished, "universities today suffer a loss of vocation" (17). Nostalgic for a culture of cooperation, Neusner and Neusner understand the research university not only as a place for individuals to pursue their own vocations but as an institution striving to consolidate a national vocation wedded to corporate capitalism and sanctified by the democratic church.[8] The rhetoric of exceptionalism, deeply entrenched within the monopoly-era university's collective vocation, fueled national opposition to the communist enemy and garnered support for national policies meant to free the world for democracy. Whether a student was acquiring vocational training, studying to be a professional, or participating in research, that student was playing a part in enhancing national success. Contrary to Flexner's assertion, neither the nation-state nor the university can act indifferently to public consent. Students, individual professionals, corporations, and corporate foundations were all heavily involved in shaping the university during this period. An examination of the specific needs of U.S. corporations clarifies some of ways that the monopolistic economy continued to thrive under its democratic aura.

Professional Cooperation, Political Consent, and the Failure of Corporate Criticism

The U.S. public research university has never been independent of corporate influence, but neither has it been a mere extension of corporate power. Instead, the university operates within the always-evolving terrain of capitalism that includes the government, major corporations, and the public. Corporate shifts within the university must simultaneously complement the democratic goals of the nation-state and meet the needs of its populace. University-sponsored corporate research accomplished this by addressing the needs of workers as well as owners and attempting to improve capitalism for the supposed benefit of all participants. For instance, the university easily adapted its curricula during monopoly capitalism in order to include new academic departments organized, in part, to study capitalist relations of production. Braverman directs our attention to schools of industrial relations, college departments of sociology, and myriad academic disciplines devoted to studying worker psychology and behavior (96). He further points out that it was in the second decade of the twentieth century when "industrial psychology and industrial physiology came into existence to perfect methods of selection, training, and motivation of workers, and these were soon broadened into an attempted industrial sociology, the study of the workplace as a social system" (96). Applied psychology, physiology, sociology, and engineering all became part of U.S. universities in the early 1920s, but the failure of these programs to provide answers to the difficult question of workplace motivation led to the even more generalized studies of "human relations" in the 1930s (Braverman 96–100). Yet most of the corporate-sponsored research that Braverman catalogues came to its greatest fruition between World War II and the late 1960s, the same years that dissenting voices focused on university transgressions in the political and cultural spheres.[9]

The nation-state certainly supported as many programs and as much research as corporations did during this period, but a culture of differentiated cooperation expressed in sentiments of national exceptionalism tended to rewrite the federally funded educational agenda within a patriotic discourse. The growing and increasingly diverse education market as well as the fact that the federal government supported individual access to higher education situated this agenda within democratic principles. Structured as a supposed meritocracy with broad access, objective assessment, and national hierarchies, the university easily assumed this democratic positionality. When reality failed to live up to such an ideal, most individuals blamed the cultural and political spheres they had been taught to identify with the university. Consequently, many radicals and progressives had cultural and political battles to fight: free speech, antiwar, and civil rights protests dominated the oppositional landscape of universities. These battles had implicit economic concerns, but they primarily centered on changing curricula, influencing social consciousness, and ending the Vietnam War, all concerns that stemmed from their dominant critique of the cultural and political limitations in the university landscape. The corporate criticisms that emerged during the monopoly era came primarily from professional insiders: academics or other scholars who were either politically predisposed against capitalism or felt constrained by their own professional structure. From World War I through the 1950s many progressive and radical intellectuals located their criticisms of higher education within corporate sponsorship rather than the government that paid their salaries or the university that trained and hired them.

The negative emphasis on corporate involvement in the university was also partially a result of the government's conscious plan not to publicize its relationship to particular university projects. Government organizers of the first area studies project, for instance, specified that they were "not to be involved publicly in developing area studies [in order] to allay suspicions that such programs were little more than 'an intelligence agency'" (Cumings 164). The government's low profile had the inadvertent effect of fueling criticism in other areas of university administration, financing, and project-building. The many criticisms that arose ranged from the way the universities were organized and functioning to their role in what commonly was termed "corporate America" (170). The critiques against a corporatized university underpinning most of these other criticisms can be taken to task in two ways. First, most criticism tended to attack corporations as the ultimate source of university bureaucracy and corruption; second, they offered no tenable solution to the problem of corporate sponsorship. The failure of these analyses to do little more than highlight problematic relationships stems, I argue, from their inability to apply an historical materialist lens to the rhetorical situation of the U.S. research university. Ahistorical critiques often missed the complex intersections among the cultural, political, and economic spheres that contribute to the relationship between universities and corporations. Rather than offering an apologia for the corporatization of universities, I merely want to emphasize that this extensive history of criticism has yielded little substantial long-term change in university-corporate relations. Little productive change comes from scapegoating corporations as wholly responsible for a complexly constructed university with government funds and wide public support—even if that corporate role appears most significant, as it does in the global stage.

Monopoly-era critiques of the university-corporate bonds were trapped within a nostalgic discourse that positioned the ideal university as somehow outside of, above, or beyond the concerns of the historical materialist realities in which it operated. Even as the number of studies leveled against corporate participation in higher education rose during this period, their basic criticisms remained nearly identical to arguments raised in the industrial era. Several well-documented studies, for instance, accused universities of working for the benefit of big business and not for the benefit of students and scholars (Cattell; Hutchins; Sinclair). In addition to their own research, these scholars all cite the Nearing Case, as it was often called, as one of the most famous declarations against corporate ties to university governing boards.[10] Scott Nearing's 1917 study of the educational board members and college trustees precedes the beginning date of my periodization of monopoly capitalism by one year, but it is worth discussion because of its long-term resonance with these later critiques. Nearing was one of two thousand people prosecuted under the Espionage Act of 1917, later amended into the Sedition Act of 1918. These acts and the disciplining of university scholarship were directly linked to a perceived need for a unified public opinion during dangerous wartime environments.[11]

Fueled by his belief that corporate involvement in universities inhibited academic freedom, Nearing placed all board members into one of three groups (business, professional, and miscellaneous) in an effort to catalogue the occupations of those governing higher education. According to his categorization, Nearing discovered that over 80 percent of the university board members were either businessmen or professionals. Nearing also studied elementary and high school board members. In those schools, he argued, "almost nine-tenths of the total number of school-board members belong in the business and professional class" (297). He suggested that the saturation of corporate involvement at all levels of education naturalized university-corporate relations. "While the predominance of business and professional men on the boards of college and university trustees is not as complete as it is on the boards of directors of banks, railroads and manufacturing corporations," Nearing argued that "it is almost equally conclusive, since these groups control so large a working majority" (299). Outlining corporate involvement, his critique provides no realistic plan to create a more responsible university administration. Instead, Nearing calls for an extrication of corporate sponsorship from universities in an educational climate wedded to the extension of corporate power vis-à-vis international area studies and the scientific research of workplace relations.[12] As the nation, and by extension the university, moved toward one of the biggest corporate booms in its history, the idea that corporate affairs be quarantined from university work was well outside the rhetorical possibilities of appropriate and tenable arguments.

Nearing, of course, was not the only university critic of this period, just the one who received the most publicity. In 1922, shortly after Nearing's study was published, Upton Sinclair—best known for his muckraking of the corporate world in texts like *The Jungle*—turned his knack for disclosing corruption toward U.S. higher education. In a tone nostalgic for the earlier individualized culture, Sinclair's 1922 *Goose-Step: A Study of American Education* critiques this new cooperative ideal in his radical diatribe against the corporate sponsorship of land-grant universities.[13]

After spending a year gathering research from universities across the nation, Sinclair concluded that "our educational system is not a public service, but an instrument of special privilege; its purpose is not to further the welfare of mankind, but merely to keep America capitalist" (18). Sinclair names major corporations, like the railroad conglomerates he relied on to transport himself from school to school, as inextricably tied to university education. From his research, he discovered that some university board members also sat on the boards of railroad companies and that several universities invested portions of their endowments into these railroads. He claimed, therefore, that each railroad was partially owned by various universities and consequently the responsibility of those institutions. In a parodic tone, he indicates this responsibility by naming universities after the railroad companies they sponsor—the Union Pacific University or the Southern Pacific University, for instance. But rather than working on behalf of any particular individual, corporation, or interest group, universities, Sinclair emphasizes, worked on behalf of American capitalism in general. It was this larger relationship between universities and capitalism that had to be terminated.

Sinclair cannot be accused of nostalgia for a past ideal, but he does fall victim to a utopian dream—a ubiquitous flaw among many socialist-minded thinkers. Sinclair believed that social upheaval was imminent and that history would simply force a change in university structures. But, he argues, if he had his way, "the trustees and the presidents should of course be laid on the shelf, for these are administrative officials, and properly removable when a change of policy is desired" (474). While his administrative housekeeping would clear out deans, directors, and department chairs up through the ranks to the university president, he would retain all professors—regardless of their political beliefs—in the name of academic freedom. The caveat was that all professors would be persuaded to teach an anticapitalist "truth" via mandatory open forums; apparently, Sinclair did not see the rhetorical bind of mandating "open forums." Even though he offers a practical solution that might aid the transition from a capitalist to a socialist political economy, the problem with this ideal, as with other more nostalgic views, is that it isolated the university from the larger political and economic infrastructure of the nation-state. Constructing the future of the university in this political economic vacuum,

Sinclair can be accused of suffering from a kind of nostalgia for a post-capitalist future rather than for an ideal past. For instance, he assumes that consensus is both possible and desirable within the university, denying the various and complex factors that impinge upon academic production. Because the U.S. public research university was constructed in collaboration with the culture of community-building, the politics of national competition, and the needs of industrial capitalism, and because corporations play a significant role in that relationship as well as its future configuration, undermining their significance in the university requires either changing the entire historical materialist landscape or altering the function of the university. Both projects necessitate structural transformation that would begin, for instance, by severing the university's relationship to professionalization and with it the U.S. public research university's primary reason for existing.

Regardless of these anticorporate critiques, corporate money continued to fund and support university research. Indeed, Hutchins asked his readers in 1936 to "think where research in any meaning of the word would be if it had not been for Rockefeller, Carnegie, and Harkness fortunes. The spirit of the age is not congenial to long-term, quiet investigations of matters remote from daily life. . . . Everybody wants the university to advance his special brand of propaganda, to join his private pressure group" (43). Hutchins acknowledges and applauds the modern university's collaboration with corporate interests as compatible with the national zeitgeist for progress, efficiency, and global leadership. Without this relationship, he supposes the nation would drift from modern affairs and retreat into the past. Clearly nostalgic for an earlier ideal, Hutchins argues for a return to the study of metaphysics—the principles on which Western higher education was founded.[14] The idea of a "return" to the study of first principles glorifies a past curriculum that would be impractical in his complex historical moment. The overlapping spheres of cultural consumption, national patriotism, and corporate production bleed into and reinforce one another to such an extent during the monopoly period that it becomes impossible to isolate any sphere from the others. The corporate economy permeates cultural understandings as well as political policies—there is no simple retreat from this structure.

Although these authors and others like them helped raise the volume on corporate dissent, they ultimately failed to initiate substantial changes in the relationship between corporations and universities. Instead, the university further adopted the corporate structure. Toward the end of the monopoly period, the professionals contained within the metaphoric ivory tower became subject to the same economic restructuring that other workers experienced. As early as the 1950s, public universities felt it necessary to significantly alter their institutional structure in order to compete against more prestigious private universities. They did this by dramatically increasing student admissions, increasing class size along with lecture hall capacity, and shifting instructional costs downward. As both federal and state funding for general education began to decrease in the 1950s and 1960s, universities increased part-time labor in an effort to be more fiscally competitive. Applied research rose, nonprofit contributions declined, and an increased effort to monitor the usefulness of research results grew. Because these structural changes rapidly accelerated in the late 1960s and 1970s, Graham and Diamond call the decade between 1968 and 1978 "the age of adjustment" (84). This adjustment, according to my rough periodization, marks the transition between the university of monopoly capitalism and the university of global capitalism.

A differentiated structure, shifts in funding from the state to the federal government, the use of graduate student teaching, and changes in educational accountability all combined to propel the university into its contemporary global stage. Christopher Simpson reinforces this claim by arguing, for instance, that "university-based development studies and overlapping projects at area studies centers in the United States, both predicted and required the worldwide triumph of modernity and contemporary forms of global capitalism" (xiv). The ideological triumph of capitalism signified by U.S. economic, political, and military success laid the foundations for area studies at the same time that such research contributed to the international extension of capitalism. Historically, both the capitalist political economy and the U.S. public research university have evolved through a corporate industrial stage (coterminous with the emergence of the U.S. research university), a corporate monopoly stage (coterminous with the expansion of the U.S. research university between World War I and the early 1970s), and are now part of a new global stage. The corporate-university relationship has acquired various forms and raised different oppositions throughout these political economic periods, but the basic relationship has always persisted. Thus, the latest form of global capitalism continues to influence, though certainly does not determine, the changes currently taking place within the U.S. public research university.

Bearing the Weight of History:
Globalization and the University, 1973–Present

Conservative and liberal critics often valorize globalization within our burgeoning technological age as the latest democratizing effort or as the triumph of the capitalist market. Indeed, globalization has brought disparate people and cultures closer together through telecommunications and advanced transportation systems. Students regularly move between national boundaries in educational exchange programs and scholars share research much more readily with the aid of advanced technology. These changes have even spawned a global education movement to standardize curriculum internationally.[15] No doubt there are many new challenges and exciting opportunities for academicians to work outside the local and national boundaries that have historically defined their scholarly commitments. However, globalization encompasses more than shrinking political boundaries, greater cultural understanding, and an improved network for academic communication. As the newest stage of capitalism, globalization has important economic ramifications. Unregulated trade, flexible labor, proletarianization of the professional classes, and advanced digital communication characterize economic globalization and significantly affect the structure of the U.S. public research university. Sheila Slaughter and Larry L. Leslie, in *Academic Capitalism* for instance, find that global economic patterns destabilize traditional notions of professional work. Professional work, they argue, previously served the public good by providing a gateway to social mobility and producing research for the betterment of society. They believe that academic capitalism—the university's participation in the market and use of market-like practices—has overwhelmed this professional project and reinvented the university as a more rigidly capitalist institution.

As we have seen, professionalized faculty in public research universities have collaborated directly and indirectly with the market economy without seeing themselves as participants in that marketplace. Thus, it is not surprising that faculty do not recognize current changes within the university structure as shifts or transitions but see only that structure crumbling apart. Against this nostalgic view of the past, I contend that cultural, political, and economic changes are all reshaping and re-professionalizing university faculty and not simply deprofessionalizing them. Faculty mistakenly think their previously pristine intellectual work is becoming deprofessionalized simply because a shift into the global political economy positions university relationships in new light, taking the formerly implicit and making it explicit. The public research university system has always been crucial to the market, but its cultural role in the industrial era and its political role in the monopoly era helped obscure this fundamental relationship; on the other hand, in the global era, the onus of this tripartite constitution falls primarily on the economic realm, illuminating the university-capitalist link. The liberal arts offers a vivid example of this move from the taken-for-granted relationship between the humanities and the capitalist political economy in the industrial and monopoly eras toward the more visible and thus more accountable role in the global era.

The primary function of the liberal arts has always been to humanize and acculturate students as departments often focus on the transcendence of material reality through the discursive realms. Canonical literature taught in English departments offered time away from the practical pursuits of business and science, ensuring that the university experience was about more than just learning a trade. Within the global university structure, however, these same professors are forced to account for the utility of their disciplinary work—often through a numerical measurement process that explicitly asks how specific educational practices will transfer to the students' future job performance. Humanities and social science departments in today's university structure are straddled with statewide assessment mechanisms as well as the increasing demand for more practical courses—technical and business writing courses, art courses in corporate identity and Web page design, speech communication courses in the rhetoric of international business, and Spanish for the workplace, among others. Although contemporary faculty are more often confronted with their complicity in the marketplace, the argument that globalization has created a fundamentally new relationship between the university and capitalism suffers from historical amnesia. Even though corporate and state economics have always been part of the university mission, contemporary scholarship suggests that, like the professional-managerial class that emerged in the late nineteenth century, a new university class seems to be developing.

This new class can be called "post-professional" in the sense that its participants pledge loyalty and self-sacrifice to projects forged and solidified in the industrial and monopoly eras even as they assume a decisively new role in the relations of production. This emerging class is post-professional because it bears the weight of professionalism's complex history at the same time that it moves beyond that history, as the example of practical courses in the humanities suggests. As a class, these new academics speak like professionals, attend professional conferences, and publish in professional journals. But many have little or no job security, lack autonomy, teach and research according to university-imposed agendas, comply with relentless assessment procedures, and receive less financial compensation. Admittedly, all of this is simply a variation on the old professional class. If the professional class has always been in bed with the corporate world, they are simply more deeply entrenched now. What is new is the relationship of post-professionalism to the production process. A more in-depth analysis of how the U.S. public research university functions differently within the capitalist relations of production will be taken up in the next chapter, but I want to emphasize that this university class both builds on earlier university relations and exists in a qualitatively new association with global capitalism. To that end, this section provides an overview of the university's contemporary historical materialist terrain as characterized by a culture of accountability, a political structure that facilitates the U.S. educational model overseas, and an economy of increased privatization.

Accountability, Multiculturalism, and the Loss of Professional Innocence

Many professionals and professional organizations have spoken out against the consequences of globalization for the public university system, yet there is certainly reason to suspect that the ideology of professionalism itself prevents faculty from being a resistant group on campus. Some theorists believe that the idea of professionalism has eroded in recent years—the proletarianization of the professional class thesis. Others believe that rather than eroding a previously protected positionality, the contemporary university has lifted the veil off professionalism, revealing its ties to the global marketplace. Without this professional cloak, one might logically forecast, as Morton Wenger does, that faculty will search for "alternative forms of occupational organization" (95). But instead of forging organizations oppositional to a privatized university, the majority of professionals participate in some kind of university-marketplace relationship even as they sometimes claim a professional identity apart from the questionable ethics of the commercial realm. More often than not, the reaction to this changing professional structure is one of adaptation. In this bifurcated university culture, faculty can criticize the representation of education as a commodity or the representation of students as consumers at the same time that they transition from intellectuals and teachers into entrepreneurs and service workers.[16] Professors write on-line software, televise lectures, market popular books, compete for corporate grant money, and develop community service projects. They do all of this in addition to their regular research, teaching, and service commitments. These transformations should not be shocking in an environment where administrators work as sophisticated fund-raisers and university presidents welcome the title of chief executive officer. In fact, university presidents are increasingly certified in the business world rather than credentialed in scholarship. The University of Colorado at Boulder's recently appointed president offers a case in point. Holding a bachelor's degree in accounting and a master's degree in law, he earned his stripes as the CEO of the Daniels Fund in addition to being a state and national legislator.

Despite these changing identities, many faculty continue to see the global economy as a shackle that can be removed to allow full professional mobility. They do not yet accept, and consequently they do not take responsibility for, the complex historical relationship between university professionals and the evolving capitalist political economy. Stanley Aronowitz summarizes this faculty position clearly: "culturally, they have introjected the values of their discipline; strategically, they tend to behave as the institution wants, and given their profound professional identification, they can never articulate these affiliations as forms of subordination" (94).[17] Departments define professional culture even though it is otherwise confined by the overall university structure, and faculty negotiate these power relations without sensing themselves subject to the university's ultimate authority. He goes on to say that faculty are so dedicated to their own disciplines that they are often unwilling to entertain new professional approaches that might entail radically rethinking their hard-won professional and intellectual status. If the ideology of professionalism has been thoroughly demythologized, faculty still cling to it, unwilling to give up a title so central to their collective sense of self. Although Aronowitz aptly identifies the problems with professional identity, he fails to offer tenable solutions. Trapped within his own idealism, he suggests that faculty and students reclaim their authority as the official university governing body. Not only does this suggest that students and faculty are the authentic and natural administrators of the university, it falls victim to the same criticisms that others received nearly a century ago: students and faculty do not have the time, the resources, or the knowledge to adequately administer the university in addition to all their other duties. Far from negotiating a space for student and faculty administration, public higher education has predominantly been modeled on corporate structures of accountability.

While the concept of university accountability expanded greatly during the monopoly stage of capitalism, the bureaucratization of that structural change has come into its greatest fruition during the global stage of capitalism. As budgets get pinched, the need to justify one's expenses as well as one's existence in the university becomes even more crucial. Not only does this relentless assessment provide the most important argument for one's place in the university, it also defers institutional criticism. The practice of increased accountability, a touchstone of the global marketplace, prevents the university from becoming too far removed from standard social beliefs because it forces units to comply with external, often commercialized standards in order to sustain themselves. To some degree this accountability demystifies academic work by making it available for quick reference by legislators, taxpayers, and individual donors. But such surveillance serves as a double-edged sword. If some research does not fit easily into the assessment criteria or if it is summarily dismissed as impractical, inappropriate, or questionable based merely on a single numerical criterion, important research could be eliminated for no other reason than its cutting-edge approach or its minority perspective. When this assessment comes from individuals without specialized expertise and is based solely on the economic bottom line, universities subscribe to the rational choice logic characteristic of the liberal free market ideology that dominates the global economy.

Academics are rightly leery of increased accountability because such assessment too often relies on a nonintellectual performance gauge. For instance, universities frequently incorporate team-oriented corporate practices such as total quality management (TQM) that rely on performance indicators "to assess and measure individuals, departments, and universities against each other by the practice of benchmarking" (Currie 4). Such systems are apparent in university rankings, Web sites evaluating professors, and end-of-the-semester course evaluation forms. TQM refocuses attention away from the opposition between management and workers, opting instead to concentrate on customer satisfaction. To the extent that faculty members succeed as professionals within this framework, they erase the class tensions embedded within their own employment structure. Faculty employees simply become team members who work together to achieve the best customer satisfaction possible. According to this logic, customers—students, that is—become the ultimate measure for most university units, inverting their role from novice into expert. While this might seem like a perfectly acceptable practice of giving students what they want, it is important to remember that students' desires originate, in part, within the marketplace. Faculty and administrators who give students what they want cannot claim to be innocent of market agendas.[18] Unable to maintain their position outside the market, professionals utilizing this team approach render traditional power relationships more ambiguous and help make corporate logic the reigning ethos of the university.

Because every unit is quantified according to how well it achieves customer satisfaction, all units become further measured by the corporate logic of profitability. Economic productivity becomes a significant determination of value. All units must make money or at least further the mission of helping both the students and the local community make money. Economic growth, of course, is not intrinsically problematic. But when the administration monitors course enrollments, degree production, and Ph.D. placement according to strict numerical criteria, it denies that education has any value outside the profit motive. Constantly promoting itself in terms of numerical accountability, the university administration has developed into the means by which the university teaching machine runs smoothly: it organizes fund-raising, solicits corporate sponsorship, files patents, manages crises such as the Ward Churchill witch hunt, and always puts forth a professional image within the local, national, and global cultural spheres. If the university administration's primary job is to raise money and manage crises rather than to ensure quality education, it is no wonder that a rhetoric emphasizing economic growth as well as individual and market freedom supports this educational era. As Spivak contends, people return to such rhetorical catchalls in order to garner popular support for transitions that disrupt the status quo and restructure social relationships. The theme of economic accountability works so well in the U.S. public research university because it pervades the national culture and supposedly invokes all individuals equally. Just as the university measures its goals by an economic yardstick, so do its students. Both reflecting and precipitating this culture of accountability, students see themselves as consumers of an educational product. The test of that education is the job and the salary it will produce. Annual surveys asking students, among other things, how much they value economic success demonstrate that students are increasingly focused on becoming financially well-off. Even though students have always seen higher education as an avenue to better job opportunities, the number of students who rated financial success as a "very important" goal rose from less than 40 percent in 1970 to almost 75 percent in 1990 (Dey, Astin, and Korn 122–23). Students enrolled in U.S. public research universities, like their fellow global citizens, work from the economic bottom line: What is this course costing me and how much money will I make with this degree?

But as citizens of the world, these students expect a broadly multicultural university experience representative of the many diverse locales brought together from around the globe. As the university increases its participation in the global economy, therefore, its nationally based cultural model necessarily incorporates a wider range of multicultural experiences. Implying that culture solidifies the relationship between universities and the economy, Masao Miyoshi argues that "multiculturalism is the urgent issue both of pedagogy and political economy in the university in the United States" ("Ivory Tower in Escrow" 43). He goes on to critique the fact that "multiculturalism, an expression of liberal open-mindedness and progressive tolerance, much too often stands in for an alibi to exonerate the existing privileges, inequalities, and class differences" (44). According to Miyoshi, multiculturalism creates a league of the elite in all regions of the world who share a common, though diverse, cultural repertoire. While ostensibly unlimited, multiculturalism includes cultural forms from different ruling classes but does not provide a mechanism for understanding the power relationship between those cultures nor for understanding what cultures are omitted from this brand of multiculturalism. Global citizens of contemporary capitalism earn their rights through the common cultural, political, and economic experiences simultaneously taking place within highly industrialized cities worldwide. The half of the world's population residing outside urban centers, often in poor rural spaces, likely cannot begin to conceive of such global citizenship nor are their concerns seriously taken into account in the dominant version of multiculturalism.

In this multicultural environment, different ideas are welcomed and accepted as potentially useful even though all ideas are often not seriously entertained beyond open discussion. Criticisms, for instance, are "repossessed by converting disagreement into preagreement, and opposition into diversity" (Miyoshi, "Sites of Resistance" 59). One example of this can be taken from the United Students Against Sweatshops organization at campuses across the nation. This student organization opposes university contracts with corporations that rely heavily on overseas labor in countries with low wages and unregulated labor. For these students, economic globalization lies at the heart of the university's relationship to sweatshops. The university, they argue, enables economic globalization by renewing contracts with the transnational corporations relying on this labor structure. Presidents of various universities repeatedly engage these criticisms by stating that the university wants the same thing as the students but that it simply has chosen another method of proceeding. They wish to work through the global channels that the students oppose such as the Fair Labor Association, which is a corporate-sponsored system of monitoring labor practices. University students want to stop what they believe to be widespread corporate exploitation while university administrations want to manage the contradiction between the human rights advocated by students and the most egregious corporate exploitation they believe to be representative of a few bad apples. Although the students and the university administrations have opposite goals for economic globalization, university administrators stealthily elide this disagreement by incorporating United Students Against Sweatshops into the university team of experts. United Students Against Sweatshops is given a voice as part of the university's multicultural pledge, but that voice is rendered impotent by ignoring its fundamental opposition to the university's goals. This strategy simultaneously maintains the appearance of inclusivity and prevents the exploration of conflicting ideological foundations.

The United Students Against Sweatshops represents a particular manifestation of the multicultural trend in university education, but it is not a unique example. The move toward multiculturalism stems from a global economy that markets cultural difference and regulates international trade. The current stage of global capitalism relies on a multicultural ideal in order to increase the profitability of transnational corporations. Globalization appropriates rather than promotes difference, passing an expanded marketplace off as openness. According to this theory, the university's engagement with the United Students Against Sweatshops has repackaged potential opposition into a sign of tolerance for diverse opinions, once again managing the teaching machine. Contrary to the consensus and cooperation promoted by multiculturalism, the culture of globalization needs to be exposed for its ultimate exclusivity and we need to "resuscitate the idea of opposition and resistance" (Miyoshi, "Sites of Resistance" 62). In the university, Miyoshi believes, we can exploit our inclusion at the academic table by challenging the larger house in which we are situated. This would require students, faculty, and administrators to challenge the culture of professionalism, but it would also require them to interrogate the relationship between global political organizations and the university. We need to speak, certainly, but we must also find ways for our voices to be heard. We need mechanisms for making those supposedly listening to our academic voices accountable to their responses and, more often, lack of responses.

From the National to the Supranational:
The Politics of Professional Globalization

Attending to the needs of global capitalism, the federal government has recently reduced its funding to universities, added more stringent specifications of how money should be spent, and passed legislation that privileges the corporate-university relationship. The federal government shifted its financial support toward individuals rather than institutions in the early 1970s at which time funding for research substantially declined and what funding remained went to student aid (Cohen 259; Graham and Diamond 89). This form of support, later developed into Pell Grants, functioned as a voucher system. Students were granted funds and were able to apply those funds to the most competitive university. Universities, in turn, could raise tuition as a method for acquiring as much of these funds as possible. This plan worked fairly well until the federal grants no longer kept pace with increased tuition. The disparity between grants to students and tuition costs became glaring in the 1980s when the government narrowed the scope of its grants and encouraged students to take out loans. The idea of student loans obviously reinforced the dual notions that education is an investment in a student's marketability and that knowledge should respond to corporate needs. Moreover, it offers a guaranteed lucrative business for banks and other lending agencies that make a significant profit off the transaction fees and interests rates.[19] To many students, educational loans are nothing more than an advance on their future salaries. If loans are high, as they often are, students demand correspondingly high future salaries and therefore funnel themselves into particularly high-paying jobs. With the high cost of student loans, the pursuit of socially and personally rewarding, but low-paying, work has become a financially impossible choice for many. Whether purposefully or not the political structure in the era of globalization overwhelmingly facilitates the relationship between corporations and higher education.

One of the most important ways the federal government has enabled the university-corporate relationship is through legislation. The critical 1980 Bayh-Dole Act, which allows universities and university professors to patent federally funded discoveries, demonstrates this well. Prior to this act, public universities filed fewer than 250 patent applications per year. In the 1997 fiscal year, universities filed for 2,740 patents (Miyoshi, "Ivory Tower in Escrow" 25). In 2003, universities were issued 3,450 patents and received nearly $1 billion in licensing revenue (Blumenstyk A27). This legislation not only encourages universities to file for patents, it also pushes university professionals to pursue work that results in corporate monopolies on knowledge as research developed in public universities turns into corporate products that often exclude large segments of the public. A patent, representing the conversion of knowledge into intellectual property, means the exclusion of others from sharing that knowledge. Not only can the public not use this information, other companies cannot produce commodities with this knowledge, artificially raising the cost of goods and creating a rather *unfree* marketplace. The government-facilitated link between universities and corporations turns universities into industry leaders that transfer technical knowledge from public hands to private hands. And as these private hands increasingly belong to transnational corporations, this transfer affects individuals all over the world. Positioned on the West Coast and adjacent to the all-important Asian market, the University of California system has become a world leader in industries dependent on specialized knowledges such as biotechnology and pharmaceuticals. In the fiscal year 2003, the University of California system filed and received more patents, formed more start-up companies, and spent more research dollars than any other university system (Blumenstyk A29). Representing the transition from the monopoly era into the global era, the University of California illustrates a shift in focus from national defense and area studies to international finance, biotechnology, and pharmaceuticals. However important the pharmaceutical and biotech industries have become, the military-industrial complex has not been erased nor fully superseded. Indeed, the military's presence in public generally, and on public universities in particular, has burgeoned since September 11, indicating the ongoing need to couple capitalism with strong military protection.

The military-industrial complex, in fact, has been central to the growth of technology-based distance learning. Universities have incorporated on-line learning as a means of reaching more students and utilizing fewer instructors. Although on-line learning is often associated with for-profit universities like the University of Phoenix, these learning environments were pioneered by public universities and only later taken over by for-profit institutions that could utilize the new technology more efficiently and increase profitability. Notable examples of public universities' on-line learning environments include the California Virtual University (CVU), Western Governors University, Penn State University's "World Campus," and Florida State University. The demand for distance education, however, has not lived up to its expected enrollments and profitability. Expensive start-up costs, low enrollment, and a general uneasiness about the economy of high technology have all contributed major stumbling blocks to public education's move into distance learning. Fortunately, says David Noble in "The Future of the Faculty in the Digital Diploma Mill," the government has stepped in to help subsidize this project. The U.S. armed services "decided to dedicate almost $1 billion to provide taxpayer-subsidized university-based distance education for active-duty personnel and their families" (29). Noble worries that such military investment will fuel further technology-based higher education and contribute to professional deskilling in the same way that Taylorism deskilled manual labors. He concludes, in a highly pessimistic tone, that the U.S. government is "now underwriting a radical restructuring of the higher education industry, at the expense of the professoriate" (29). While no restructuring will completely deskill the university-based professionals, Noble is certainly correct to register caution. As part of the professional restructuring of higher education, on-line learning environments utilize new and increasingly rigid technological formats to which individual pedagogical styles must conform. Blackboard, one of the more popular prepackaged courseware formats currently available, allows students and faculty to alter insignificant aspects of the site like color choices, but does not allow them to alter teaching and assessment structures that rely on quantifiable tests and quizzes rather than open-ended, problem-solving, or explorative assignments.[20]

Rather than signaling the demise of professionalism, such a trend seems to be in line with the historical function of the university. Utilizing on-line resources combines the professional role with the latest technical skills needed to support the global capitalist structure, helps prepare students to work in that economy, and maintains the link between the university and the marketplace. Just as industrial capitalism bred the professional-managerial class, the infrastructure of the global economy—digitalized production, telecommunications, and the growth of culture industries—depends on a new breed of university professionals for its continued innovation and maintenance. While the federal government continues to serve a critical role in higher education by legislating and funding this kind of university-based training, it is increasingly willing to share or defer that role with corporations or other nongovernmental organizations. As a major institution of corporate production, U.S. research universities must move, adapt, and expand to the scale, scope, and needs of capitalism. Global capitalism requires movement overseas and alignment with international laws and trade regulations. Consequently, supranational organizations, trade agreements, and international finance reinforce the U.S. public research university system as the globally dominant model. The global stage of capitalism, that is, encourages the internationalization of the well-matured U.S. public research university system.

Because the U.S. public research university has successfully forged a unique tripartite relationship among universities, the government, and corporations, it provides the obvious example for the rest of the global economy to emulate. Indeed, this is already happening in many of the most industrialized nation-states. According to Slaughter and Leslie, for instance, the last twenty years have created "a remarkable degree of convergence in higher education and R&D policy" among Australia, the United Kingdom, and the United States (61). While this struggle between convergence and independence certainly results from the global economy and interdependence of nations, it is also, at least partially, the result of advice disseminated from supranational organizations like the World Bank and the Organization for Economic Cooperation and Development (OECD). Acquiring some of the dominance of the nationally focused philanthropic organizations, these organizations have been providing education advice since the early 1960s. Both organizations' many publications on university education tend to support a model of higher education based on the U.S. public research university system. The World Bank's 1994 *Higher Education: The Lessons of Experience* advises nation-states to shift university dependence from the state onto multiple private sources, especially individuals in the form of higher student fees and corporations in the form of donations and research contracts. A homegrown practice in U.S. public research universities, this funding strategy is foreign to other national cultures. In similar ways, agreements like the North American Free Trade Agreement (NAFTA), the General Agreement on Trade and Tariffs (GATT), and the European Community (EC) all represent international legislation that sets economic agendas dependent upon national educational institutions restructuring to fit into a model created by the U.S. public research university.[21] The use of these supranational organizations to extend the model developed by the U.S. public research university into other nations stems, primarily, from the economic imperatives of the transnational corporations. Expanding training facilities worldwide allows corporations to work in cheap labor markets while maintaining the professional expertise needed in the so-called information age.

Corporatized Professionalism and the Consequences of Academic Capitalism

Although many academics criticize the increasing corporatization of the university, both national and international policy promote this aspect of higher education, setting it up as an example for other nation-states to follow. Roger Noll, editor of the Brookings Institute's *Challenges to Research Universities,* states that "a frequent complaint about university education in other countries is that it does not adequately prepare students for jobs as technologists in private industry because it is too theoretical" (11). In the United States, however, this is not a problem. Federal support for fundamental research is diversified among the leading research universities, both public and private, as well as industrial parks, think tanks, and government organizations so that research follows the same competitive logic as any other industry. Noll's study suggests that two notable qualities of the U.S. public research university—its partnerships with the government and the corporate world—make it a model for other nation-states to follow (16). The idea of the university as an arm of corporate and government interests has become naturalized in the U.S. public university system over its more than 150-year history. That such partnerships serve national economic and security issues goes without saying. But what Noll does not add in this endorsement is that these qualities have conflated social good with the profit incentive and turned supposedly autonomous professionals into major corporate players.

The economic restructuring of the university has led to what is by now a familiar, and at times even naturalized, labor structure where underpaid part-time adjuncts and graduate students replace full-time faculty members, where corporate sponsorship replaces government support, and where students, faculty, and administrators adopt market-like roles. Richard Ohmann explains that in this new economic structure, state and federal funding have been reduced "from roughly half of [public universities'] budgets in the early 1970s to less than a third" (9). At the same time, and as a consequence, "part-timers doubl[ed] from 1970 to the 1990s as a percentage of the workforce; [and] full-time, tenure-track hires amount[ed] to only about one-third of all hires" (7). These numbers will shock no one familiar with the university: faculty know how precarious the system is and students know that access to a tenure-track professor often requires pushing past graduate students, postdoctorates, and other temporary faculty. This professional hierarchy keeps instructional and research costs low at the same time it keeps tenure-track faculty free to pursue their research agendas. This system of adjunct and part-time labor was once considered temporary, but it is now structurally integral to the contemporary university.

This is not to say that part-time employees are underpaid because professors are overpaid. On the contrary, with the exception of a few "stars," most professors take home fairly modest pay in comparison to other professionals. Derek Bok in *The Cost of Talent* states that professorial salaries, in relationship to other occupations, peaked in 1973 and hit a low in 1981. During the 1970s and 1980s, professorial salaries could not even keep pace with the rate of inflation (54). Apparently true of lawyers and doctors, this trend hits faculty especially hard. In the humanities, faculty often go through years of school, acquire substantial student loan debt, and, if they are lucky, earn salaries that keep them living just a notch better than when they were struggling students. This predicament, certainly not unique to humanities professors, was not lost on students whose interest in business-related careers soared during the 1970s and 1980s. During that period, for instance, "the proportion of all undergraduates majoring in management climbed from 13.6 percent to almost 25 percent" (Bok 45). Just as the global university reshapes faculty professionalism, it also reshapes the brand of professionalism that students wish to acquire. The high cost of education coupled with a university structure that privileges high-tech job training encourage students to seek high-paying professional jobs.

Structured to support corporations, universities, partially supported by the state and federal governments, nevertheless absorb all the risk while private corporations and a limited number of individuals acquire most of the benefits. When corporations provide university faculty with grant money, those funds do not cover the entire cost of a project. Faculty salaries are usually covered by the individual's home institution, most of the costly equipment already exists in good research labs, and corporate grants are often matched with state money as an incentive to seek such grants. State and federal tax dollars subsidize enormous start-up costs that help generate university inventions subsequently licensed or contracted to commercial developers. Furthermore, corporate contracts to university research labs often result in the migration of university professors—especially those in the sciences—into business and industry (Slaughter and Leslie 132). Through their research, professors come into contact with a corporate sector that offers significantly higher salaries and better benefits than do universities. This professional movement out of the university is even greater for the graduate students who are highly concentrated in these labs. Through this informal employment structure, corporations can help determine the professionalization of future employees and elide some of the costly and time-consuming aspects of the hiring and training processes. At the same time, they retain the highly specialized knowledge and skills of veteran professors on an as-needed contractual basis. Although this may seem like a win-win system, such enthusiasm should be tempered by the knowledge that complicity in the larger global political economy means participation in a system in which there are many who lose. This system minimizes the time and resources available for open-ended research, drains university labor, and generally ignores questions of social, political, and economic inequities.

Nostalgia and the One-Dimensional Evaluation of University Education

Contemporary scholarship too often fails to include historical materialism among its methods for studying the university. Subsequently, as the corporatization of U.S. public research universities becomes almost impossible to deny, the common response from many academics, especially in the humanities, has been a superior and indignant stand against the contamination of the professional ideal by tainted corporate interests. Though it is certainly tempting to assume that recent discussion over how universities function in service to global capitalism stems from a fundamental change in the university's relationship to society, it is important to remember that this university system emerged by, through, and in service to a capitalist political economy that unevenly combines corporate, state, and civic interests. Recent discussion surrounding the state of the contemporary university system nevertheless suggests that the value of professionalism stems from a culture of social equity and a politics of democracy as opposed to globalization's focus on the economics of technological and scientific progress. Therefore, I want to end this chapter by discussing how we often dichotomize the contemporary and historical values of the public research university in such a way that the cultural and the political stand in opposition to the economic.

Assigning value, whether cultural, political, or economic, might appear to be an easy enough task, but such evaluations of higher education are fraught with contradictions and complications. According to Joan Scott's essay "The Rhetoric of Crisis in Higher Education," all levels of U.S. education have been justified almost exclusively by a vision of democratization even though they have been simultaneously constructed by the economic needs of corporate capitalism. The mutually reinforcing notions of social equity and democracy suggest that public universities are designed to produce and to disseminate a wide spectrum of knowledge, to teach citizenship, to provide socioeconomic mobility, and to be universally accessible to all interested students. The constant gesturing toward these political and cultural goals implies that this education works to improve national public good and not to bolster the interests of any one section of the population. Yet economic expansion, whether led by the nation-state or by corporate foundations or more often both, has always been at the heart of university-based technological and scientific progress. Adding to the university's democratic reputation, Scott contends, "the marriage of business and academe—the corporate penetration of the university—has [also] made instrumentalism [a] reigning ethos" of university work (299). Professional work is clearly intended to fulfill practical economic needs as well as everyday social problems, as both fall within the jurisdiction of instrumentalism. For Scott, the foundations for the many crises that emerge in higher education lie precisely within this contradictory logic wherein culture and politics stand in diametric opposition to economics even though they collaboratively define the central project of university professional work.

Scott offers a challenge to those who see corporatism as a new phenomenon that has compromised the university's democratic innocence. She demands that such scholars recognize the interpenetration of supposedly exclusive university components. I wish to push this even further by challenging academicians to understand democracy and corporatism as two parts of a triangulated historical materialist foundation of higher education. While social equity, democracy, and economic progress work together within the dynamics of capitalism, the overlapping and interdependent tripartite structure of the historical materialist setting for the university allows different areas to surface as most apparent while the other constituent parts weave into a nearly invisible background cloth. This structure, for instance, enables the U.S. public research university to prioritize corporate interests as part of the unseen and unspoken background at the same time that it foregrounds the democratic discourse of professional training. The contradiction between what the public university purports to accomplish and how it spends its resources becomes practically resolved through the language of professionalization and the discourse of democracy.

Once we recognize that the inadequacies in our contemporary university system do not result from a lost responsibility to our professional past but to the complexities of the current stage of capitalism, we can begin to more fully address the multifaceted relationships between globalization and the cultural, political, and economic realms of education. We cannot, however, create viable solutions as long as we fall back on nostalgic calls for a return to the purity of our past democratic mission. Nostalgia has a romantic appeal, but it also has a long history that we must combat. Take, for instance, Veblen's 1918 critique of higher education. Writing at the boundary between the industrial and the monopoly eras, Veblen skillfully identifies the structural and ideological problems of corporatism within the ideal of higher education. But his argument relies on an educational design that cannot be achieved within the historical materialist terrain on which the U.S. public research university was built. He held business exigencies responsible for the "unreflecting propensity to make much of all things that bear the signature of the 'practical'" and explained that "'practical' in this connection means useful for private gain; it need imply nothing in the way of serviceability to the common good" (*The Higher Learning in America* 193). Veblen, like others after him, rigidly distinguishes the economic and the practical from the democratic and reflective nature of professional work. Not surprisingly, he accused higher education of attracting only those "pragmatic spirits within whose horizon 'value' is synonymous with 'pecuniary value,' and to whom good citizenship means proficiency in competitive business" (196). While this might be true, it belies a reductionist logic that flattens a three-dimensional structure into nothing more than a singular perspective of economism. Universities and students exist within capitalist terrains that must be negotiated rather than simply ignored. Negotiation requires cracking holes in the walls that separate the multiple cultural, political, and economic foundations constituting the parameters of legitimate professional behavior. Further, it requires moving outside these porous parameters to invent new foundations and new structures.

Veblen hits upon a critical thread in higher education and uncovers what Scott sees as the underlying contradiction between democratic presentations and capitalist motivations. Nonetheless, this powerful insight is quickly undermined when he fails to take full account of the interdependencies among the valuation processes within the cultural, political, and economic realms as well as the outer rhetorical boundary erected from these exchanges. In a critique nearly identical to current discussions of higher education, Veblen claims that corporate influence turns education into nothing more than "a merchantable commodity, to be produced on a piece-rate plan, rated, bought and sold by standard units, measured, counted and reduced to staple equivalence by impersonal, mechanical tests" (222). Again, not unlike contemporary scholars, Veblen concludes that "the intrusion of business principles in the universities goes to weaken and retard the pursuit of learning, and therefore to defeat the ends for which a university is maintained" (224). Because he argues that the economically determined value of education betrays a more authentic educational mission, Veblen falls into the same nostalgia that prevents some of the best contemporary theorists from working toward comprehensive solutions to the problems of higher education. An answer that asks the university to extricate itself from these capitalist connections is not only naive. It is simply impossible given that the U.S. public research university is comfortably seated within the most successful capitalist political economy in history. Instead, we need to theorize the university as a subset of a larger system, one built through the rhetorical valuations that affect both material structures and human relationships within those structures. Such research will begin to reveal where and how we can intervene in and undermine the problematic socioeconomic relationships compounded by this structure of higher education.

While the valuation of professional work tends to isolate one or two attributes, an historical materialist lens insists that all constituent parts and their effects be visible. Valuation processes must simultaneously include cultural, political, and economic components. However, because of an uneasy relationship between culture and politics on the one hand and economics on the other, evaluations of higher education too often overemphasize or underemphasize economics. Against this trend, the last two chapters have analyzed the U.S. public research university through the hermeneutics of valuation I have been calling historical materialism. The history I sketched resists suggesting that the university is a unified whole acting on behalf of any single ideology or interest. Instead, I have shown that at particular historical junctures various organizations and individuals found value in a new kind of structure that created and re-created the public research university system. This system took up and reworked different strands of higher education in order to offer an institution that better supported the different and sometimes disparate needs of a changing capitalist political economy. The U.S. public research university was and is a fractured and loosely bound component of a larger political economic system.

Working from this rhetorically constituted historical narrative, the second part of the book more thoroughly engages the complexities of the university in the period of global capitalism. Since the early 1970s the political economy of globalization has been defined by multiculturalism, neoliberal politics, and the economics of finance capital. Chapter 3 takes these arguments further and contends that the university engages the larger capitalist political economy and reconfigures itself in order to contribute to alternative methods for producing surplus value. My analysis has dual conclusions. First, the university exploits both faculty and students as a source of free labor and dramatically changes the valuation of university education; second, this new structure forges opportunities for individual and collective agencies that might lead to significant social change. Chapter 4 follows with an in-depth case study of the globalization of the U.S. public research university system and its construction of the post-professional.

II

3

The Collusion of Economic and Cultural Systems
Globalization and the University

Chapters 1 and 2 demonstrate that the relationship between the capitalist political economy and the U.S. public research university is both complex and historically contingent. Just as the industrial stage of capitalism created a new research model of education and developed new disciplines to foster that research, the monopoly stage of capitalism initiated new departments—area studies and workplace psychology, for example—in order to help train professionals in scientific management and develop the knowledge necessary for cold war maneuvering. Although these structural changes were never direct instantiations of a simple democratic ideal, they responded to and perpetuated various democratic values. An individualized version of democracy helped forge the university as a necessary economic component of disparate local communities during the industrial period while the nationalized democratic vision of the monopoly stage justified huge expenditures on university-based military research. Currently, I argue, a new consumerized notion of democracy—the idea that individual freedom derives from one's ability to access and purchase a variety of commodities—contributes to the increased privatization of this university system. The values and production processes of global capitalism, however, have not erased earlier ideologies and modes of production. Instead, industrial, monopoly, and global capitalist structures exist simultaneously and in cooperation, both inside and outside the U.S. public research university system.

Because these capitalist shifts imply continuities as well as discontinuities, the U.S. public research university has been able to maintain an intimate collaboration with the corporate sphere amid considerable structural change. Given this commitment to participation in the corporate sphere, it should not be surprising that many economically motivated organizations of globalization are looking toward this university system as the ideal for higher education worldwide. Indeed, as mentioned in chapter 2, supranational associations such as the Organization for Economic Cooperation and Development (OECD) and the World Bank as well as international agreements like NAFTA, GATT, and the General Agreement on Trade and Services (GATS) are globally redefining national higher education according to a model forged by the U.S. public research university. The U.S. public research university is no longer simply one national system among others; instead, it is increasingly becoming the hegemonic model worldwide. A theoretical understanding of globalization will provide insight into the contemporary university system and help illuminate the university's future path. For this reason, this chapter offers a broader explication of the global political economy as a heterogeneous assembly of cultural, political, and economic values. Specifically, the chapter unearths the democratic valuations of globalization to demonstrate how the structural combination of industrial production, monopolistic management, and global consumption enables new methods for producing surplus value.

Surplus value, in a traditional Marxist analysis, is the profit that results from the capitalist mode of production. According to Marx, the value of a worker's labor becomes objectified within the products one produces; workers transfer value into commodities through design, creation, or assembly—what economists call value-added procedures. Marx believes that wages are not determined by the amount of value a worker transfers into commodities, as one might suppose. Instead, salaries are determined, often at a lesser value, by the socially necessary cost of sustaining a worker's livelihood—what we currently refer to as a living wage. The excess value created by the unequal exchange between workers and the corporations to which they sell their labor constitutes surplus value. Relying on this definition, however, many theorists overemphasize the economics of globalization, stressing its ability to increase surplus value through an accelerated production cycle, a worldwide assembly line, and reduced national regulations. While we cannot neglect these important economic factors, we also cannot forget that changes in the economic sphere have social and cultural consequences. Individuals who engage in labor are not just classed subjects but also nationalized, racialized, gendered, and sexualized subjects. Relationships based on nationality, race, gender, and sexuality vary significantly according to the economic exigencies of globalization. For instance, *maquiladora* factories along the U.S.-Mexican border reinscribe patriarchal domination and thereby change the cultural makeup of host cities.[1] With a high percentage of female workers displaced from agrarian spaces and placed into unfamiliar urban factory work and with male bosses who are taught to devalue these women and the work they do, there is little wonder that a significant number of sexual abuse cases have caught the attention of human rights activists. As horrific as these crimes are, what I want to stress here is that economic globalization in twin factories would look different if gender and race relationships were altered. The cultural, political, and economic are inextricably linked.

An equally important cultural effect of economic globalization is the fact that the general public increasingly assumes responsibility for the profits, successes, and failures of private corporations. As the recent bankruptcies of Enron, Worldcom, and a string of airline companies demonstrate, individuals might lose their life savings when the stock market fluctuates, but corporations and corporate leaders often escape these crises relatively unscathed. This double-edged sword means that individuals acquire the burden of corporate risk, but it also means that they retain some authority over the shape and structure of corporate rule. The 1994 Zapatista resistance to NAFTA, the 1999 Seattle battle against the World Trade Organization (WTO), the continuous protests at G8 summits, and global demonstration against the U.S. invasion of Iraq all suggest that individual and collective social critique flourishes even amid the proliferation of corporate power. The public sphere includes various movements that position themselves against the neoliberal free market economy of globalization, whether they take the form of corporate exploitation, deregulated free-trade zones, summit meetings among the leaders of the world's wealthiest countries, or an unjust war waged to protect future markets.

Consumers, in fact, might gain political leverage in the global era of capitalism. Take, for example, the current popularity of reality-based entertainment where "private" activities such as one's everyday life or one's personal trauma are manipulated, commodified, and broadcast through radio call-in shows or television programs. Wages, in this context, are transformed into opportunities and prizes—privileges rather than rights.[2] Without paying working actors, the producers of these shows continue to sell prepackaged consumer audiences engaged in individual leisure time to advertisers.[3] As volunteer laborers, contestants cannot organize in the same way that workers can, but the consumers of these shows, if they constituted themselves as a united community, might be able to exercise influence over the economics of this labor as well as its cultural productions. In one such instance, consumers blocked CBS's plans to air a reality television show based on the hit series *The Beverly Hillbillies.* A script that called for transplanting a poor, rural family from the Appalachian Mountains into a Beverly Hills mansion drew serious complains from the Center for Rural Strategies, which organized the campaign that eventually prevented the program from moving forward. Together with the Rural Education Special Interest Group of the American Research Association, it formed the Rural Reality Alliance specifically to protest the proposed television series. In a full-scale campaign, they developed an informative Web site, distributed a petition, ran editorials in newspapers across the country, and encouraged others to contact legislators. The group's power no doubt resided in its ability to garner consumers or nonconsumers of this television network.

The non-wage-paying labor exemplified by the entertainment industry can also be found in university programs as ostensibly benign as service learning, peer instruction, and unpaid internships. These programs pass off the free labor of students, whether performed in the nonprofit sector, the business world, or the university, as opportunities for self-improvement and civic engagement. Technologically supported self-management, such as computer or telephone course registration and fee payment, furthers this economy by replacing paid university employees with non-wage-earning labor. The rhetoric supporting these new university structures often suggests that they will save time and provide new cultural experiences. Indeed, this rhetoric implies that together technology and philanthropy will bring democratic privileges to all. However, as many theorists have suggested, democracy does not necessarily follow such technologies (Hirschkop; Braun). While I do not disagree with these theorists, I maintain that the expansion of such technology does allow for new methods of negotiating economic and cultural terrains. Individual participants in these university programs have opportunities to actively intervene in the educational system as well as the capitalist landscape. For instance, United Students Against Sweatshops offers another excellent example of how consumers—in this case, consumers of university degrees—can exert pressure on producers—in this case, corporations that produce products with direct and indirect ties to the university. But before we can conceive of possible avenues for intervening in and reshaping economic and cultural globalization as well as the university's role in that process, we need to better understand the capitalist stage of globalization.

Following theorists like Frederic Jameson, I am cautious about celebrating the political economy of globalization as national decolonization, ethnic and racial inclusion, or the demise of the nation-state. Certainly the bilateral standoff between superpowers like the United States and the former Soviet Union no longer animates international politics, but the former Soviet empire cannot itself account for all cultural, political, and economic struggles of nation-states worldwide. Quite the contrary, according to Jameson, "the transnational system itself" should be held responsible ("Notes on Globalization" 74). Because the transnational system re-creates colonial power relations under the guise of multiculturalism, the next section uses postcolonial, cultural studies, and Marxist analyses of the interrelationship between the cultural and economic spheres to explore globalization. I emphasize the increasingly intimate connection between the cultural and the economic values embedded within the global political sphere, follow this with an outline of four constitutive processes of globalization, and end with a short discussion of how these global processes impact the shape of the U.S. public research university. Such analysis, I believe, will help individuals better understand their participation in the university and in globalization. In turn, they may choose to become more active forces, consciously participating in the rhetorical deliberations that simultaneously construct the U.S. public research university system and secure its role within the era of global capitalism. I turn now to the historical materialism of globalization: the politics of neocolonialism, multicultural commodity circulation, and the expansion of finance capital.

Multicultural Appropriation, Neocolonialism, and the Politics of Subversion

The cultural, political, and economic terrain—the rhetorical boundary of legitimate action—ubiquitously labeled globalization has been developing since the early 1970s within the United States and the spaces affected by U.S. policy.[4] The 1970s initiated the world into globalization through a process that Marshall McLuhan, as early as 1964, had the foresight to call a cultural "implosion" (71). According to McLuhan, the accelerating effects of electronic communication and the rapidly evolving transportation system pressured the traditional center-margin structure of industrialism until the world simply collapsed under the weight of instantaneous communication, high-speed travel, and increased interconnectivity. Rather than simply enlarging, the network of communication eventually falls into itself and creates several small but related localities. The world, not unlike the one Michael Hardt and Antonio Negri construct in *Empire,* transitions into a "global village" of many independent sites virtually connected by advanced technology (5). In this globalized state, contact between disparate people and places cannot occur outside the commodified structure of a technologically advanced communications industry.

Global cultural production might appear to be a simple humanist project promoting respect among various national and ethnic communities, but it is important to remember that cultural production comes into existence through economically oppressive functions. The world's wealthiest population, for instance, can experience the luxury of Caribbean vacation spots only because the international tourist industry has imported hotels, restaurants, and entertainment into some of the world's most impoverished spaces. The importation of these resorts does not add to the local economy but competes with it, often selling commodified imitations of the local culture within corporately owned all-inclusive resorts that quite literally prevent vacationers from interacting with local culture, learning about local politics, and spending money in the local economy. As only one example among many, the tourist industry reflects the way that globalization has deprived culture of its larger web of interrelated significations. Tourists consume reified objects and experiences with no clear relationship between those cultural texts and the political or economic systems that produce them.[5] Subsequently, the cultural sphere carries within itself a mark of innocence that erases its complicity with economic exploitation. Culturally, the world appears closer than ever, but this apparent proximity operates through a neocolonial politics that continues to subjugate previously colonized nation-states by imposing global economic structures. Neocolonial politics begins with, and then transcends, the nation-state without moving beyond nationalized forms of cultural appropriation (themed resorts that sell indigenous experiences without local consultation), political manipulation (tax-free zones that privilege foreign corporations), and economic exploitation (sweatshops and other underpaid employment practices).

The interdisciplinary work associated with the Birmingham Centre for Contemporary Cultural Studies often took for granted the notion that culture was nationally defined. Indeed, its methodology necessitated the nation-state as a key component of analysis. Consider, for instance, such seminal works as Raymond Williams's *Culture and Society* (1958), E. P. Thompson's *Making of the English Working Class* (1963), or even Dick Hebdige's *Subculture* (1979). Each of these texts examines a particular group, or concept, from the standpoint of "Englishness." In many ways, this emphasis on the nation makes sense since England of the 1950s, 1960s, and into the 1970s was significantly constituted by its receding national imperialism in relationship to an increasingly decolonized world. Nevertheless, this notion of the nation-state unproblematically determining cultural difference has been thoroughly critiqued by scholars of various disciplines—especially those in postcolonial studies. Texts like Benedict Anderson's *Imagined Communities,* Partha Chatterjee's *Nationalist Thought and the Colonial World,* and Homi Bhabha's edited collection *Nation and Narration* demonstrate the fallaciousness of a nationally homogenous culture. Collectively, these authors argue that nation-states do not contain homogenous groups, do not determine the identities of individuals, are not easily delimited by the geographical boundaries, and do not determine the possibilities of decolonial movements. Perhaps inadvertently, they also shift the focus of analysis from the national to the global.

Although early cultural studies work often assumed that a dialectic between the local and the national produced cultural texts, theorists now argue that culture results from a movement between the local and the global. The expansion of this dialectic to subsume a larger geographical space, however, has not fundamentally altered academic interpretations—scholarship continues to fall into two opposing schools of thought. Either globalization is an exciting new phenomenon, frequently associated with the emergence of the postmodern and the celebration of difference, or globalization exists as a mask for cultural imperialism, erasing difference and promulgating a universal, homogenous, and often North American identity. Roland Robertson, an early scholar of globalization, defines this debate as the difference between divergent and convergent theories. The theory of convergence suggests that all societies are moving toward the same cultural apex, albeit at different speeds. Alternatively, the theory of divergence emphasizes different routes to and forms of cultural achievement (11). Most educational scholarship tends to fall solidly within one of these two camps. Those who favor current globalization practices believe that local difference can outweigh the imposition of world standards (Waghid; Mok; Mok and Lee). Antiglobalization theorists, on the other hand, fear that homogenous education practices will erase unique local cultures (Im; Torres and Schugurensky; Pinto). Others struggle to promote some combination of these two positions (Habu). Nevertheless, the two poles of homogeneity and heterogeneity serve to enclose and encapsulate the majority of debate within cultural and educational globalization.

Deliberations about the value of one universal culture as opposed to many particular cultures repeat themselves, I believe, because they operate within a binary structure that prevents their resolution. Theorists such as Edward Said (*Culture and Imperialism*) and M. M. Bakhtin ("Discourse in the Novel") argue that multiple cultures, whether national or global, are constantly engaged in a hegemonic struggle to secure economic and political interests within a particular time and place. While one specific culture will always achieve dominance in any spatio-temporal matrix, other cultures continuously compete for legitimacy, recognition, and power. The perpetual movement between homogenous and heterogeneous cultural forces invites scholars to alternatively emphasize a singular dominant culture and multiple competing cultures; we might, however, arrive at different interpretations if we reconceptualized this process as multiply constructed and exchanged valuations that constitute the rhetorical boundaries of particular historical materialist landscapes. Such an analysis helps us understand contemporary phenomena within an historical framework that has been constructed from collaborating social spheres rather than from a corporate power that cannot be contested. Further, historical materialism offers maps of power relationships that indicate points of vulnerability and opportunities for change. Even if those opportunities pass, this interpretation keeps the conversation moving forward, laying the groundwork for future change.

Unfortunately, many theorists have foregone analysis of cultural and economic complexities and (mis)appropriated McLuhan's notion of the global village in order to celebrate the current state of globalization as a friendlier, more intimate, and more economically beneficial era.[6] Valorization of the so-called global village is most prominent within the politico-economic sphere. For instance, the Brookings Institute's research on economic globalization definitively states that "the age of globalization brings a major shift away from power relations and towards greater cooperation" ("America in the Age of Globalization" 1). This promotion of globalization fails to mention the policies that support, and sometimes enforce, such cooperation. It simply elides the fact that globalization often mandates cooperation in the form of deregulated trade policies, the reduction or elimination of import and export taxes, and the creation of what Saskia Sassen calls "the global assembly line" (*Losing Control?* 7). The international extension of production along with the absence of regulatory systems increases competition between transnational conglomerates and wipes out local production while the Brookings Institute's emphasis lies almost exclusively on cooperation. Certainly authors like Thomas Friedman and Joseph E. Stiglitz have tempered the wholesale endorsement of globalization coming from economists and theorists like Milton Friedman and Francis Fukuyama, but these critical perspectives represent only another variation of the same free market logic. The difference between the two approaches can be characterized by degrees and not by entirely different notions of interacting as a global community. Apparently, for those like Stiglitz, it is better to drown inch by inch than by one quick plunge.

Although the Brookings Institute claims to be an independent organization devoted to nonpartisan research, its promotion of global cooperation mirrors conservative sectors of the U.S. political and economic spheres as part of the carefully constructed coordination of economic discourse. An example of this resonance can be found in an Associated Press release from April 2001 in which Federal Reserve Chairman Alan Greenspan explicitly critiques the anti–World Trade Organization protestors in Seattle. Unlike the supposedly naive protestors, Greenspan believes "the best single action that the industrial countries could actually take to alleviate the terrible problem of poverty in many developing countries would be to open, unilaterally, markets to imports from these countries" (quoted in Crutsinger). The products potentially imported from these developing countries would be primarily owned by transnational corporations headquartered within the world's wealthiest countries, particularly the United States, but Greenspan does not include this information in his comments. Nor does he mention that free trade usually secures international markets for corporations based in these industrially advanced nations. With less expensive overseas production costs resulting in less expensive consumer products, transnational corporations can close out competition and still claim to support free and open markets. When Greenspan, the Brookings Institute, or any other organization argues that developing "countries need more globalization, not less," they forget the important caveat: "if they are to be economically useful to developed countries" (Crutsinger).

Some theorists, however, oppose this economic view by emphasizing cultural ramifications of global production systems such as the exploitation of the people, customs, and knowledges of developing countries. Political activist A. Sivanandan, for one, denounces the 1994 Uruguay Round of GATT for securing policies that legitimate the exploitation of cultures located in poor nation-states. As a result of this GATT agreement, he says, "northern agribusiness and pharmaceutical companies were allowed to patent products and processes based on genetic material derived from Third World crops and wild plants and sell them to the Third Word, while

Third World countries were forbidden to develop their own local equivalent of western products on the grounds of technological 'piracy'" (12).[7] In this example, globalization subjugates culture to an economic system that appropriates local knowledge and indigenous products for their possible profitability—local culture is patented, marketed, and commodified according to the logic of transnational corporations. These same market processes prevent the original cultural owners from sharing in the profits derived from this corporate system, even when that cultural knowledge is critical to the health, economy, or religion of local populations. In short, cultural appropriation initiated by wealthy nations is acceptable according to this agreement while economic reappropriation of poorer nations is clearly off limits.

Enabled by global policies like this GATT agreement, wealthy countries often appropriate local cultures of poorer countries in nearly the same way that they once raped their lands of natural resources and raw materials. Such a strategy tends to interpret participation as approval, so if non-Western people watch Western television or work in Western factories, we understand these individuals as endorsing the neocolonial structure rather than as acting within the social limits as they currently exist. Against such limited interpretations, John Tomlinson believes that the cultural sphere—including cultural approaches to agriculture and medicine—provides opportunities for intervention into, rather than acquiescence to, the homogenizing process of economic globalization. Equipped with advanced technologies and enabled by rampaged consumer practices, cultural production offers a rich site for local cultures to maneuver in what Tomlinson calls "global cultural politics" (30). The dialectical relationship between the cultural and the economic creates, he contends, "at least the possibility for local intervention in global processes" (26). Because culture has become increasingly valuable within, and hence increasingly connected to, the economic sphere, individuals can use cultural apparatuses to disrupt global economic processes. For instance, many movements resistant to globalization have relied on its postmodern technologies. The Zapatista movement used Internet communication and publicized itself through international media outlets while the movement against the Iraqi war made its message known through an Internet demonstration that took place on February 13, 2003.[8] While these technology-supported global movements have yet to disrupt the economic production of globalization in any significant way, they do affect specific global events, if often minimally.

Affecting global outcomes from one's local positionality suggests, according to Tomlinson, the possibility for global citizenship. This citizenship requires a cosmopolitan sensibility or "a cultural disposition which is not limited to the concerns of the immediate locality, but which recognizes global belonging, involvement, and responsibility and can integrate these broader concerns into everyday life practice" (185). Tomlinson claims that such cosmopolitanism is on the rise as a result of consumer practices that allow individuals to come into contact with foreign fashion, ethnic food, and multicultural entertainment, at home or abroad. Consumer spaces, offering a smorgasbord of difference, encourage disparate nations, cultures, and people to engage in historically unprecedented ways and enable individuals to build communities around commodified cultural texts rather than national or identity categories. Tomlinson suggests, for instance, that "the complex hybrid nature of contemporary global youth cultures organized around music, dance and fashion" creates the possibility for conscious and active consumer groups that transgress old ideological limitations (200). These new groups form most easily within audiences that already function as a community—Internet, religious, music, and intellectual communities, for instance. As organized collectives, individuals ranging from university professors to music fanatics make decisions that significantly enable global processes. Acting together to persuade members to purchase (or not purchase) a product or to understand events differently, these collectives could potentially impact the niche market to which they belong.

Still, because global culture is almost exclusively connected to the research, transportation, or communications industries, Tomlinson argues that these emergent consumer practices bear the historical traces of modernist ideologies. In fact, he believes that no matter how globally conscious they are, these communities often contribute to "global modernity," or the worldwide acceptance of modernist ideologies (32). Active primarily between 1890 and 1945, modernism ideologically justified European colonization of non-European people and lands. But for Tomlinson, modernity also justifies today's cultural imperialism exemplified, for instance, by the seizure of indigenous cultures for the production of agri-business and pharmaceutical processes that are then sold back to those cultures for a profit. Without too much resistance, the modernist values of enlightenment, reason, progress, and development make the extension of market apparatuses and cultural appropriation appear acceptable and even necessary. Tomlinson contends that modernity, rather than dying out, has simply evolved along with changing forms of imperialism. He nevertheless maintains hope that the advanced technologies associated with our current global age will create opportunities to displace modernity "from its dominant conceptual-discursive position" (45). Unlike consumers of the nineteenth and twentieth centuries, consumers today have instantaneous communication with people and products from around the globe. Aided by this technology, individuals are more likely to acquire a cosmopolitan view of the world—an ideology necessary to the progressive politics of global citizenship. For instance, I purchase my coffee from Dean's Beans, a fair trade coffee roaster that not only delivers organic French roast coffee to my door but regularly sends me e-mail updates on the labor struggles of coffee growers worldwide. Similarly, my long-distance phone company, Working Assets, provides phone service but also sends me information on social justice projects and publications. In this fashion, consumers can rely on such alternative companies for cultural, political, and economic reports from around the globe.

Arjun Appadurai also believes that globalization provides occasions for resisting modernist ideologies and transforming global structures. Echoing Tomlinson, Appadurai locates globalization within the ongoing project of modernism, favors cultural difference, and argues that globalization does not necessarily or even frequently imply homogenization or Americanization. He proposes that the multicultural and overlapping cultural flows of globalization require an examination of how "locality emerges in a globalized world, of how colonial processes underwrite contemporary politics, of how history and genealogy inflect one another and how global facts take local form" (18).[9] Five dimensions, or cultural flows, compose this complex order of globalization. These flows, Appadurai suggests, occur in and through the growing disjunctures among the spheres he labels ethnoscapes, technoscapes, financescapes, mediascapes, and ideoscapes. Communities of people make up ethnoscapes; scientific and technological development constitute technoscapes; mediascapes take into account mass communication; financescapes are determined by economic exchange; and ideoscapes are "comprised of elements of the Enlightenment worldview, which consists of a chain of ideas, terms, and images, including *freedom, welfare, rights, sovereignty, representation,* and the master term *democracy*" (36). Appadurai emphasizes these Western themes, as opposed to others, because they originated within the same nation-states that project their political philosophies onto other nation-states through colonial and postcolonial capitalist structures. As the predominant ideological frames worldwide, these ideologies dominate the political flows of globalization. Ideoscapes and mediascapes obviously connote rhetorical work, but the other "scapes" should be understood as equally implicated in the rhetorical valuation process constituting our current world structure. Ethnoscapes provide the basis for waging specific arguments, forming identifying strategies, and garnering collective action; technoscapes offer the most significant medium for instantaneous, up-to-date communication and deliberation across vast distances; and financescapes fund the whole process.

Appadurai defines all five flows as building blocks of imagined communities, which is reminiscent of Benedict Anderson's description of nationhood. Appadurai sees these "scapes" as fluid, irregular, changing, and open to various perspectives. These categories and their fluidity are useful for understanding how structures of feeling, belonging, and responsibility create communities dedicated to activism and social change. Because the various, contradictory, and uneven flows of globalization tend to redirect identification away from the nation-state and onto other, often virtual or imagined, communities, opportunities for social change exist in cultural groups rather than in traditional citizenship. For instance, Appadurai believes that "forms of computer-mediated communication have created new possibilities for transnational forms of communication, often bypassing the intermediate surveillance of the nation-state and of major media conglomerates" (194). If financed independently and dedicated to progressive political as well as cultural values, media productions can have a subversive edge that crosses national and cultural barriers. By way of example, he cites the increasing number of film and music productions that cross over national, language, and cultural barriers. Such productions have the ability to alter individual perspectives on race, gender, ethnicity, and nationalism. These changed perspectives might, in turn, compel individuals to alter the economic structures of globalization.

Though it does not account for all global phenomena, a postcolonial lens with its focus on economics, power struggles, and political configurations allows individuals to invent new ways to participate in the current political economy. A particularly useful discussion of such agency can be found in *Culture, Globalization and the World-System: Contemporary Conditions for the Representation of Identity*. This collection of essays, edited by Anthony D. King and first presented in 1989 at an international symposium on cultural globalization, advocates postcolonial analysis as a means to better comprehend the cultural and economic intersections of globalization. In his introductory essay, King states that because globalization causes national deterritorialization, we need theories that transcend the nation-state. Paying attention to historical and cultural change rather than technological transformations, he uses "post-colonialism as one distinctive prism through which some contemporary phenomena can be approached" (5). A postcolonial analysis, especially when enhanced by Marxist and cultural studies perspectives, enables us to view local phenomena in relationship to large global processes that exploit not only labor and natural resources but also people and cultures. It helps us trace, for instance, the multiple and contradictory implications of how university apparel is produced. A sweatshirt with the name of a major U.S. university stamped across the front might signify college sports, public education, and even access to democratic privileges. But it also signifies, to a much less recognizable degree, the labor of poorly paid overseas workers with their own economic and democratic hopes. Democratizing the messages and styles written onto clothes or any other commodity cannot erase this second signification. Instead of diversifying niche products, we need to examine these dual economic and cultural meanings through the multiple theoretical apparatuses of postcolonial, Marxist, and cultural studies analyses.

As the university apparel industry suggests, textiles and other goods are often produced or assembled in previously colonized spaces in order to be imported back into and marketed in more industrialized locations. But these previously colonized spaces also provide opportunities for the appropriation of cultural artifacts. Cultural theorist Stuart Hall emphasizes how globalization enables the appropriation of postcolonial cultures. In his assessment, the capitalist crisis of the 1970s resolved itself by creating and expediting access to new global markets, both commodity markets and financial markets. This new economy "not only links backward sections of the third world to so-called advanced sections of the first world in a form of multinational production, but increasingly tries to reconstitute the backward sectors within [the First World's] own society" ("The Local and the Global" 23). Multinational corporations connect industrialized nations with less developed nations by appropriating and patenting their products, simultaneously incorporating those sectors into the world market and alienating that population from its own production. This appropriation reconstitutes cultures by imposing a capitalist mode of production and its attendant infrastructure onto local production at the same time that it represents those cultures within a normalized capitalist structure that might appear significantly foreign to the original culture. According to Hall, local populations and their distinct cultures irreparably transform into isolated slices of a nearly homogenous, mass-produced multicultural aesthetic.

Besides extending production into new and larger markets, multicultural inclusion offers a safe mechanism for addressing, or appearing to address, cultural difference. Economic globalization must negotiate with the interests and values of diverse localities. Because the world is not culturally homogenous—as Appadurai and Tomlinson stress—commodity production must represent cultural differences if it is to be accepted. Thus, global production must "incorporate and partly reflect the differences it [tries] to overcome" (Hall, "The Local and the Global" 32). If subjugated individuals have avenues for inclusion, no matter how minimal or inconsequential such opportunities might be to the larger structure of dominance, these individuals will be more likely to accept an unfair social structure as the signpost of a democratic future. Counterintuitively, globalization dominates cultural production via the incorporation of heterogeneous cultural texts. Although different in appearance, these cultural texts are homogenous in terms of their commodity production and economic valuation. The fact that nearly all individuals can see representations of themselves and their lives in the marketplace does not signify the failure of imperialist homogenization; rather, it suggests the successful commodification of a multicultural aesthetic and the extension of dominant market forces.

As the current outgrowth of this neocolonial struggle for representation, the negotiation and subsequent inclusion of difference—often called neoliberalism—constitutes the ideological justification for globalization. According to Hall, liberalism is "intimately connected with the birth and evolution of the modern capitalist society" and its liberal tenets change along with the evolving needs of capitalism ("Variants of Liberalism" 38–39). The celebration of cultural difference currently functions as one of the key neoliberal tenets maintaining global capitalist structures, perhaps accounting for the fact that the libertarian doctrine espoused by such authors as Charles Murray (*The Bell Curve*) and Ayn Rand works so well within the current free market reign of global capitalism.[10] This celebration appears to be explicitly against the interests of capitalist agents who wish to ensure their own cultural and political sovereignty. However, multicultural inclusion is actually necessary to delimit and contain resistance from subordinate groups. Transnational corporations enlarge their influence by absorbing specialized markets, commodifying culture worldwide, and appealing to as many different groups as possible. Instead of universally securing its particular ideological and structural positions, this corporate hegemony simply defines the limits within which we can act, whether in acquiesce or in struggle. By defining the rhetorical perimeter of acceptable behavior, hegemony determines the boundaries of discussion so as to include as much as possible without ever threatening the dominant structures it functions to maintain. Today, the processes of cultural appropriation and commodity distribution define culture and politics through an ideological struggle that primarily takes place within the sphere of consumerism and much less so within official political spheres. Individuals, that is, are more likely to purchase their political participation by shopping in the global marketplace than by engaging in more substantive political deliberations. Contrarily, I believe, globalization will be understood better as, and potentially changed through, the negotiation of cultural, political, and economic valuation processes—processes with the potential to alter corporate hegemony over the rhetorical boundaries of individual and collective agency.

This cultural, political, and economic valuation process necessitates new methods for understanding conflict and engaging in change. On the one hand, the production of cultural valuation articulates to democratic consumerism. The availability of multiple and different products ensures that individuals have the freedom to customize their identity, create consumer groups, and resist hegemonic ideologies. On the other hand, the production of economic valuation signifies exploitative labor processes and structures of appropriation. Processes of political valuation have the unsavory duty of managing the multiple contradictions between the cultural and the economic. Economic exploitation and cultural emancipation represent two opposing values built into the political structure of globalization. Cultural value, economic value, and political value are not analogous overlays of the same principle; instead, they are enmeshed within one another and mutually complicit with the global cultural, political, and economic structures they collectively construct. At the heart of both the cultural and economic dynamics of globalization, then, is the question of value.

Economic and Cultural Globalization: Valuation and the Ties That Bind

Turning to Frederic Jameson allows me to more clearly trace the interdependency between the economic and cultural threads of this neocolonial regime. According to Jameson, "globalization is a communicational concept, which alternately masks and transmits cultural or economic meanings" ("Notes on Globalization" 55). As a communicational concept, globalization is for him fundamentally rhetorical; its rhetorical production does not occur at the hands of a group of conspiring individuals but simply responds to changes in the capitalist mode of communication. As print, broadcast, and electronic media expand, they tend to proliferate the ideology necessary to the maintenance of capitalism. The communications industry, that is, forms an ideological state apparatus that contributes to the capitalist relations of exploitation. Because this industry produces messages in commodity form—a form that can, according to David Harvey, "conceal as much as it can reveal about their social meaning"—the vast field of communications never overtly reveals its capitalist interests (Limits 17). Served in bite-sized commodity pieces, global communication provides some information while ignoring other data. Think, for instance, about the commodification of U.S. patriotism following September 11, 2001. What do we learn about U.S. culture when an individual wears a red, white, and blue T-shirt with the words "united we stand" printed on it? Does the T-shirt signify support for a unified nation or support for military attacks in Afghanistan and, later, Iraq? Does this prototypical individual include Arab Americans, Mexican migrant workers, or recent Russian immigrants in his or her sense of a united stance? Along with these questions about the cultural meaning of this T-shirt, further questions can be asked of its production. Was it manufactured in the home of a local resident or by a poorly paid laborer in Thailand? The commodified text remains silent on these questions even as the vast reserve of patriotic rhetoric multiplies. No one can fully read the answers to these questions in a T-shirt whose signification can be coded and recoded in so many different ways. In fact, commodification is most marketable when a cultural text, such as this T-shirt, contains enough meanings to appeal to a wide spectrum of consumers. Cultural texts are purposely ambiguous and rhetorically open-ended.

Because economic practices are obscured when culture is served in commodity form, analyses of global culture can fall short if the economic and the political are not overtly emphasized. Indeed, such an overdetermination of the cultural allows people to slip into what Jameson laments as "a postmodern celebration of difference and differentiations" ("Notes on Globalization" 56). This is one of the dangers of Tomlinson's theory. Because he enthusiastically offers the cosmopolitan as a unique subject capable of overthrowing modernism, he risks overlooking the economic strings that tie modernist ideologies together. Falling into a similar trap, postcolonial critics like Homi Bhabha ("The Commitment to Theory") and Gloria Anzaldúa often contend that the postmodern hybrid subject is specially qualified to oppose the oppressive structures of capitalism. These theorists, according to Jameson, lose their oppositional edge to the extent that their various versions of resistant subjectivity eschew the material and the economic.[11] Certainly both Bhabha and Anzaldúa discuss the relationship between economic structures and cultural production, but they nevertheless privilege postmodern culture and its hybrid subject as the key agents of social change, arguing that such postmodern subjects are not contained by space or positionality and can, therefore, engage in myriad oppositional tactics. Jameson, on the other hand, contends that it is only through the interrogation "of economic and social institutions that, in [his] opinion, the postmodern sublime can alone be adequately theorized" (*Postmodernism* 38). For Jameson, economics and culture are indissolubly connected and must never be analyzed in isolation. This emphasis on the economics of globalization is critical to understanding not only how culture circulates but also why it moves the way and in the form it does.

Multiculturalism and postmodernism's hybrid subject often extend and partially conceal the economic homogenization into which global culture intertwines. The widespread economic effects of cultural globalization, according to Jameson, are "deeper than anything known in earlier forms of colonization or imperialism" ("Notes on Globalization" 58). In the United States, he argues, this trend toward homogenization is exacerbated by our "our tendency to confuse the universal and the cultural, as well as to assume that in any given geopolitical conflict all elements and values are somehow equal and equivalent" ("Notes on Globalization" 59). Cultural texts communicating various ideological agendas enable this slippage between the universal and the particular because they function through an always-expanding chain of signification. Slavoj Žižek explains that the universal exists as an empty signifier and only "acquires concrete existence when some particular content starts to function as its stand-in" ("Multiculturalism" 29). Žižek contends that the logic of multinational capitalism succeeds because it appropriates diverse texts worldwide for its project of expanding commodification. In his analysis, multiculturalism represents the ideal form of ideology for global capitalism. Under the ideological guise of multicultural inclusion, cultural globalization justifies and masks an economic project that exploits increasing numbers of people. The globalization of culture appears to offer inclusion, representation, and equality; but, in the final analysis, culture only globalizes to the extent that it is economically beneficial to transnational corporations.

Modernist concept metaphors, such as freedom, rights, democracy, value, and other Enlightenment terms critiqued by Appadurai work especially well as conduits for passing off the particular as the universal. For instance, value—a concept metaphor used for the assessment of capitalist commodity production—universalizes diverse local texts by evaluating all aesthetic artifacts as equal contributions to a multicultural world or by categorizing texts quantitatively according to price rather than qualitatively according to use. All texts contain both an exchange value and a use value. An exchange value corresponds to an item's price while a use value denotes the value an item has for its owner. An exchange value fluctuates according to different markets; a use value, however, can be determined by sentiment, applicability, or aesthetics regardless of market value. A high-priced HDTV with an equivalently high exchange value might have little to no use value for someone without electricity; a low-priced political button might have high use value for someone who worked on a memorable campaign. The concept metaphor "value" serves as the shell into which specific economic, cultural, moral, and aesthetic meanings take shelter, often in unpredictable ways, but almost always separating the exchange value from the use value. The way to resist the effacement of economic labor structures built into cultural value classifications, says David Harvey, "is to replace the fixed idea of 'values' with an understanding of 'processes of valuation'" (*Justice, Nature, and the Geography of Difference* 11). Because value is maintained in different forms throughout the circulation of capital, understanding the process of valuation, rather than the specific nature of value in any given form, is critical to an analysis. The benefit of Harvey's suggestion can be seen in the rhetorical hermeneutics of valuation that offered an historical materialist reading of the U.S. public research university in chapters 1 and 2. Greater complexity of the university system was revealed through this reading process and its historically contingent valuations than could be gleaned from cultural, political, or economic perspectives alone.

Given the important role value plays in the production and consumption of commodities, Gayatri Spivak offers a parallel conception of this process of valuation by combining Marxist and deconstructionist analyses. In "Scattered Speculations on the Question of Value," Spivak divides the question of value into its Marxist materialist and its poststructural discursive schools of thought. For a Marxist, labor power determines value; alternatively, a poststructural argument cites consciousness or language production as determining value. Marxists believe in the materiality of value while poststructuralists believe in its discursivity. Both of these theories, however, escape a precise explanation of what value is—what Spivak calls the onto-phenomenological question. Rather than critiquing this evasion, she valorizes it as a potential point of commonality between Marxism and deconstruction.[12] For instance, Spivak argues that "Marx makes the highly sophisticated suggestion that the development of the value-form separates 'word' and 'reality'" (167). This separation of word from reality or sign from referent signifies what Spivak, in a different essay, calls catachresis.[13] Used oppositionally, catachresis parodies and makes perverse a trope or metaphor in order to highlight its limitations. To make this oppositional move, catachresis necessitates "a concept-metaphor without an adequate referent" ("Poststructuralism, Marginality, Postcoloniality and Value" 204). Although Marx explains how value is produced and poststructuralists explain how value is consumed, both avoid analyses into the ontological nature of value. Value is not a predefined characteristic but determined by various social processes. The lack of any clear ontological origin confines valuation within various catachrestical interpretations. The value of democratic higher education, for instance, lacks a clear referent even though it is often coupled with the U.S. public research university. Catachresis offers us a method for mocking this rhetorically constructed linkage and calling the present boundaries of democratic university education into question. Such a parody might include a campus bake sale to help fund a doctor's visit for an adjunct professor without health insurance or it might include teach-ins that visually represent the complicity of universities in sweatshop labor. Both rhetorical performances revalue educational practices in unconventional terms that mark the limits of our current institutionalization.

Because value signifies catachrestically, one can make use of these multiple significations without finally determining a specific inflexible referent corresponding to value. For this reason, Spivak argues that "it is possible to put the economic text 'under erasure' to see, that is, the unavoidable *importance* of its operation and yet to question it as a concept in the last resort" ("Scattered Speculations" 168). In the preface to Spivak's translation of Derrida's *Of Grammatology,* she tells us that to put something under erasure is to acknowledge that it is both inaccurate and necessary (xiv). Adjunct labor and corporate apparel contracts have become necessary components of the contemporary university system and yet these components disrupt the ingrained notion of universities as exemplary sites of democratic practice. While Spivak no doubt advocates poststructural notions of value, she also recognizes that "to set the labor theory of value aside is to forget the textual and axiological implications of a materialist predication of the subject" ("Scattered Speculations" 172). An economic understanding of value is important to the extent that it bears witness to the human relationships underlying the exchange of any text. For her, all cultural artifacts exist as multilayered texts that appear culturally as if in isolation from previous economic inscriptions even though these economic marks are bound up with the cultural. So conceived, value not only makes economic exchange and profit possible, it enables all exchanges, all communication, and, indeed, all social practices. A Marxist perspective, therefore, needs to be inseparable from a poststructuralist understanding of value, if individuals hope to change not only the appearance but also the experience of globalization.

Regardless of how useful this Marxist and poststructural catachresis might be, cultural value is often discussed without reference to economic value. Since at least the 1980s, multiculturalism has been promoted as the neoliberal doctrine of cultural inclusion, wearing the mask of equality and using the rhetoric of appreciation, difference, and democracy. This multicultural doctrine succeeds because it overshadows the fact that cultural inclusion frequently perpetuates inequality when the economics of globalization are taken into account. Market inclusion values difference by making it accountable to the logic of capitalism. But when a text becomes valued according to that market, it often becomes unavailable—and hence devalued—among the people whose history and whose labor produced that text. Thus, Jameson defines cultural freedom and democracy, the logics supporting multiculturalism, as "a zero-sum game in which my freedom results in the destruction of other people's national culture industries" ("Notes on Globalization" 61). Take global patent laws again, for example. International patent laws allow "transnational corporations to claim ownership of the Third World's agricultural heritage and then sell it back to the Third World for profit. Eventually, rising prices could put this heritage out of reach of its original inventors" (Kundnani 67). As soon as common cultural knowledge is valued according to the global capitalist system, it becomes inaccessible to its original owners even though it is often redistributed within the all-inclusive rhetorics of multiculturalism and the global market. In this sense, value—determined by a static cultural or economic assessment—insufficiently defines the processes of globalization.

Instead, we need to examine the economic and cultural processes (as well as the political regulations) by which globalization materializes and acquires value. These economic and cultural processes of globalization have been discussed in disciplines as different as anthropology, literary and cultural studies, political science, sociology, and economics. Whatever the critical differences among these disciplinary foci, several characteristics of globalization are repeatedly highlighted. Attuned to cultural and economic valuation, I examine four of them: the creation of digital technologies that accelerate information transmission; the development of transportation technologies and physical infrastructure that allow for a global production line; a reduced service industry replaced by technologically assisted consumer labor; and the increased sovereignty of transnational corporations proportional to the reduced sovereignty of the nation-state. These innovations represent the most widely discussed phenomena of economic globalization, and they are intimately connected to new processes for increasing surplus value. Together these technologies create the highly sophisticated structure of globalization. Outlining the threads that explain what is new about this global structure enables me to better explicate how globalization localizes within the U.S. public research university.

Building the Global Political Economy: The Cornerstones of Transformation

Surplus value, as I have already mentioned, consists of the extra value created from the capitalist mode of production, specifically through the process of wage labor. According to Marx, surplus value manifests because workers add value to the commodities they produce. Workers enhance a product through the labor they add to it and therefore that product accrues the value of their labor. A computer chip has more value when assembled onto a board and placed inside a computer. The value associated with the labor it takes to build the computer transfers from the worker to the marketable product. But this valuation process is not unique to assembly work. A history professor who writes textbooks adds value to the historical information by explaining and clarifying these ideas into a book marketed to potential readers; a service worker in the student union adds value to raw food by cooking it for customers. Rather than calculating wages according to the value transferred from a worker to a product, a worker's wages are determined by the value required to sustain one's ability to work. If the value added to commodities exceeds the value paid out in wages, then surplus value emerges (*Capital* 268). According to Marx, surplus value can be increased in only two ways: extending the workday (absolute surplus value) or increasing worker productivity (relative surplus value). Extending the workday increases surplus value in absolute terms but does nothing to disrupt the socially determined rate of profit—the ratio between surplus value and the cost of maintaining workers. Factory workers would assemble more computers, the professor would write more books, and the cook would make more food, each creating more surplus value in real terms but not proportionally. In a completely different way, relative surplus value (or an improved rate of profit) derives from increased productivity. Because wages as well as retail prices are partially determined by social norms—the equalization of wages, the homogenization of production processes, and access to markets—corporations constantly compete to beat the social average and increase their rate of profit. Capitalist competition, therefore, demands perpetual technological innovations in order to increase productivity and accelerate the circulation of commodities. There is one catch: this process will only produce increased surplus value for one company during the short period of time it takes for an innovation to become standardized. The first store to ask people to carry a discount card, allowing them to track consumer purchasing patterns, was able to lessen the cost of market research, lower prices, and strategically still make more profits than the competition. This innovation created extra surplus value for that store, but once store cards became standard and prices equalized, that store no longer produced extra surplus value through this innovation.

Regardless of how surplus value manifests in the labor process, however, profit only arises if surplus value can be transformed into money. Because consumers must purchase commodities within a specified period of time in order for profit to be realized, the transformation of surplus value into profit requires that consumption keep pace with production. Unless production is complemented by consumption, the circulation of values stalls and crisis ensues. Consequently, capitalism requires the speed of this circulation cycle to constantly increase "because to do so is to increase both the sum of values produced and the rate of profit" (Harvey, *Limits to Capital* 86). Technological innovations in the realm of production must be matched with similar innovations within the consumer sphere. One can produce VCRs more cheaply, but no profit will be garnered unless there are consumers willing to buy the VCRs within the time it takes to renew the supply. If a market is saturated, new markets need to be created—surplus production must find a consumer market or no profits will be realized. If no new markets are available, companies need to generate material and rhetorical reasons to convince consumers to update old equipment with new products. Companies need to break into the previously untapped Chinese market or get traditional markets to replace VCRs with DVD players. Rhetorically, this is done by providing "extras" only available on DVDs, by touting picture quality, and by making new VHS releases hard to find. None of this will happen unless there are ways to produce constant innovations, to instantaneously access consumers, and to quickly transport products around the globe. The speed of circulation finally requires technologies that transform capitalist structures and ease the mobility of information, of commodities, and of people.

Technological innovations within production have always been part of capitalism and have always played an especially important part in the transitions between its various stages. William Tabb argues that the transitional periods among the first, second, and third industrial revolutions parallel each other. Each revolution was precipitated, he argues, by technological innovations that reduced the cost of, and therefore accelerated the rate of, production. The first industrial revolution of capitalism occurred in the eighteenth century and resulted from steam power; the second industrial revolution, in the late nineteenth century, came about through the use of electricity and the electrical motor. The growth and speed of transportation and digital technologies, he argues, currently enables the third revolution (24). Digital and transportation technologies—both developed from a system of capitalist competition—are two of the most important processes necessary for global consumption. Digital technologies keep individuals across the globe apprised of the latest and most popular consumer products vis-à-vis the Internet, cell phones, and satellite TV while high-speed transportation systems bring those products into homes. Instantaneous contact with consumers and the ability to deliver goods within days go hand in hand in the global marketplace to help create more and more surplus value that can be transformed into greater and greater corporate profits.

With these technologies, globalization facilitates the creation of both absolute and relative surplus value. Globalization extends the workday, often surreptitiously, through the use of cell phones, home computers, and mandatory long-distance travel, to name only a few of the technologies contributing to this extension. If you provide a worker with a cell phone, he or she becomes continuously available to field questions and solve problems even while attending a child's soccer game or eating at a restaurant. These technologies along with other innovations in production also increase productivity. Computers have exponentially increased the speed of production. For instance, police officers frequently carry small wands that can read a suspect's fingerprint and match it against a database of previous offenders to expedite the incarceration process. But globalization distinguishes itself from earlier stages of capitalism by its ability to extract surplus value beyond these two traditional methods. The four cornerstones of globalization I will now examine suggest that the global capitalist landscape creates a new type of surplus value—one best described as virtual surplus value. Because the contemporary political economy weaves together global consumption, monopolistic management, and industrial production, virtual surplus value both requires material production and operates irrespective of that materiality. This apparent contradiction begins with the creation of digital communications.

The Creation of Digital Communications

Digital communication—coding and decoding information using the binary logic of 1s and 0s—enables the nearly instantaneous transmission of information and increases "the economic efficiency of networks by allowing them to be shared more thoroughly and effectively among many users" (Schiller xv).[14] These networks of information accelerate rates of investment and contribute to greater communication among different groups of people. The increasing speed of investment turnover is especially evident in the currency markets. According to historian Jerry Harris, "foreign currency transactions are so volatile that 66 per cent [of investors] hold money for less than seven days" (25). Clearly, an investor who withdraws his or her money after only seven days is not interested in expanding the growth, stability, or strength of a national currency. Such an investor can only be interested in short-term profits on speculation and not future material production. Although speculation has been part of the capitalist system since the creation of the joint-stock company in the nineteenth century, the methods for speculative investment have become much more sophisticated with digital technology. As a result of this new form of speculation, an investment can easily make profits without having any relationship to current or future production. For instance, many individuals reaped huge profits from a short-term investment in the Mexican peso made immediately prior to its 1994 devaluation. Investors who pulled their money before the peso fell secured enormous profits from a short-lived increase in the value of the peso even though Mexico never experienced any material benefits. The peso's increased valuation resulted from economic hopes associated with NAFTA while its decline derived from the subsequent Zapatista uprising in Mexico City—neither of these events was directly tied to innovations within the productive sphere. On the contrary, both events were rhetorically constructed for global media outlets. Given our interconnected world, it is no wonder that similar currency devaluations followed. Thailand's bath fell in 1997, triggering waves throughout Southeast Asia that resulted in South Korean, Malaysian, and Indonesian devaluations. *The Lexus and the Olive Tree* by Thomas L. Friedman chronicles this story from Asia to Russia and into the United States. His assessment that each economy impacted the other rings true, but I want to stress that these valuations and devaluations resulted from global rhetorical processes as much as financial speculation.

While Marx argues that profits from speculative investments like this represent the distribution of surplus value and not its creation, the new global structure indicates that profits accrued from digitalized information have an unusual relationship to the creation of surplus value. Because surplus value is located in production, earlier forms of capitalist investment supported long-term corporate growth in order to advance technology and potentially increase surplus value. Significantly different, this new form of short-term speculation has little or no interest in the material conditions of companies or nation-states. In place of the material conditions of production, the immediate transmission of information—necessary for the precise timing of investment—acquires primacy within the global economy. Instantaneous information has an ability to add value as never before. If television, magazines, and newspapers all inform us of NAFTA and its great potential to industrialize Mexico, they are adding value to the Mexican peso. The simple fact that currency values fluctuate according to a floating rather than fixed rate further indicates its circulation within a system of virtual valuation. This change has an enormous impact on capitalist production as the investment dollars that once translated into better material conditions for workers, however unevenly, no longer offer the same means for improving material realities. Detached from the material sphere, money can circulate from investment to investment in the virtual world of e-trade without ever attaching itself to any material landscape. Yet as the example of the rise and fall of the Mexican peso illustrates, the material world fluctuates according to these investments. Encouraged to invest by the promises of NAFTA and encouraged to withdraw that investment by the Zapatista threat, currency traders profited while the people of Mexico underwent a devastating economic depression.

One consequence of these accelerated investment cycles, then, is the creation of a false currency. False currencies, or what Marxists call fictitious capital, consist of "money that is thrown into circulation as capital without any material basis" (Harvey, *Limits* 95). The extension of credit, for instance, constitutes a false currency. Information technology as it has evolved within globalization creates another false currency. In this global paradigm, the false currency of virtual money replaces traditional forms of money. Digitalization actually transforms the economy so that virtual money acquires an exchange value and can be bought and sold for a price just like any other commodity. Economist Elinor Harris Solomon defines virtual money as a currency "without any reserve base or monitoring or measurement feature of the customary banking kind" (9) or simply "computer money with no immediate interface with conventional money" (201). Virtual money can circulate, by virtue of the Internet, buying and selling commodities around the world without staying in any one account for very long. In this virtual economy, corporations can sell their products back and forth to internal corporate divisions in order to inflate their value. The consumer ultimately pays for this inflated value in sky-high prices, but no one puts extra labor into the product to increase its value and justify its price. Unlike traditional surplus value that accrues on the backs of workers, virtual surplus value accrues on the backs of consumers. In a traditional scheme, owners of corporations have to attract buyers before they can transform surplus value into profit, but digitalization helps overcome this glitch to profits by constructing surplus value within a virtual economy. It is only later, when customers come into play, that this house of cards crumbles with the big investors safely out and their profits secured.

Investments made with virtual money have the potential to generate surplus value by outdistancing, rather than superseding or replacing, productive labor. According to Solomon, "the electronic money transfer message moves very fast. The legal and institutional mechanisms don't always work that fast, especially when many currencies, languages, and laws enter in. The result is fast-as-light money flow but not quite so fast balance sheet transfers through a string of banks and wires" (203). Virtual money quite literally moves so quickly as to be unaccountable to, untraceable within, and disconnected from traditional economic structures. It makes and breaks fortunes before the earnings derived from material production, distribution, and consumption are even figured into the equation. But, to underscore, virtual money and virtual surplus value cannot exist irrespective of the material foundations of telephone wires, computer cables, and video screens that enable instant digital communication. Nor can virtual investing continue without someone laying the wires, attaching the cables, building the computers, and maintaining the phone lines. Industrial production, an integral part of globalized consumption, forms the foundation on which this new economy operates, even though globalization rhetorically denies the persistence of an industrial era. In this sense, global capitalism privileges a false economy both because it creates false currencies that enable greater profits and because it denies the real currencies of production that require accountability and responsible action.

Take America On-Line (AOL) as an example of the false economies constructed through global rhetorical practices. AOL was able to buy Time Warner in January 2000 specifically because its stock traded at fifty-five times its earnings—because "AOL was 'worth' nearly twice as much as Time Warner as their stock was valued in the marketplace, *they could use it as currency*" (Tabb 45, my emphasis). Artificially inflated stock prices function as currency, regardless of any value-added process, and falsely determine a company's worth. Tabb places the word "worth" in quotes to signify that this value is fictitious. In this virtual economy, AOL had an exchange value equivalent to that of Time Warner even though the two would be drastically unequal within a traditional monetary economy. That is, this stock market value far outpaces the company's earnings and must, therefore, be determined by something other than a company's ability to make profit. In this case, the information that AOL has cornered the market on Internet service providers and that the Internet is the marketplace of the future add value to AOL regardless of its actual profit margin.

Value has severed its ties to any clear material referent, even though material structures are needed within this valuation system. AOL could not have sold its shares without causing a panic and disrupting the whole market, but using its own inflated valuation, AOL traded its stock for ownership of the lower valued but more profitable Time Warner. Because these shares could not be converted into cash at the same rate as they could be exchanged for acquisition of Time Warner, the value must be operating within a different economy. AOL exchanged rights to a portion of its future profits—determined by the information that AOL will increase in value—for ownership of the material assets of Time Warner Corporation. This exchange differs from traditional speculation because the precision of digital technologies produces the illusion that this information is somehow infallible rather than speculative. The consumers of stock—increasingly, working professionals whose retirement has been privatized and placed into futures accounts—have been told that their nest egg will be there even though such an outcome is uncertain. Making probable judgments about uncertain future outcomes has always been the domain of rhetoric; and now, in the global era, rhetoric and economics converge more than ever as valuation in the virtual economy relies more on the communication of information rather than on the production and consumption of material goods.

The new digital economy manufactures virtual money that can buy and sell major corporations without significant concrete backing, but it also enables the connectivity of greater numbers of people across greater distances. To be sure, such connectivity does represent a major effect of globalization. Sassen points out that stock markets worldwide have become globally integrated since the 1980s (*Losing Control?* 12), and Tomlinson argues that telecommunications have created a new sense of proximity across borders (181). This economic and cultural interconnectivity is necessarily bound together within a capitalist system that requires the transgression of always larger socioeconomic boundaries for its own survival. As early as the *Grundrisse,* Marx claimed that a precondition of capitalism was "*the production of a constantly widening sphere of circulation*" (407). As that sphere widens, capitalists need to be in communication with and economically connected to one another across greater distances. Indeed, political scientist Jonathon Nitzan argues that the high number of mergers and acquisitions within our current economy "reflects the progressive breakup of socio-economic 'envelopes,' as dominant capital moves through successive amalgamation at the industry, sectoral, national, and finally, global level" (226). With the transgression of each barrier comes increased communication. Although Marx predicted the global spread of capitalism, he did not foresee the way that this nearly instantaneous communication would affect the circulation of money and the production of surplus value. Digitalization, like other linchpins in the global terrain, represents a new phenomenon that builds on old structures. The transportation system, another key component of the global political economy, also constructs new phenomena from old arrangements.

High-Speed Transportation

Just as digital technologies circulate information almost instantaneously, other technologies circulate people and commodities more quickly than ever before and thus make the dispersal of production across national boundaries possible. As I noted earlier, the new technologies of globalization primarily result from the need to speed up the circulation of commodities in order to increase profits. With this goal in mind, globalization has tended to divide production into smaller, more discrete cycles, creating what many call the global production line. Harvey explains that "the splitting of a production process into many different phases and firms through market exchange appears to be highly desirable, since it diminishes the turnover time" (*Limits to Capital* 132). These many different phases, he argues, fit into the two divisions of capitalist production. The first division sells fixed capital to the second division, which uses those items to produce commodities it later sells to retailers. In other words, the first division is made up of the production and sale of commodities between capitalists prior to consumer commodities entering the global marketplace whereas the second division consists of commodity production for the general retail market.

In the global economy, the international production and sale of commodities between capitalists occurs more easily and more quickly through the creation of export-processing zones. Within these zones, tariffs and taxes between countries are reduced or eliminated. Such production zones allow "firms, mostly from high-wage countries, to export semiprocessed components for further processing in low-wage countries and then to re-import them back to the country of origin without tariffs on the value added through processing" (Sassen, *Losing Control?* 7). Moving between countries with unenforced safety regulations, minimum wages, and other labor policies allows transnational companies to produce items more cheaply. The unevenness of many national labor policies encourages twin factories on two sides of a border dividing high- and low-wage countries such as the U.S.-Mexico border. This deal is only sweetened by tax and tariff incentives. Free-trade zones (NAFTA, for instance) and export manufacturing zones (unregulated, low-wage areas) further allow corporations to avoid local taxes. The economic advantages accrued from dividing up the production process in this way compel companies to develop new technologies that allow for the increased mobility of products and people. The division of the production process across large spatial boundaries simply could not exist without significant technological and physical infrastructures that enable the convenient movement of products across borders. International travel necessitates a productive sphere to assemble, repair, maintain, and replace airplanes, ships, cars, trains, and other mass transit systems. That same industrial labor process also constructs the buildings and stations in which such transportation is housed. Clearly, global consumption significantly depends on industrial production.

Because of this industrial scaffolding, people are also moving across national boundaries with much greater frequency and in greater numbers than they were prior to globalization. This is true of workers, students, and travelers. Harris notes, for instance, that "foreign-born students in the U.S. account for 50 per cent of all mathematics, computer science and engineering graduates" (28). He also points out that "40 per cent of all new patents in the computer field are from immigrant workers and in Silicon Valley almost half the workforce of many corporations is of foreign origin" (28). Certainly there are myriad reasons for this kind of mobility—economic necessity, political asylum, and educational opportunities as well as social and familial incentives. Such mobility could not take place without advanced technologies that connect some people in both physical and virtual spaces at the same time that such technologies subjugate others to the work of industrial production. The high population of immigrant workers in Silicon Valley includes foreign-born computer scientists and engineers who are likely well connected with the communities they left behind; but the immigrant population also includes low-skilled wage workers who assemble computer parts in what is often called Silicon Alley—these workers are much less likely to have easy and reliable contact with distant others.

The industrial technology that propels commodities and laborers via large-scale transportation systems as well as the less visible industrial workers who assemble these technologies force us to remember that we do not occupy an exclusively postindustrial era as theorists like Jean-François Lyotard and Daniel Bell suggest. Against this characterization of the global economy, Spivak insists that "the entire economic text would not be what it is if it could not write itself as a palimpsest upon another text where a woman in Sri Lanka has to work 2,287 minutes to buy a t-shirt" ("Scattered Speculations" 171). The internationalization of the labor process creates this palimpsest of postmodern written over modern written over premodern, she says. Even postindustrial information exchange requires a large material infrastructure that is built and maintained via traditional industrial labor processes. For instance, as advocates of rural subsistence farmers, the Zapatistas represent this "premodern"; as sophisticated manipulators of global technologies from international news outlets to the Internet, the Zapatistas represent the "postmodern." Both works are intertwined and bound together in the current historical materialist map of globalization.

Because of this complex global scene and its subsequent uneven development, the equalization process—the ability of all people to benefit from capitalist labor—is disrupted within and between various geographical regions and little commonality exists among wages, products, and markets across a country or within a given geographical space.[15] The commonalities that do occur between two places are not geographically determined. Instead, they are determined by financial functions. Certain "global cities" have more in common with each other than any one of those cities might have with other cities in its own nation-state. As major metropolitan sites, these cities and their heterogeneous culture depict a multicultural world rather than a national one. Global cities—New York, London, Tokyo, Paris, Frankfurt, Zurich, Amsterdam, Los Angeles, Sydney, and Hong Kong, as well as Bangkok, Seoul, Taipei, São Paulo, Mexico City, and Buenos Aires—bind major international financial and business centers (Sassen, *Cities in a World Economy* 4–5). While globalization has certainly added new nodal points to the traditional centers of capitalist production, the power relations of globalization continue to privilege major centralized locations over the vast majority of other spaces. Indeed, the increased dispersal of production around the globe necessitates an increased centralization of financial headquarters. Such centralized functions take place primarily in global cities where corporate headquarters as well as specialized financial, legal, accounting, managerial, and executive functions exist. Global cities house a specialized service industry to accommodate the specific financial needs of transnational corporations as well as the luxury services desired by their upper-level management.

A Shrinking Service Industry

There is reason to suspect that the overall service industry, unlike the global city's service industry, is beginning to shrink. I believe the general service industry is declining as consumers, aided with technology, are increasingly doing the work of that industry. In order to claim that the service industry is shrinking, one must first acknowledge the historically ambiguous categorizations and incorrect definitions of service work. Traditionally, much of what has been categorized as service is more closely related to production. Arun Kundnani states unequivocally that "for as long as the concept of services has been in use, it has been plagued by definitional problems" (52). Service sometimes includes mental labor while other times mental labor falls under the category of management. Another definition, which includes software development, suggests that the service industry produces intangible goods. Yet most software is sold in tangible forms like compact discs. A music concert might provide an intangible good, but the lighting and stage crew construct quite tangible products, as do the workers who make T-shirts and other souvenirs. In this way, the numbers involved in the service industry often remain deceptively high because of an imprecise definition that includes everything from restaurant workers to musicians, software engineers, lawyers, and accountants. Even without clarifying these categorical slips, a significant numerical reduction can be found in the service industry.

Contrary to much of the economic literature addressing a vaguely defined service industry, Sassen argues that production jobs are increasing in numbers greater than those in the service industry. She states that by 1978 the largest percentage of female workers in Singapore, for example, was not in service as it had been previously. Instead, the greatest number of jobs was in production and related areas. Although the service sector in Singapore, like all sectors, has increased in absolute numbers, "its percentage of all jobs declined from 34.7 percent in 1957 to 14.9 percent in 1978" (*Globalization* 113). Reduced by over half, this drop is extreme. The U.S. service industry followed a slightly different trajectory but has also undergone a significant decline. Even though the sources for U.S. statistics vary according to fluctuating criteria, the 1930s, 1940s, and 1950s indexes show a generally stable service industry that occupied 10 or 11 percent of the workforce. That figure rose to 13 percent in 1960, 16 percent in 1970, and nearly 20 percent in 1978. However, by 1990 the percentage of service workers in the United States dropped to somewhere between 11 and 13 percent (*Handbook of Labor Statistics; American Labor Sourcebook;*

U.S. Census Bureau; *1990 Census of the Population*). In short, U.S. labor trends of the 1950s, 1960s, and early 1970s show a rising service industry. This trend peaked by the late 1970s and then began to fall as the transition into the global political economy solidified.

One way to account for this surprising trend is to recognize another trend: beginning in the late 1970s, consumers increasingly took on the work traditionally performed by the mid-level service industry. Braverman states that monopoly capitalism's key function was to absorb masses of unproductive labor—labor that does not create surplus value—into its wage system. Child care, food preparation, and business accounting, all of which once occurred in the unpaid sphere of the home, became absorbed into wage-labor systems and helped extend the reaches of surplus value (287). Global capitalism has transformed much of that labor, which predominantly falls within the service category, by encouraging the customer to perform this work him- or herself. Monopoly capital absorbed certain forms of work into its wage system to produce more profit. In turn, global capitalism increased that profit by maintaining management of service work while shedding responsibility for paid wages. In this new structure, service work is performed for the benefit of capitalist production but brilliantly goes unpaid. We begin to fill our own sodas at fast food restaurants, deposit our own checks at ATMs, make payments directly into corporate accounts via electronic banking, answer our own questions by browsing the Web, and even collect and deposit demographic information by carrying and swiping grocery store cards. The culture industry and television producers have paired up to create a plethora of shows that use unpaid amateurs to sing, design, model, act, and dance for the viewing public. TV producers get cheap programming and the culture industry gets free advertising as well as a potential star. Specialty areas, like stock market brokering, have also adopted a similar unpaid structure by allowing consumers to establish their own brokerage accounts to do their own buying and selling on-line. If the service industry is decreasing, we can attribute at least part of it to consumers who freely assume the duties that were previously performed by paid labor.

Yet, as I indicated, corporations maintain their ability to supervise these unpaid consumer laborers. Digital technologies, characteristic of globalization, enable businesses to track consumer habits and control consumer laborers from a distance. Corporations use new technologies that monitor consumers and create individual profiles as a means to "manage" customers. Internet technology is critical to this new activity as it surveys our shopping habits while on-line, catalogues this information in databases, and sells it to marketers. Those with a profile indicating potential profitability are given customer service while those unlikely to generate profits for the company may find themselves with high fees and no customer support. In global capitalism, customers as well as employees are managed according to strict numerical information. Tabb calls this management practice "the new world of customer apartheid" (169); David Broad calls it the "informalization of labor" (27); Mark Andrejevic names it the "digital enclosure" (35–36). Regardless of the specific nomenclature, the point remains that unpaid consumer labor coupled with corporate-managed technologies creates surplus value in unprecedented ways. This new process for creating surplus value includes any task performed outside traditional workspaces from which a corporation might profit but for which the work goes unpaid. In this new arrangement corporations retain the right to manage consumer workers and shed responsibility for remuneration.

Consumers accept this additional labor for many reasons but especially because this new consumerism appeals to notions of convenience, efficiency, and independence. Like other supposedly time-saving technologies, these innovations are presented to the public within the rhetoric of democracy and efficiency. We will not have to stand in line as long at the grocery store if we help with the bagging and fee processing; we will not have to leave home to make travel arrangements if we do it ourselves online. Though these changes certainly save corporations money, they do not always save consumers time. But there are reasons for alarm beyond the truth-value of efficiency claims. The shrinking service industry has significant ramifications for other national institutions that must absorb the large numbers of displaced workers. Take checkout counters, for instance. As large chain stores introduce self-serve checkout counters, they eliminate or reduce the number of cashiers. Wal-Mart and other major retailers have recently introduced self-serve checkout stations where customers scan their own groceries and pay via machine. Four of these self-service stations are supervised by one cashier who helps if there are problems, makes sure all items are scanned, and watches to see that proper payment is entered. Not only is this worker asked to do more, three other workers have been replaced by a process that requires customers to labor for free. If the service industry shrinks, so do the number of jobs, but this seems to fly in the face of reported statistics that the United States maintains exceptionally low unemployment rates. Where are all these displaced workers?

While U.S. unemployment rates remain deceptively low, the university population grows and our prison populations swell. Universities graduate, on average, 9 percent of its working-aged population compared to the 2–4 percent in most European societies. According to Stanley Aronowitz, higher education plays a role in "cushioning the effects of recessions, job-destroying technological change, and the frequent shifts and restructuring in the American economy" (28). Prisons offer another institution for the housing of surplus labor. The prison population has steeply risen since the 1970s transition into globalization, perhaps cushioning the national joblessness rate. Ruth Wilson Gilmore demonstrates that although violent crimes and drug use have declined, the legal system has produced an increase of 1.4 million inmates between 1982 and 1998. The state of California created what antiprison advocates call the prison-industrial complex by investing a "portion of [state] revenue flows into the prison system, at a level nearly equal to general fund appropriations for the State's two university systems" (185). The prison-industrial complex, like the university, includes both the private and public sectors and provides many businesses with a low-cost, low-risk labor force. Not surprisingly, Gilmore understands this huge rise in the prison population as deeply connected to the restructuring required by the global political economy. Whatever the specific links, it is worth noting that this 500 percent increase in the prison population between 1985 and 2000 has gone relatively unnoticed within the mainstream press. With such little stir over a significant reduction in the free working population, we should at least consider the possibility that universities and prisons function, in part, to absorb the recent reductions in the service sectors. With the service industry declining and international production jobs on the rise, the transnational corporation becomes one of the central cogs constructing the historical materialist boundaries of globalization.

Increased Corporate Sovereignty

The fourth, and final, cornerstone of globalization I wish to discuss is the often-cited fact that nation-states appear to be receding in importance as transnational corporations increase in stature. Although the nation-state retains much of its authority, transnational corporations do play an increasing role in dictating how nation-states exercise that authority. Unlike earlier historical periods when military occupations and political control of nation-states constituted imperialist practices, globalization works through an economic imperialism that empowers transnational corporations to determine many of the relationships between distant people and places. One measure of this can be traced through the changing patterns of investment in developing countries. Transnational corporations (TNCs) have become the major source of foreign direct investment— superseding investment by nation-states. This transition developed momentum after the foreign exchange market opened itself to international investors in the mid-1970s. Subsequently, transnational corporations "emerged as a source for financial flows to developing countries. . . . In some respects, TNCs replaced banks" (Sassen, *Cities in a World Economy* 18). Earlier capitalist relationships necessitated national banking systems that standardized currency and offered security against stock market fluctuations, natural disasters, as well as the ebb and flow of speculation. When national currencies were opened to foreign speculation, however, the strength of this banking system gave way to funds from transnational corporations that possessed the surplus capital to finance projects in developing nations. Because these projects mean larger market shares and cheap labor, transnational corporations were eager to take up this new financial role.

In addition to financing the industrialization of developing countries, corporations are increasingly extending themselves into spaces previously excluded from the corporate sector. For instance, health care, education, and prisons were all designed to serve the public interest and were therefore not-for-profit ventures subsidized by state and federal funds. Even though many individuals profited by working in these sectors, the institutions themselves were supposed to serve the public good rather than any particular private interest. With a solemn pledge to eliminate superfluous spending, hiring, and bureaucracy, corporations have exploited the opportunity presented by the current global era to take over schools, hospitals, and prisons in order to make a profit. Given these changes and the extension of corporations into the public sector, Malcolm Waters believes "it is impossible to deny that multinational or transnational corporations are frequently more powerful than the states whose societies they operate in" (33). With tentacles in multiple nation-states, the freedom to operate without tariffs and often without taxes, transnational corporations can avoid the hard-won labor policies of one nation by simply taking its business elsewhere. Transnational corporations are even able to make profits off of civil rights—securing exclusive textbook contracts in public schools and turning elections into televised dramas—as well as the denial of those civil rights—producing surveillance technologies and privatizing prisons.

This power shift from the nation-state to transnational corporations requires a similar shift in strategies for resistance. If transnational corporations have acquired some of the authority once reserved for the nation-state, as consumer laborers, we have the power to demand that corporations be responsible to the public they claim to represent. Within this new structure, individuals need to pressure corporations—using their power as consumers—to ensure that individuals are given rights and protections. Sassen believes, for instance, that we must consider the possibility that there exists a form of economic citizenship that empowers and can demand accountability from governments. According to Sassen, this economic citizenship belongs to "firms and markets, specifically, the global financial markets, and it is located not in individuals, not in citizens, but in mostly corporate global economic actors. The fact of being global gives these actors power over individual governments" (*Losing Control?* 38). Citizens living in a sovereign nation, at least in theory, are governed by the will of the people. In turn, that government provides rights and protections to its citizens. This notion of citizenship is fundamentally called into question if the sovereignty of a nation-state succumbs to corporate rule. In such a situation, Sassen contends, "firms operating transnationally need to ensure the functions traditionally exercised by the state in the national realm of the economy" (*Losing Control?* 14). In fact, Sassen argues that transnational corporations have emerged as important governance mechanisms whose authority is not centered in the state but in the market logic of globalization. Thus, oppositional agency might emerge in two distinct ways: we could contest the foundational logic of globalization in order to undermine corporate sovereignty or we could demand that these corporate citizens take responsibility for their actions. Though the site for lodging complaints and demanding accountability for one's rights may have shifted from the nation-state to the transnational corporation, the will of various locally grounded individual communities still maintains authority for maneuvering, negotiating, and participating in one's day-to-day activities.

If individuals possess as much power as they always have, they must endorse corporate power—along with the rest of the national structure—in order for such corporations to have widespread legitimacy without appearing to overextend their authority. Rhetorical boundaries of acceptable behavior are constituted through individual and collective action within cultural, political, and economic realms. It is critical to remember, then, that this power shift in favor of corporate sovereignty signifies "*an abdication of state power,* not a lack of that power" (P. Marcuse 25). While the general public acquiesces to this shift, that same public could always exercise its interests differently. Corporatization ideologically and structurally encourages individual complacency; but this does not make it so. Consider the centralization of national power in response to the September 11, 2001, terrorist attacks on the World Trade Center and the Pentagon. After this event, the nation-state chose to reclaim its authority and the general public endorsed that decision through a heavily manufactured, extremely commodified patriotism that included flags, bumper stickers, buttons, and music, to name only a few of the new products that emerged. In keeping with the sociopolitical boundaries of globalization, this movement existed primarily within the consumer sphere where political support can be bought, sold, and negotiated but not voted upon and especially not debated. Voting rights remained within the U.S. House and Senate where they authorized the PATRIOT Act, military action in Afghanistan, and the Iraqi war—initiatives broadly supported by the concomitant consumer campaign rather than thoughtful rhetorical deliberation. Regardless of the merit of this commercialized patriotism, it leaves little doubt that the nation-state remains a powerful means of uniting people across distances and legitimizing globally significant actions from military attacks to the encroachment of domestic freedoms.[16]

Unfortunately, though, this national patriotism does nothing to address the decline in trade unionism, the individualization of resistance within the marketplace, and the emergence of corporate citizenship. In fact, rather than collectively working for change, Waters argues that people who exert their agency as consumers tend to "extend trust to unknown persons, to impersonal forces and norms ('the market,' or 'human rights') and to patterns of symbolic exchange that appear to be beyond the control of any concrete individual or group of individuals" (63–64). The possibility for collective change within this cultural-economic milieu seems dismal. Whether through a sense of complacency or a sense of hopelessness, individuals give up the idea of collective agency to some loosely held belief about the inevitability of globalization. Waters is not alone in this gloomy forecast. Other scholars, like Carl Boggs in *The End of Politics: Corporate Power and the Decline of the Public Sphere,* similarly bemoan the loss of civic participation that seems to have disappeared with the advent of globalization. For Boggs and others leery of globalization, this retreat from the public sphere significantly limits progressive work. Indeed, relatively few citizen outcries resulted from the voting inconsistencies of the 2000 presidential election and only a murmur of dissent resulted from revelations that President Bush and his staff manufactured its case to justify war against Iraq.

Against this political paralysis, Sassen advocates that we theorize local arrangements that might impinge on global structures. She believes that theoretical work should do the following: decompose the nation-state into discrete places and analyze specific localities as complete components in collaboration with the larger national tapestry; refocus analysis away from single corporations and instead include organizations of corporations, networks, and structural arrangements; and focus on place, materiality, and physical infrastructures (*Globalization* 213). In the spirit of these suggestions, the next chapter refocuses on the U.S. public research university as a specific scene within a larger national and international landscape. It analyzes particular universities in a network of relationships with other universities but also in relationship to the cultural and economic flows of globalization. I end this chapter with a brief discussion of the emergent global university and its articulation to the four key characteristics of globalization. Chapter 2 discussed the general shape of the U.S. public research university within the global stage of capitalism; the following section will emphasize how the four major components of globalization play out in the university.

Connecting Global Capitalism to the Global University

Even though the global political economy reduces and potentially eliminates service labor, such labor—unpaid and performed by consumers—increasingly participates in the production of surplus value. The elimination of service labor from the arena of wage work results, in part, from the fact that digital communication technologies such as cellular phones, home computers, Internet connections, and satellite television enable, and sometimes require, extended workdays. With these technologies in many U.S. homes, the traditional boundary between work and leisure comes into crisis as individual leisure time becomes an arena for the production of surplus value. The need for some instructors to use technology at home in order to be in communication with their colleagues and their students in a nearly continuous fashion exemplifies one way this blurred boundary has become naturalized in the form of listservs, e-mail communication, and interactive Web boards—technologies that are often purported to serve democratic and inclusive learning environments. As instantaneous communication becomes the norm, the extended workday based on the immediate fulfillment of student needs also becomes standard. Surreptitiously extending the workday, these technologies increase absolute surplus value—more journal articles and books are written, more student papers are graded, more experiments are run, more grants are submitted, and more patents are filed. Relative surplus value is also created, as these new technologies demand on-line work at sites that track and catalogue educational services. This information can be sold to companies interested in the hot college-aged market as well as to the increasingly profitable courseware industries. Such technologies allow greater surplus value to be extracted from the same labor process—at least until the practices become standardized, markets adjust, and corporations look for new ways to create surplus value.

A number of other changes within the university's labor structure are made possible because of new transportation technologies designed to move people as well as consumer products quickly and efficiently. Relying on the speed and ease of local and international travel, the university has become an expert in what Broad calls the casualization of labor, which he defines as "the expansion of part-time, short-term, contract, and other sorts of casual labor" (27). The new global university makes use of casual labor in myriad ways. Teaching is now increasingly the domain of graduate students, adjuncts, and other part-time workers who are paid on a per course basis. These teachers, however, cannot sustain themselves on a part-time salary when they need to pay rent, make student loan payments, and buy their own health insurance. In order to survive, some instructors secure jobs at several universities and become what many people in California call "freeway flyers." Representing another creative employment option, the overflow of graduates from university Ph.D. programs sometimes temporarily leave the country to teach English for higher wages and with significant tax breaks in Asian and Eastern European countries. These options construct a safety value for the overflow of graduate students for whom there are no jobs at the same time that they deter graduating Ph.D.s from critiquing a system that overproduces doctoral candidates in a shrinking job market.[17] Without the advancements in transportation brought about by globalization, such a safety net might not exist.

Similarly, the fluidity with which people are able to move across borders allows large numbers of foreign students to travel to the United States for graduate and undergraduate educations. If the cost of an education at public universities is growing out of reach for lower- and middle-class students in the United States, such universities increasingly seek upper-class students from other countries. Masao Miyoshi writes that that many foreign students "are now actively recruited for the tuition they bring from rich families in the Third World" ("Ivory Tower in Escrow" 36). Although this trend is not new, it is on the rise. The ease with which information, commodities, and people are moved across great distances has certainly impacted the structure and makeup of U.S. public research universities. A university can now teach more students without placing pressure on its physical infrastructure through technically supported distance learning; a university can temporarily hire greater numbers of graduate student teachers who can later export their skills to other countries; and a university can attract foreign students when the number of eligible tuition-paying domestic students dries up. In short, global capitalism's drive to produce surplus value through unpaid or underpaid labor has contributed to the displacement of a generally secure university professoriate by students and insecure, part-time faculty.

Even undergraduate students are introduced into the trend of casualized labor through courses in service learning, required, nonpaying internships, and the payment of peer instruction in course credit rather than in wages. Much of this student labor is also extracted on a voluntary basis with the explicit mission of training students into democratic and civic participation. In addition to the promise of higher grades and a better understanding of course material, such experience can be highlighted on résumés and in job interviews. Resonating with the world outside the university, this phenomenon of students teaching students represents the replacement of a paid service industry with unpaid consumer labor. Students who are awarded credit for life experience often do their own teaching as well. At the University of Phoenix, for instance, "students fill out their degrees by earning credit for life experiences. Parenting, Family Life, and Loss and Bereavement were among one student's retroactive 'courses'" (Nelson and Watt 5). Without assigned coursework and without an instructor to help these students critically interrogate their experiences, students must presumably make sense of this coursework themselves. Although the University of Phoenix is a private, for-profit university, it is an important example because public research universities look to such schools as models of economic efficiency within the new economy. Public universities also compete with these institutions to attract and retain students. This competition compels universities to adopt the most innovative structures in order to advance beyond their peer institutions, secure a reputation, and attract a large student body.

Often these practices include privatizing public education according to corporate models. Indeed, as the government reduces its economic support to universities while corporations increase theirs, these corporations become increasingly influential. Corporate needs change quickly and they require universities to adapt just as quickly. For instance, the flexible work structure discussed earlier exemplifies how universities adapt to the corporate philosophy of just-in-time production. Adjunct faculty members are retained, in part, to supply instruction for courses that may or may not fill with students. Some instructors are offered jobs as late as the first day of classes. This kind of flexible labor, according to Cary Nelson and Stephen Watt, characterizes "an institution devoted to serving the semester-by-semester training needs of corporations" (2). Certainly the U.S. public research university was established, at least to some degree, to perform corporate research and train corporate employees, but the new global form of this university nevertheless distinguishes itself by changing research, curricula, and even its own infrastructure on an immediate, and as-needed, corporate basis. While it is easy to draw such an analogy because university and corporate structures are so similar, I resist the temptation to argue that these structures are the same. Rather than being identical, they are distinct, dependent, and complicit. Drawing analogies is a place to begin, but we also need to come to terms with the unique historical materialist landscape of the university if we are going to understand how it actively participates in and cooperates with the corporate world. If the global university is instrumental in the creation of an international post-professional class of managers and technical intellectuals who identify themselves with the transnational corporation, then an historical materialist analysis must study the internationalization of the U.S. public research university.

So far this book has focused on developing an historical materialist picture of the U.S. research university as it emerged in the industrial era, developed throughout monopoly capitalism, and matured within the age of globalization, with particular emphasis on the current structure of globalization. Moving away from corporate analogies, chapter 4 fleshes out specifically how the regulatory policies embedded within the global stage of capitalism have impacted and transformed the contemporary university as an international structure independent of but related to the globalization of transnational corporations. Policy in one delimiting sense exists at the level of officially transcribed and legally binding legislation within governments, corporations, universities, or other authorized institutions. Yet, according to Cynthia Enloe, author of the groundbreaking *Bananas, Beaches, and Bases* and a critic of international politics, policy also includes any standard practice whether it is officially constituted or not. Like discourse, policy is determined by everyday activities and is only effective if it is constantly enacted. If one wants to determine and analyze policy, he or she must assemble a given policy from its concrete practices. Therefore, in order to determine how globalization becomes concretized within the contemporary U.S. public research university, the next chapter analyzes the rhetoric of university missions and the global circulation of that rhetoric as it secures worldwide hegemony for the U.S. public research university model of higher education.

4

The Rhetoric of University Missions

Globalizing Economic Consent, Commodifying Multiculturalism, and Privatizing the Social Good

The messages contained in the market economy discourse on education are powerful tools of social persuasion. They shape conceptions of reality by framing discussions of ideas, values, and actions associated with education within arbitrarily established boundaries of acceptability. . . . When individuals live inside the linguistic confines of one discourse, that is, the market economy version, they are defined and limited by the particular world view it promotes.

—Emery J. Hyslop-Margison, "The Market Economy"

This chapter explores the relationship between globalization and the rhetoric of U.S. public research university statements of mission. I argue that the mission of the university is not only increasingly saturated by the discourse of economic globalization but that the rhetoric found in these statements is made manifest in various nation-states across the globe, defining and delimiting the material realities for much of the world's population. The mission statements I examine in this chapter have been revised at least once in the last twenty years and all tend to reflect the needs of global capitalism. While I am interested in these changes, I do not wish to prove that these revisions derived from the dynamics of U.S. capitalism. Similarly, I believe that a gap exists between what universities perform and what university mission statements claim, but I will not use this chapter to demonstrate this. Instead, I explore the actions performed by the statements themselves and think about what consequences result from the movement of these statements. Mission statements express the goals, visions, duties, and even the responsibilities of a university. Having both religious and military connotations, the language of mission statements can be quite powerful. I seek to analyze that power, explore its various material manifestations, and call for an intervention into its global cycle of production.

To be clear, I agree with higher education expert Emery Hyslop-Margison. The movement of market discourse—enabled and enclosed by the rhetorically constructed historical materialist boundaries of globalization—within the educational domain contributes to a particular worldview and, in fact, a specific kind of world. The idea that language helps construct reality has disputed and lengthy origins that can be traced back to the Sophists. The popularity of this idea within contemporary theory, however, is most often linked to a range of poststructuralist thinkers, including such prominent theorists as Jacques Derrida and Michel Foucault. Poststructuralist theories of language frequently subjugate the role of communication to less structured, less clear, less mappable notions of power, preferring to proffer one cognitive map undermined by others in an indefinite play of language. Derrida, for instance, challenges J. L. Austin's speech act theory, which designates only some language, in special contexts, with the power to perform actions beyond simple communication. He suggests that "a context is never absolutely determinable, or rather, [he explains] why its determination can never be entirely certain" and culminates this critique with a call to undermine traditional concepts of language through deconstruction (3). Destabilizing commonsensical beliefs and radically questioning the ontological and epistemological justification for Western cultural, political, and economic knowledge, deconstruction offers one means of exploiting language production for social change. This work necessitates negative and positive steps—what is torn down by radical language games must be built anew. Imagining a new society with new ways of legitimately participating in that society must, I believe, include deliberation and rhetorical practices, but it must also include exploration and change within the materiality of our world. By itself, then, deconstruction does not adequately attend to the material exigencies of capitalist production, consumption, and reproduction.

Foucauldian discourse analysis, on the other hand, requires attention to both materiality and discursivity. While many scholars practice discourse analysis without paying attention to political or material processes, Foucault provides the much-needed framework for linking textuality with materiality. His methodological text, *The Archaeology of Knowledge and the Discourse of Language,* and his 1977 interview "Truth and Power" both argue for a discursive intervention into materiality. Foucault explains that historical discontinuities change "ways of speaking and seeing, the whole ensemble of practices," and that these new practices signify "a modification in the rules of formation of statements" ("Truth and Power" 112). Historical fissures, for Foucault, offer opportunities for exploring how language has the power to shape and transform the way we see the world as well as the way we act in that world. Examining these discursive moments reveals the boundaries of possibility in action, speech, and institutional practice: rhetoric, that is, helps constitute materiality. Changes in linguistic practices not only indicate "a different mentality, but transformations in a practice, perhaps also in neighboring practices, and their common articulation" (*Archaeology* 209). As I indicated in the introduction, the process that Foucault calls discourse formation functions analogously with the concept of rhetoricality that I borrow from John Bender and David Wellbery. Through these similar conceptions of language, we can understand a change in the representation of and discussion surrounding the university to reflect altered practices as well as new material organizations of society. Something as apparently trivial, inconsequential, or mundane as a mission statement produces power-effects— rhetorically constructed enclosures within which material reality can be acceptably designed. Speaking specifically about the discourse of education, Foucault implies that a statement of mission in its "distribution, in what it permits and in what it prevents, follows the well-trodden battle-lines of social conflict" (*Archaeology* 227). This chapter attempts to assemble some of the various effects of those powers in order to strategize methods for interrupting the present cycle of economic globalization and replacing it with more useful forms of globalization.[1]

Interested in texts through which the university consciously defines itself (its goals, work, and purpose), I focus primarily on university mission statements. However, I also analyze other texts that specify this larger mission for a particular college, department, or academic organization. My goal is to explore changes in the research university's explicitly stated mission in order to examine how these changes articulate to broader power relations and are concretized within multiple layers of local, national, and international practices. For instance, these university rhetorics provide the educational model endorsed by the Organization for Economic Cooperation and Development (OECD).[2] Major lending organizations, like the World Bank, rely on statements by the OECD in order to define, shape, and develop higher education in countries less industrialized than the United States. In fact, most funds for higher education worldwide are contingent on a country's adoption of the OECD plan for higher education. While I do not claim that the U.S. public university system is the origin of all this rhetoric, I do want to point out that these universities are a linchpin in the circulation of a market-focused rhetoric among systems of higher education as well as international organizations throughout the globe. By examining the connection between various supranational organizations and the rhetoric of globalization within research universities, I believe this study refocuses theories of higher education onto material consequences. Just as education helps constitute the historical materialist terrain of a nation-state, the fact that the U.S. public research university system's revised missions set the agenda for worldwide educational practices suggests that this language impacts historical materialist conditions of nation-states around the globe.

While I have already explored the rhetorically constructed historical materialism of the U.S. public research university at different historical moments—including the moment of globalization—I now map the historical materialism of globalization by tracking the rhetoric of U.S. public research university mission statements and its various movements through national, international, and global organizations. Rather than attempting to create a blanket statement about this rhetoric as a uniform discourse, I explore how it takes local forms. My analysis is influenced by Foucault's technologies of knowledge theory as well as the theory of postcolonial critic Arjun Appadurai, which explains how global phenomena localize according to various "scapes" in order to emphasize the circulation of texts as well as their concrete, local forms and effects. According to Appadurai, "the complexity of the current global economy has to do with certain fundamental disjunctures between economy, culture, and politics" (33). With a commitment to the historical materialist realms of culture, politics, and economics, Appadurai looks to different kinds of exchanges to understand these realms. He believes that various global forces circumnavigate the globe but that disjunctures emerge when different personal and institutional identifications compel individuals to design uniquely inspired versions of those global flows. To see these disjunctures, we need to track cultural, political, and economic activities through a more refined lens such as that of Appadurai's "scapes." For instance, university mission statements outline the way a university seeks to create and disseminate knowledge. Consequently, mission statements clearly illustrate the movement of ideas—they sketch out a university's ideoscape. Although the movement of ideas should be expected within a university, university discourse also contributes to the movement of people, technologies, money, and images. These various and complex "scapes" in conjunction with Foucault's technologies of knowledge theory explain how the "idea" of the U.S. public research university and its professional subjectivity—to borrow a phrase from John Henry Newman's 1852 *The Idea of a University*—has been transported, translated, and reassembled within disparate localities worldwide.[3]

Professional training and certification exist as one way individuals develop knowledge about themselves and share that knowledge with others. Like aristocratic titles, a professional title signifies something about its bearer. This signification allows professionals to claim the right to both a certain kind of job and a certain form of prestige. Indeed, the use of professional titles opens the educational terrain to questions of work, labor, and economy as well as questions of individual subjectivity, identity, and consciousness. According to Foucault, professional training in Western culture represents one of the "techniques that human beings use to understand themselves" ("Technologies" 18). Professions create knowledge through four technologies: sign systems, production, power relations, and notions of the self. In the following sections, I show that examining these four technologies in relationship to Appadurai's "scapes" and situating the pairs within the four aspects of globalization I outlined in chapter 3 can help us understand the increasingly globalized model of the U.S. public research university and its subsequent creation of a post-professional class. This framework, as I see it, describes four multivalent and cooperative realms for circulating values within the global world: Foucault's technology of sign systems links with Appadurai's ideoscapes and requires digital communications; the technology of production relies on financescapes and requires increased corporate sovereignty; the technology of power interacts most prominently with technoscapes and necessitates high-speed transportation systems; and the technology of the self develops new ethnoscapes that reshape the service industry. Combining Foucault and Appadurai with my assessment of four key global shifts, I focus on the creation of a post-professional class and its circulation outside the United States. Additionally, I look at how the post-professional comes into being both inside and outside the United States in relationship to rhetorical challenges stemming from these mission statements and conclude the chapter by emphasizing that this rhetoric and its globalization represent a neocolonial boundary of higher education that subsequently constructs a neocolonial post-professional class. Before I do so, however, I briefly explain the method by which I construct this case study.

Building a Case: A Nonprobability Sample of U.S. Public Research Universities

The Carnegie classification system, the standard typology of U.S. universities, began in the early 1970s along with the emergence of the global political economy. Its original goal was to help individuals, policymakers, and other organizations locate and fund the many diverse functions of higher education. Until its revisions in 2000, the criterion used by the Carnegie Foundation to classify a research university was dual: the number of doctoral programs and the amount of federal funds. According to the Carnegie Commission, their 2000 classifications "discontinued the use of federal support as a basis for classification. In its place [they] have extended the previous use of doctoral field coverage" ("Background and Description" 5). The recognition that federal support is only one economic resource as well as the National Science Foundation's decision to cease reporting data used by the commission to determine federal funding prompted these new assessment criteria. Even with these changes in the Carnegie classification, research expenditures remain a critical factor in determining the mission and goals of universities. Including, but not limited to, federal support, I use total research expenditures as one of the key characteristics of my sample of universities. With an emphasis on research money and a goal of being geographically representative, I selected nine universities for this case study.

This data set represents what social scientists call a "nonprobability sample." Nonprobability sampling includes several different methods such as quota, judgment, convenience, and snowball samples. I use a nonprobability judgment sampling, which allows for a detailed study based on specific characteristics. According to H. Russell Bernard, "researchers don't usually pull research sites—communities, hospitals, school systems—out of a hat. They rely on their judgment to find one that reflects the things they are interested in" (176). After choosing and analyzing one's own data set, a researcher attempts "to generalize about cultural data" while allowing the intracultural variations within a set to complicate his or her conclusions (147). Rather than ignoring difference as anomalous or allowing difference to undermine conclusions, a nonprobability sampling allows for claims about continuity as well as difference. Using this nonprobability judgment sampling, I chose universities that were representative of different geographical areas—the East, Midwest, and West—as well as universities that represented a broad range of research and development expenditures, ranging from $104 to $550 million annually. The different geographical areas, to some extent, determine the local interests of universities and hence how they implement larger national and global trends while the different amounts of research funds should, at least in theory, determine the extent to which these universities can participate in the national and global research mission. I selected representative institutions that might offer a picture of the way that broad historical trends around the globe concretize differently within research universities, offering an opportunity to map worldwide educational convergence as well as divergence.

Unlike a random sample that might provide a disproportionate number of extremely well-funded or extremely poorly funded institutions, this method covers a range of research institutions. Without the burden of an all-inclusive study, it also ensures that all major "types," if not all institutions, are represented. Of course, this choice in sampling is not without its problems. Because the sample is not completely comprehensive, I risk omitting important exceptions to the conclusions I draw. My analysis examines nine institutions from Carnegie's total set of 102 public research universities nationwide.[4] These nine universities represent different characteristics among research universities, but as less than 9 percent of the total population, this sample cannot claim to represent the whole.

For this study, the University of South Carolina (East), the University of Nebraska (Midwest), and the University of New Mexico (West) represent institutions within the low range of research spending. As public research universities, however, these institutions are by no means impoverished. Indeed, they are among the top one hundred most funded universities, public and private, in the United States. Their annual expenditures on research and development average between $100 and $150 million, a budget exceeding that of many small nation-states. The University of North Carolina (East), Ohio State University (Midwest), and the University of Arizona (West) constitute the sample of institutions within the medium range of research expenditures. These universities are among the top forty most funded public or private universities in the country. Their expenditures on research and development range between $250 and $400 million annually. The three most funded institutions in my sample are Pennsylvania State University (East), the University of Michigan (Midwest), and the University of Washington (West). These institutions are among the top eleven most funded universities in the United States with annual research and development expenditures totaling between $400 and $600 million.

The highest-funded schools all have a student population of around 40,000 while the least-funded schools have a student population slightly below 25,000. The universities in the mid-range do not cluster around the same-size student body. These student populations ranged from 24,000 at the University of North Carolina to 35,000 at the University of Arizona to 48,000 at Ohio State University—one of the largest campuses in the nation. There seems to be some evidence that as research dollars increase, so does the size of the student population. Yet such a correlation is by no means uniform. Regardless of the amount of research dollars or the number of students, the founding dates of these universities cluster around the late nineteenth century. Six of the nine institutions were founded in the second half of the nineteenth century, two were founded in the first half of the nineteenth century, and only one was founded late in the eighteenth century. At least one university in each dollar range is a land-grant university. Given their institutional status as public research universities, these founding dates are not surprising. Nor would I be surprised to find that these universities have histories similar to the ones outlined in chapters 1 and 2, nor that their present configurations reflect particular responses to the current global stage of capitalism. Toward this inquiry, I turn now to my analysis of the rhetorical valuation of globalization within these universities and the exchange of that valuation between and among these institutions and the supranational organizations that regulate globalization. I begin with the category of ideoscape/sign system enabled by digital technology as the changing ideological landscape that helps determine how language shapes social policy as well as how individuals enact that policy.

Global Citizenship and the Uncertain Ideoscapes of Higher Education

Funding agencies and governing boards function according to what they interpret as the needs of society, say educational theorists Howard Buchbinder and Pinayur Rajagopal. They argue that universities, regardless of national origin, make these interpretations "public through their academic plans and/or mission statements" (284). A mission statement publicizes the ideological landscape—the ideoscape—of a particular university and explains its self-proclaimed relationship to the broader historical materialist terrain. While such relationships appear individualized, the frequency of global communication has opened the door for what Foucault calls the technology of sign systems to move virtually anywhere on earth. Circulating around the globe and in the midst of changing cultural, political, and economic regimes, the doctrine of liberalization and free trade exemplifies this fluidity. The notions of market centrality, private sector efficiency, and the dangerous growth of big government have infiltrated educational spheres worldwide (Buchbinder and Rajagopal 294).

While this neoliberal doctrine stems from the U.S. system of higher education, the global hegemony of its sign system reshapes higher education in the United States as well as in European, Asian, Latin American, and African countries.

By examining both the discourse of research university mission statements and the way the rhetoric of these mission statements reappears internationally, I argue for a more complex understanding of what it means to create a worldwide system of higher education derived primarily from the U.S. public research university. Rather than wholeheartedly accepting claims that such an educational model will enhance national economies and promote democracy around the world, I believe that the goal of globalizing a capitalist cultural, political, and economic system plays an equally important role in this restructuring of higher education. For instance, the OECD's *Policies for Higher Education* suggests that societies worldwide are developing free market strategies and that "the movement toward mass higher education will contribute to this fundamental democratization of society" (92). Higher education serves the rhetorically necessary function of developing discourses and training professionals, both of which redraw the boundaries of society to match the needs of an evolving capitalist structure. Just as in the history of the U.S. public research university, this rhetorical work articulates to democracy while obfuscating its capitalist functions. Indeed, the OECD suggests that the U.S. "establishment of different sectors of higher education reflecting the status hierarchies in the larger society is a more effective way of using higher education to buttress rather than undermine the class structure" (*Policies for Higher Education* 78).[5] The stratification of higher education represents a perfect solution to the problem posed by increasingly democratizing an educational system whose research agenda is narrowly focused on a limited number of market-driven projects, at least according to the OECD. U.S. higher education—the model being reproduced around the globe— might extend a form of democracy, but it also preserves a capitalist class system. These dual roles exist within the nation and they will continue to exist as this system moves increasingly overseas.

Mission statements make these ideologically antagonistic functions of the U.S. public research university appear to be natural extensions of each other rather than contradictory partners. Dominating the mission statements of U.S. public research universities, a unified mission of teaching, research, and service suppresses the complex and dialectical nature of these institutions at the same time it eases the tension between providing broad access to higher education and specializing in discrete research agendas. According to a typical research mission, vast amounts of money can be pumped into a single, potentially marketable project, whose goal is removed from the interests of the local community as long as the teaching mission somehow accommodates that community. Consequently, students from the local community as well as from around the globe accept the primacy of market-based research because of an ever-expanding teaching mission that offers job training under the nomenclatures of lifelong learning and continuous accreditation at the same time it encourages the exploration of cultural differences within its service components. The service mission—including various university outreach projects, public programming, and cultural events—teaches these students that the world needs to be shaped in the image of corporate capitalism and that individuals, rather than corporations or nation-states, need to take responsibility for solving social problems like class antagonism and poverty, racial hatred and civil rights, or sexism and violence against women.

A close examination of the nine sample U.S public research university mission statements reveals how this three-pronged strategy largely contains student and local activism within university-sponsored, highly bureaucratized, and easily monitored projects. Enveloping local and global communities within its mission, these statements contain rhetoric that undermines the dominant contradiction of U.S. higher education—it serves the democratic interests of teaching for citizenship at the same time that it serves the interests of corporate capital that often fail to recognize the rights of citizens—in two distinct ways. First, mission statements unify the goals of teaching for citizenship and pursuing market-driven research. Second, and as a variation of the first, mission statements mediate the tension between producing good citizens and accumulating wealth by the democratic mark of a land-grant tradition. Significantly, the rhetoric of citizenship in both approaches elicits the powerfully egalitarian notion of mass education that overwhelmingly justifies the university's expensive research initiatives. The global movement of ideoscapes embedded within this sign system constructs the post-professional as an increasingly specialized intellectual linked to the land-grant mission but dedicated to the activity of research.[6] Similarly, universities represent the post-professional as a resource for local, national, and international community building but primarily depend on the post-professional for income-generating activities.

The University of South Carolina's statement, for instance, clearly announces its three-part mission but emphasizes the production of good citizens. Its primary goal "is the education of the state's diverse citizens through teaching, research and creative activity, and service."[7] Noting the fluctuating historical moment, the university instructs students on "the values necessary for success and responsible citizenship in a complex and changing world." Following such a configuration, the university defines service as a public commitment "to its community, state, nation, and the world." Economic globalization, according to this mission, functions as an apparently benevolent process whereby U.S. institutions like this public university retain the power to offer service to those without such agency. Because economic growth necessarily improves the general standard of living, the university can be "dedicated to using research to improve the quality of life for South Carolinians" and still pursue whatever market research yields the most profit. The citizen not only acknowledges and assimilates into the new world order, he or she also provides the defense of its structure. In the name of its citizens, universities rely on this trickle-down ideology reminiscent of the progressive arguments lodged by Robert Hutchins and Abraham Flexner during the monopoly stage of U.S. public research universities. As old and as thoroughly bereft of concrete success stories, the trickle-down theory nevertheless remains as strong as ever as long as the citizenry are the ultimate proposed recipients. To endorse a university structure because it names your interests even though it rarely delivers your interests represents a significant power-effect determined by the rhetorical boundary of ideoscapes such as democratic education and service to the citizenry.

Revised in 2001, the University of New Mexico's two-page statement similarly invokes citizenship as a strategy to explain its research mission. Among its visions, the University of New Mexico wishes "to serve as a significant knowledge resource for New Mexico, the nation, and the world; and to foster programs of international prominence." To achieve this service mission, the university attempts to "provide students the values, habits of mind, knowledge, and skills that they need to be enlightened citizens, to contribute to the state and national economies, and to lead satisfying lives." In this list, contributing to the economy, being an enlightened citizen, and leading a satisfying life function as equivalent and connected values. This equivalence erases significant differences between, for instance, the drive for capitalist accumulation and the potential valuation of self-worth outside economic parameters—a strategy that connects, in classic American fashion, market economies to spiritual fulfillment. Even more explicit than the University of South Carolina, the University of New Mexico claims to enhance its state's "quality of life and promote economic development; [as well as to] advance our understanding of the world, its people, and cultures." Creating wealth, producing citizens, and serving the world all fall under the single theme of university work.[8] Each promises to offer greater individual opportunity, the potential to reap economic rewards, and the possibility for individual fulfillment. These mission statements function through a rhetoric that unites a diverse audience of social justice advocates, individualists, and economic climbers through identification with the university and its professionalizing mechanism.

Relying on this same equivalence between notions of an enlightened citizenry and market-driven research, the mission statements of both the University of North Carolina and the University of Michigan imply that although research takes primacy, it informs the university's other missions of teaching and service. Instruction at the University of North Carolina is committed "to those values that foster enlightened leadership for the State and the nation." The university not only extends "knowledge-based services and other resources of the University to the citizens of North Carolina," it also addresses, "as appropriate, regional, national, and international needs." Notice how the word "appropriate" modifies the scope of North Carolina's service, making these endeavors at least disconcertingly flexible if not entirely empty. This ambiguity is even more distressing when linked to the needs of literally anyone on earth. Apparently, university educated citizens can take responsibility as they see fit for any event, from the local to the global, as they have been professionalized to take leadership worldwide. Perhaps revelatory of the strength of this service in the humanities, the American Council of Trustees and Alumni (ACTA) recently released a report that indicts this university as well as the entire state system. According to the report, the system of higher education in North Carolina requires restructuring, including a move that would vest the governor with full appointing capacity. The appeals to social needs that justify North Carolina's research initiative cannot fully manifest because they might threaten the corporate research agenda. This claim that North Carolina's citizenship training produces world leaders repeats itself in the University of Michigan's mission. Revised in 1992, the university's mission "is to serve the people of Michigan and the world through preeminence in creating, communicating, preserving, and applying knowledge, art, and academic values, and in developing leaders and citizens who will challenge the present and enrich the future." At its heart, this statement suggests that service necessitates advanced knowledges. Its students, as the bearers of this knowledge, will lead the state, the nation, and the world. The language of this statement implies that without this research agenda, individuals and nation-states would search aimlessly for order and leadership. The rank of the university and the status of its students need no further articulation. Scour any of the U.S. public research university mission statements and you will find this same sentiment. These universities see themselves as instructing the body of leaders most capable of ruling not only the state, not only the nation, not only the "free world," but the entire surface of the earth.

The University of Washington's mission statement just as clearly assumes its prestige as a research institution by emphasizing the pursuit of scholarship and suggesting its filtration into the subordinate missions of teaching and service. According to its 1998 statement, "the primary mission of the University of Washington is the preservation, advancement, and dissemination of knowledge." This research mission is balanced by a commitment to extend the reaches of the university's education and service missions. Attempting to counter the historic animosity between prestigious universities and the communities in which they are located, the University of Washington uses its teaching mission to reach deep into the local community. The university "seeks broad representation of and encourages sustained participation in [the local] community by its students, its faculty, and its staff. It serves both non-traditional and traditional students. Through its three-campus system and through educational outreach, evening degree, and distance learning, it extends educational opportunities to many who would not otherwise have access to them."

This multifaceted approach to the local community recalls the original mission of the U.S. public research university. Since the late nineteenth century, public universities have diversified their functions in order to appeal to a greater number of students, quell the public distrust of higher education, and recover some of the high costs of research. Schools such as the University of Washington continue this practice by extending hours of operation, broadening coursework, and recruiting nontraditional students. In part, this kind of outreach can be attributed to the notion of professional schools as practical and locally oriented. For instance, this mission states that although "the academic core of the University of Washington is its College of Arts and Sciences; the teaching and research of the University's many professional schools provide essential complements to these programs." The college of arts and sciences, traditionally associated with elite liberal arts education, needs to be infused with the practical, business-focused education of the professions in order to garner broad public support. Articulating the liberal arts with professional programs, like law and business schools, serves a double signification: first, the humanities need to be coupled with practical knowledge to avoid slippage into an idealistic and unproductive ivory tower; second, the professional schools are never as heartless and as partisan as their free market rationale might imply as long as they work adjacent to and in harmony with the humanities. Ultimately, the mission statement rhetorically secures an elite and increasingly privatized research agenda by diversifying its teaching and service according to the commonsensical and utilitarian needs of the professional world.

At many universities, the practical character of this professional education is specifically associated with a land-grant mission. Public research universities as diverse as Pennsylvania State University and the University of Nebraska proudly advertise their land-grant heritage. Pennsylvania State's newly revised mission statement, for instance, opens by defining itself as a "public land-grant university that improves the lives of

people in Pennsylvania, the nation, and the world." The university's activities "promote human and economic development through the expansion of knowledge and its applications in the natural and applied sciences, social sciences, arts, humanities and selected professions." Since
the Land-Grant Act of 1862, public universities have utilized statements
like this to emphasize the role of mass higher education: to expand the
scope of the university and make research practical as well as economically viable. In fact, reference to land-grant status functions as one of the
most effective topoi for making precisely the same argument as that of
the University of Washington; highlighting land-grant status is, therefore,
a common trope within university systems. Positioned within this tradition, the University of Nebraska's 1991 statement claims that its institutional strength derives from its ability to simultaneously value the democratic mission of its land-grant origins and the goal of economic growth.
Specifically, the University of Nebraska recognizes "the values of combining the breadth of a comprehensive University with the professional
and outreach orientation of the land grant University." This structural alliance, it contends, allows "the people of the state unique opportunities
to fulfill their highest ambitions and aspirations." Personal aspirations, in
this configuration, cannot be understood outside the goal of amassing individual wealth. Consequently, the University of Nebraska attempts "to
focus teaching and research on specific societal issues" at the same time
that it tries to "enhance [student] ability to compete in world markets."
The fusion of democratic citizenship and capitalist production within one
mission allows the friction between the two opposing functions of the
university to wear through the thin boundary between public service and
economic production until they appear to be the single, unified goal of
public higher education. The proposition that democratic and social justice issues might be at odds with free market logics exists outside the rhetorically constructed institutional boundaries of these universities, and is
therefore less accessible to those who live within the rhetorical confines
of this educational landscape.

Constructing professionalism as a united and all-powerful identity
over and above the diverse identities of various citizen groups helps universities compete unabashedly for prominence in the global markets of
finance and education. Ohio State University defines its mission as aspir-

ing toward "international distinction in education, scholarship, and public service." It legitimates this goal by combining "responsibility for the advancement and dissemination of knowledge with a land grant heritage of public service." While striving for economic profitability in research, the university provides "education for qualified students who are able to benefit from a scholarly environment in which research inspires and informs teaching." As this example illustrates, research mission statements frequently qualify the all-inclusive discourse of citizenship by ability, redefining democratic citizenship through merit-based achievement. In a university meritocracy, the most able students rise to the top while the vast majority of students pass through a generalized curriculum. The idea of a meritocracy helps smooth over a different contradiction than humanities versus professional schools. This second important contradiction exists between research needs and teaching needs, which allows research to prevail because it can wrap itself within a history and discourse of land-grant status that invokes the democratization of education and teaching according to community needs.

The majority of those who pursue a general education are an integral component of the professional marketplace. Appealing to these numbers, the University of Arizona effectively builds on the democratic ethos of the land-grant tradition by highlighting the practical, everyday applicability of university education. Its mission succinctly states that as a public, land-grant research institution, "the university prepares students for a diverse and technological world while improving the quality of life for the people of Arizona, the nation, and the world." The university integrates its teaching and research as well as its "achievements of regional, national, and international significance into everyday life." Its objective is "to collaborate in linking educational, research and public service programs to local, state, national, and international needs." Rhetorically deferential to the needs of the citizens who support and fund the university, this statement connects the specialized knowledge necessary for remaining competitive in the new global economy with the concreteness of everyday activities and strategically aligns those who want education to be practical with the corporate leaders who increasingly determine the focus of university research. Like the other statements, it manages deep antagonisms within the overall mission of public research universities by revaluing key professionalizing functions and thus redrawing the appropriate boundaries of university, professional, and corporate work.

Along with the other sample mission statements, Arizona's statement illustrates the tenuous relationship between teaching or serving the public and collaborating with industry on economically productive research. Because this discourse advances research as the fundamental factor for building economic profitability and improving the quality of life for individuals and nation-states throughout the world, it forms the ideological basis for the U.S.-led discourse on global higher education. In its updated *Policies for Higher Education in the 1980s,* for instance, the OECD requires that universities include "representatives of the world of work in course design" and that universities promote "the exchange of staff between higher education and industry" (39). It further suggests that universities build research parks, patent discoveries, and pursue research that demonstrates economic profitability. Universities should cooperate with industry to develop "strategic research aimed at promoting technological and industrial innovation" (*Policies in the 1980s* 53). Unlike this research mission, which follows the most sophisticated, cutting-edge agenda, however, the OECD recommends that teaching focus on the practical needs of individuals—job training and other life skills. The OECD believes that education should impart "a more practical orientation to studies and [be] more accessible to adult students" (36). While universities focus research on high technology and high profitability, their instruction simply reproduces the status quo of low-paying and routine-driven workplaces. Lifelong learning, continuous accreditation, and distance learning reinforce the historical materialist terrain of capitalism by augmenting rather than challenging the dominance of its research agenda.[9] And they do this in the name of democratic educational values—the prevailing ideoscape of higher education loosely centered in the United States and extending around the globe.

Although there have been challenges to the hegemony of this corporate-influenced signification of education, the U.S. public research university's diverse ideological foundations as well as its institutional structure remain the most reproduced educational model in the world. A significant reason for this success lies in its ability to incorporate and contain multiple and sometimes opposing agendas. Eliding challenges from community organizations or identity groups, such a diversified mission includes a wide variety of interests at the same time that it subjugates nonprofitable functions to the goal of advanced research. This strategy is explicitly endorsed by the OECD, which claims that "the politicization of the university is a familiar problem in almost all advanced societies and is the theme of much current literature. Its solution may be linked to the larger problem of devising structures that sustain educational diversity within an emerging system of mass higher education while allowing its component institutions and units to preserve their own unique identities, a narrower range of functions, and staff and students who share attitudes and values appropriate to their own institution" (*Policies for Higher Education* 71). As an exercise in hegemony, the OECD advises that some institutions serve the people so that others can pursue the interests of global capitalism. The U.S. public research university leads the world in education because it serves both functions within a single institution. The fundamental ideologies of the U.S. public research university (to extend economic profitability through market research and to diversify the student body through broad teaching and service missions) have merged into a single unwritten policy for including, containing, and thus undermining political disagreements. By absorbing political and cultural differences, this diversification clears the way for corporate capitalism. The various university campuses that litter our landscape exist as the material embodiment of rhetorical boundaries that name, separate, and contain: nonprofessional locals stay clear of all university campuses, regional students and faculty stay clear of the main campus, and humanities students and faculty at research campuses stay clear of their professional and business colleagues.

According to the OECD's representative study of U.S. universities, *Higher Education in California,* the University of California system has gone further than any other public university system in sketching out these rhetorical and material boundaries. Like the other mission statements I examine, California's 1960 master plan and its subsequent revisions define the mission of higher education as the interplay between "the forces of citizenship responding to popular political demand and of accommodation to class interests through market strategies" (*Higher Education in California* 21). On the one hand, this university system "prepares young people for the unequal and authoritarian relations of capitalist production, but on the other it socializes children for citizenship in a democratic society" (22). In addition to offering paid services, creating an adult education market, and securing research contracts with technology industries, universities in California also "developed science parks, business affiliates, elaborate patents policies, and even created 'university-owned enterprises' with a view to developing more active technological transfer between industries and universities" (54). Conscious of the global terrain of education and "mindful of California's frontier position vis-à-vis the labor supply and trading relations with Latin America and the countries of the Pacific Rim," its universities prepare students "with the skills required by modern international, national, and local labor markets" (17).[10] As a means of teaching for citizenship in a global economy, the labor market necessarily determines the skills required of students. If California were geographically close to Eastern Europe, apparently its educational mission would shift accordingly. Within this discourse, universities appear to address the will of the people at the same time that they allow corporate interests to set the curricular agenda.

Attempting to complicate our investment in the altruistic functions of higher education, my analysis offers one reason why so many still cling to this nostalgic view of the public education: the mission statements of U.S. public universities tend to unify the bifurcated functions of research and teaching within a diversified institutional structure. These mission statements are not inconsequential; they are not merely empty or unfulfilled rhetoric. Instead, the very fact that we take these statements for granted demonstrates that we have internalized and accepted their contradictions. According to Foucault, our benign acceptance, our indifference, and even our dismissal of their significance reveals the power of mission statements to affect individual "acts, attitudes and modes of everyday behavior" ("Truth and Power" 125). Rather than fundamentally challenging the power of a unified university system, the rhetorical union of a diverse structure within a single system of signs creates "a multiplication and reinforcement of their power-effects" (127). This multiplication takes us from ideoscapes to financescapes. While the ideoscape of citizenship valuated within mission statements explains how this diversified structure is justified through appeals to the public good, the movement of financescapes supporting global production illustrates how this diversified structure is enforced. In other words, various and fluctuating ideoscapes reveal the ideology of the post-professional, but the financescapes involved in this rhetoric show how the university-produced post-professional moves outside the United States through the same channels that enable corporate sovereignty to move freely around the globe.

A diversified educational structure, for instance, represents a condition on which many loans are issued to nation-states for the restructuring of higher education (Chossudovsky; Pannu; World Bank, *Lessons of Experience*). Without this diversification, the World Bank predicts that "many countries are destined to enter the twenty-first century insufficiently prepared to compete in the global economy" (*Lessons of Experience* 25). The World Bank goes on to argue that "strong student activism and weak governments have prevented the introduction of critically needed reform" (25). The World Bank, the IMF, and the OECD have developed a large body of literature about higher education that offers strategies for convincing nation-states worldwide to endorse a unified higher education structure compatible with economic globalization without acknowledging globalization's inequitable distribution of resources and benefits. According to Phillip Brown and Hugh Lauder's analysis, emphasis on "the universal consensus highlighting education and training systems as holding the key to future prosperity has obscured fundamental differences in the way nations are responding to the global economy" (5). A uniform education system, with technical and economic progress as its justification, suppresses such differences as the uneven economic development that solidifies nation-states into rigid positions within the global economy. Based on the theory of comparative advantage, global capitalism looks to some nations for cheap labor, some for natural resources, some for markets, and others for the financial infrastructure. The quality of life within a nation-state is influenced, in part, by its position within this global system of production. The movement of financescapes demonstrates how a global system of publicly and privately funded higher education enforces this system of production and moves the U.S. model of education around the globe with the help of the supranational organizations and international treaties. In short, Foucault's technology of production coupled with the movement of financescapes and increasing corporate sovereignty provide the infrastructure to take the U.S. model of higher education overseas.

Global Financescapes and the Internationalization of the U.S. Public Research University

U.S. public research universities, especially those with a land-grant heritage, were heavily funded by the post–World War II welfare state and its Keynesian economic scheme (Cohen; Graham and Diamond; Noll). This state-funded higher education proliferated in the 1950s and 1960s as nontraditional and first-generation students filtered into universities across the country. By the 1970s, however, Keynesian economics began to be dismantled as the emerging global political economy started privatizing social welfare programs such as health care and education.[11] In this new economy, universities took their cue from and assumed an international authority, argue Buchbinder and Rajagopal, by reinforcing the language of treaties such as the 1994 NAFTA and GATS agreements as well as global funding institutions like the World Bank (296). With historical antecedents reaching back to the post–World War II restructuring of the imperialist world, these treaties utilize a rhetoric that displaces and adjusts previous discourses of monopoly capitalism onto the new landscape of globalization. That is to say, the interplay among international trade agreements, monetary institutions, and university-sponsored discourse constitutes a new financescape and a revision of the historical materialist terrain of global capitalism. In this section, I argue that the discursive relationship between international financial organizations and the U.S. public research university constructs the scaffolding that supports the global university's raison d'être: post-professionalization must participate in the creation of surplus value.

Examining the language of these financescapes as it encroaches on the world of higher education reveals how the economic landscape rhetorically produces boundaries of possibility that both enable and limit possible action. These rhetorically constructed boundaries serve "as a constraint and a parameter for movements" in the discourse on post-professionalism as well as in everyday life (Appadurai 35). For instance, chapter 12 of NAFTA, "Cross Border Trade in Service," identifies education and professional certification as critical services within the capitalist mode of production. It states that as producers of a free market service, institutions of higher education should "liberalize quantitative restrictions, licensing requirements, [and] performance requirements" in order to foster international economic exchange (Article 1208). In an annex to Article 1210 titled "Professional Services," the agreement also encourages countries "to develop mutually acceptable standards and criteria for licensing and certification of professional service providers." These standards include accreditation of schools, universalized examinations, and recertification or continuous education. In short, NAFTA contributes to a global economic regime through the language of liberalization, the standardization of best practices, the creation of new tax regimes, the delegitimation of the nation-state, and the establishment of nongovernmental regulatory boards. Once the U.S. model of university education takes root worldwide, the international movement of post-professionals from one corporation located in one global city to another will take place with ease and efficiency. This, of course, is already in play and increasingly so every day. A May 2004 study reports that the computer programming/software engineer industry is the largest service sector currently outsourced. Computer programming and engineering outsourcing is followed by jobs for accountants, lawyers, insurance representatives, real estate agents, chemists, and physicists. In ten years, the projected job loss in these industries is expected to reach 432,500, totaling a loss of $1.18 trillion in wages (McCarthy). While outsourcing has been common since the 1970s, the inclusion of professional jobs in this movement adds new wrinkles to the equation, requiring international agreements that regulate how trade in both the productive and service sectors will function.

Emerging from the World Trade Organization's 1994 Uruguay Round, GATS also serves to standardize education in such a way as to enable the smooth operations of capital—both within and outside education. It mandates, for instance, "that education providers from all foreign countries which are members of the GATT must be treated the same" (Buchbinder and Rajagopal 288). According to Buchbinder and Rajagopal, this directive could result in an elimination of locally focused curriculum, the funneling of all research through the same competitive mechanisms, and the uniformity of educational standards. Indeed, they suggest that "taken to its logical conclusion GATS could translate into a global educational system" (288). Such a system would, according to many experts, imitate a model carved out over the first one and a half centuries of public university education in the United States (OECD, *Development of Higher Education;* Guthrie and Pierce; Spring, *Education and the Rise of the Global Economy*). This model can be characterized in several ways, but most prominent are its diverse funding sources, its stratified institutional makeup, its relative independence from state power, and an autonomy balanced by significant accountability and surveillance mechanisms. Although these trade agreements provide the framework for global educational policies, monetary organizations do not necessarily look to them for guidance. Instead, they look to the various U.S. public research universities where this discourse and structure not only exist but also have successfully incorporated the needs of global capitalism into their system of higher education.

Discursively similar to international trade agreements, the rhetoric of U.S. public research universities indicates how the global circulation of local knowledge and the creation of international links facilitate the flow of capital and reinforce the language of globalization. For instance, South Carolina's *Institutional Planning and Assessment 2000–01 Fact Book* asserts that "The University's efforts in the international area, particularly important to the state's development of foreign trade and investment, continue to expand. Academic exchange programs and research linkages have been established with European, African, and South American universities, as well as with China and Japan." Mimicking the doctrine of international treaties, universities argue that research links and professional standardization are critical to local development in the global economy. For this reason, the University of South Carolina's Moore School of Business offers a Global Track that "focuses on the political, economic, and business factors affecting the investment climate of various regions throughout the world." The track provides an internationalized curriculum, encourages an understanding of non-Western cultures, and requires six months of overseas work experience. Not unlike mission statements claiming to produce world leaders, this program purports to "give students the competitive advantage they need in today's workplace." Specifically, it claims to create "future global managers, who can apply their expertise anywhere in the world." Business goals, here, are remarkably aligned with the university mission statements I explored in the previous section, reminding us of the interpenetration of these technologies, "scapes," and spheres. Rather than leading the world into an equitable partnership, this professional school trains internationally savvy corporate post-professionals who can use their cultural knowledge to exploit the economic conditions of nearly any location worldwide.

Besides incorporating U.S. business strategies into overseas locations, some research universities attempt to localize various strategies derived from their myriad global relationships. Take, for instance, the University of Washington's Interdisciplinary Global Studies option. This program claims that "it has become imperative for citizens in this country to understand better the complex and disparate global interactions involving trade, politics, immigration, the environment, technology, and culture." Thus, it offers students the opportunity "to pursue area studies that focus on particular regions of the world, such as Asia or Europe, human rights, political economy and cultural studies." Although area studies is best known as the university apparatus accompanying monopoly capitalism, such programs have evolved along with the needs of a changing landscape of capitalism. According to David Ludden, direct of the Area Studies Center at the University of Pennsylvania, this field will only survive "to the extent that it makes a case for itself in the constellation of interests that converge on globalization" (6). In fact, he believes that the global political economy "provides many new opportunities for area studies to serve the social sciences, business schools, public policy institutes, medical schools, NGOs, United Nations organizations, private enterprise, and governments" (6). Failing to align itself with dominant political economic agendas, area studies has recently come under fire for advocating supposedly anti-American political positions. This attack only further reveals the significance of area study programs to the geopolitical interests of the corporatized ruling elite. Its programs keep the university, financial, and technological economies in motion as they offer important knowledge about linguistic, cultural, and social differences that are necessary components for tailoring market products and procedures to new locations. Area studies knowledge has become flexible enough and accrued a sufficient exchange value, says Ludden, to "allow practitioners of all the disciplines *to expand their powers to operate anywhere in the world*"

(6). Transformed by the age of globalization, area studies now trains post-professionals to lead the world, no matter what their business needs are or where their worksite might place them—a goal commensurate with university missions rather than cultural understanding.

Like the University of Washington, both the University of Nebraska and the University of North Carolina clear the way for financial movement by connecting the local and the global. These universities expand the traditional boundaries of academic space in order to train a post-professional class unencumbered by national boundaries. According to its International Affairs mission statement, the University of Nebraska's World Campus—its distance learning initiative—"provides overseas coursework integrated into the UNL curriculum." Similarly, the University of North Carolina has a nonprofit Global Center with the stated mission of "helping organizations and individuals function effectively in the global environment." The center divides its mission into two parts: providing global training and creating global connections. Both units are intended to "help people understand other cultures in order to work and live more effectively with the growing cultural diversity that comes from our changing workforce and expanding business horizons." At the same time that these programs operate under the altruistic label of cultural diversity, expanded access, and intellectual freedom, they also perpetuate a discourse that reinforces the financial movement of capital and legitimates uneven economic structures. The focus of international research links often revolves around business, finance, and trade while cultural diversity, area studies, and distance learning frequently lay the groundwork for future capital transfer within this complex global landscape.

Within such a structure, policy decisions follow profitability rather than any ethic of social good, nationally or internationally. This economically driven ideology clearly informs the restructuring of policies such as California's tax reform. Rather than relying heavily on state tax dollars to fund education, California revised its laws so that less tax money is spent on education. Instead, the state encourages corporate and individual donations through significant tax deductions (OECD, *Higher Education in California* 55). In this way, individuals and private firms finance education, purchase a stake in the shape of that education, and are reimbursed for their generosity. The monies granted to universities frequently come with strict instructions for its use—instructions that might very well benefit the donor. Even as this philanthropy provides cultural capital in the form of public relations and advertising, it also provides indirect economic capital in the form of tax breaks and future intellectual knowledge. Advocating such policies, the OECD frankly states that "California laws, rather than any miraculous generosity, explain why so much private money flows into the independent colleges and public institutions" (*Higher Education in California* 122). Such policy amounts to continued, though indirect, government support. Because less revenue will be derived from these donors in the form of tax dollars, the government concedes profits on the condition that others directly fund education. This gives the corporate world greater access to and control over the university and it builds a positive corporate image, simultaneously taking care of both its research and advertising needs.[12]

In addition to providing such incentives for higher education funding, national governments are central to the process of making the U.S. public research university model the international standard in higher education. The OECD functions as the greatest advocate for linking universities with the global economy (Hyslop-Margison 204). Yet this supranational organization operates from a budget publicly funded by its member countries—historically, the world's most industrialized nations. According to its mission statement, the OECD is devoted to "economic growth" and the "expansion of world trade on a multilateral, non-discriminatory basis in accordance with international obligations." With such a mission emanating from highly industrialized, capitalist member states, there can be no doubt that this government-supported organizational interest in higher education rests primarily on its goal of expanding an evolving capitalist system. Its close cooperation with the World Bank, which works on a one dollar, one vote policy, further suggests the economic exigencies of these global organizations can be traced to specific geopolitical locations. No one can claim that the World Bank, regardless of its purported interest in alleviating poverty and disease, works on behalf of any interest other than the expansion of free market capitalism. Even such liberal economists as Joseph Stiglitz, once a senior vice president of the World Bank, admit that the bank and its sister organization used rigid ideological devotion to economic laissez-faire capitalism rather than democratic debate to determine its course of action. While he blames the IMF and its disinterested, statistically driven research methods for this failure, Stiglitz readily admits that the economic programs were both disastrous for individual nation-states and good for transnational corporations.

Besides the OECD, the other main financial engine for a U.S.-led global educational scheme is the World Bank. Two implications of World Bank funding to higher education are noteworthy. First, "implementation of human capital ideas are given more force by being tied to education loans. Second, the World Bank's education efforts frequently reflect the current school proposals in the United States" (Spring, *Education and the Rise of the Global Economy* 180). Indeed, R. S. Pannu argues that most non-Western nations receive global doctrine "not only in the form of textbook knowledge or as academic theory, but also as prepackaged policies they must follow in order to tackle the debt and balance-of-payments crises" (94). The World Bank's structural adjustment loan—loans designed to alleviate the debt crisis of the most impoverished nations by propelling them quickly into the contemporary global marketplace—requires the implementation of several reforms including the privatization of government programs such as public education (Chossudovsky 2531). Michel Chossudovsky, director of the Center for Research on Globalization, roughly dates the eruption of globalization's economic discourse in academic and research institutions throughout the world from the 1980s. As a consequence of the merger of global economic discourse and higher education, he argues that "critical analysis is strongly discouraged, [and] social and economic reality is to be seen through a single set of fictitious economic relations which serve the useful purpose of concealing the working of the global economic system" (2531). Regardless of whether the market acts as a real, independent force or functions as a constructed illusion, Chossudovsky's point is worth reiterating: the monolithic principle of market freedom underlies the expansion of these U.S.-influenced educational reforms.

Even while reforms in global higher education have to be traced through a complex chain of international treaties, policy organizations, and economic institutions in order to arrive back at the U.S. public research university, the discourse persuading these reforms strategically employs the rhetoric of diversity as a means to further obfuscate this series of relationships. For instance, because the World Bank overwhelmingly relies on non-U.S. examples that mirror the U.S. model of effective university structures, it appears to appreciate a variety of national educational programs at the same time that it displaces the role of the United States in these reforms. Yet these non-U.S. examples have all, at one time or another, adopted U.S.-inspired educational policies. To take only one example, the World Bank highlights Singapore for reforming higher education as a stepping-stone to greater participation in the global economy. The international lender claims that "Singapore put in place a market-driven but state-controlled, three-tier higher education system to support its private sector–driven economic modernization strategy." The bank especially emphasizes Singapore's "diversified, flexible education system" as well as the fact that its "size, quality and course offerings are based on labor market needs" ("The Singapore Experience"). A decade earlier, as we have seen, the OECD praised California's three-tier educational structure and suggested that it should serve as the ideal for the rest of the world. Specifically, the study encouraged California's model of "open access to the three public segments [as] one within which there are differentiated advantages of tracking through what we have characterized as a tripartite system" (*Higher Education in California* 71). Just like its structural mentor, Singapore has developed strong ties with industry, focused on market technology, and created a diversified open access system that simultaneously allows mass education and high-tech specialization. The World Bank's desire to represent educational success through Singapore illustrates how the complex circulation of ideoscapes can deflect U.S. associations through a multicultural doctrine. With this strategic positioning of examples, the financing of higher education by these lending institutions has the appearance of broad acceptance, diversity, and even democracy.

The financescapes that facilitate this discourse also help create a global educational system that itself functions as a technology for the circulation of funds and ideas, creating a global higher education industry primarily based on the U.S. public research university. This educational technology, mandated by international lending agencies, ostensibly rests on sound scientific research. Multiple, purportedly nonpartisan organizations study national systems of higher education worldwide, citing sources, offering documentation, publishing and disseminating study after study. Within this research framework, the redolent political ideology of any group (equally including corporations and human rights advocates) has been thoroughly cleansed from the proposed findings. Nonetheless, Pannu argues that the U.S. public research university "bears the systematic imprint of the doctrinal, theoretical, and methodological choices that inform its overall agenda" (92). This agenda, of course, is the accumulation of capital within strategic spaces. Consequently, these reforms have created an internationalized system, what Pannu calls the "intellectual-financial complex," that enables the transfer of both digital and discursive technologies (99). I turn now to an examination of how the U.S. public research university has evolved into a complex system for global technological transfer that requires a high-speed transportation system for its efficient movement. Such a system functions as what Foucault calls a technology of power and relies on the use and production of technoscapes.

Global Technoscapes and the Intellectual-Financial Complex of Research Universities

The World Bank states that investment in higher education yields economic returns. Specifically, they say that investments in higher education contribute to increases in labor productivity and to greater long-term economic growth. But they are adamant that "quality improvements and enrollment expansion in higher education will have to be achieved with little or no increase in public expenditures" (*Lessons of Experience* 3). Instead, universities should seek funding from corporations and alumni. They should also implement student tuition and fees as well as "pursue income-generating activities such as short-term courses, contract research for industry, and consultancy services" (7). According to the World Bank, the global system of higher education should follow four main directions: differentiation of institutions and institutional tasks; redefining the role of the state; diversification of funding apparatuses; and the creation of accountability mechanisms (viii). In short, the World Bank promotes the U.S. model of higher education. Transforming the U.S. public research university into a technology of power that can be imported and exported easily, this educational model requires the use of technoscapes—the high-speed movement of "technology, both high and low, both mechanical and informational," to connect a complex structure ranging from international treaties and world lending agencies to non-profit organizations and individual institutions (Appadurai 34).

The U.S. public research university has nearly perfected the World Bank's four key aspects of higher education in order to transform elite education into a post-professional education, an institutionalized knowledge that trains both the upper echelon and the everyday worker. The Extended University of the University of California, for instance, aims "at the penetration of a network of prestigious establishments by a system of new educational patterns, rather than the creation of a non-traditional institution parallel to an existing one" (OECD, *Policies for Higher Education* 31). According to the OECD, there are two processes occurring in higher education. First, elite universities—both public and private research universities—are expanding; and, second, elite universities are transforming. In order to broaden the scope of higher education and increase its consumer appeal, elite universities must accommodate practical and applied research agendas. "Institutions are still preparing elites," argues the OECD, "but a much broader range of elites which includes the leading strata of all the technical and economic organizations of the society . . . their chief concern is to maximize the adaptability of that population to a society whose chief characteristic is rapid social and technological change" (64). Indeed, the proportion of students enrolled in higher education "depends mainly on the extent to which the universities have been capable of absorbing equivalent institutions originally created outside the university" (*Development of Higher Education* 25). As the only country to exceed mass higher education (approximately 50 percent of the population) and approach universal higher education (approaching 75 percent of the population), the United States, predicts the OECD, will lead this technological transformation (63).

Because partnerships with other institutions and organizations help universities compete in the technology industry, research universities are working to secure their place within this global nexus. As of spring 2002, for instance, the University of New Mexico has been in the process of developing an international initiative. According to its "Strategic Direction on Preeminence," the goal is to create a unit that is "distinct among higher education programs in international studies, that makes a significant contribution in this domain, and that builds on [their] distinct New Mexico resources." Its focus will be topical, its scope will be global, and it will have "potential for national and international prominence." One of seven strategic directions, this plan attempts to "provide an environment that cultivates and supports activities of global preeminence and impact." As a result of such programs, the university believes that "partnership opportunities with other universities, with the National Laboratory sector, and with industry will increase." In particular, they hope this strategy will lead to "global partnerships" and will "play a major role in the economic development of their regions." Global partnerships, according to this initiative, signify the merger of university technologies with markets from agribusiness and pharmaceuticals to computers and communications. No specific department nor particular area of research is identified; but in the current era of globalization, it is considerably more likely that this globally competitive university knowledge will come from science, technology, or business departments than from either the social sciences or the humanities.

One of the biggest global businesses—and one of the most often discussed industries—in the current global economy is the high-tech industry. Recognizing the importance of tapping into this industry, Ohio State has been working on its technology network by investing in its large industrial park, TechPartners. TechPartners boasts "world recognized medical, business, agricultural, engineering, education and arts colleges." A value-added, technology-based, economic development network, TechPartners consists of "seven university and non-university organizations, aligned toward Ohio State's goal of elevating Ohio State to a best practice technology partnerships university." TechPartners is an organization intended to create "the alignment necessary to join business with the assets of a large, public research institution like Ohio State University." Through its motto, "connecting knowledge with a global marketplace," Ohio State makes clear its intention to move technology from the university into the private sector and around the globe. Such partnerships not only perpetuate technological advances worldwide, they also reconstruct the post-professional as one who is both multiculturally literate and academically specialized within discrete industries. The university, as a technology of power, commissions and develops research within these industrial parks as a crucial component of economic globalization.

While these industrial parks are an invention of the late nineteenth-century U.S. reforms in higher education, their popularity and importance have skyrocketed due, in great part, to the importance of the high-tech industry. The supposed need for global transfers of technology, in fact, has naturalized the triangulated relationship among corporations, the government, and the university found in research parks. Reinforcing this normative link, Pennsylvania State explicitly articulates the mission of its research park, Innovation Park, as providing "access to Penn State researchers and facilities, and business support services that help companies transfer the knowledge within the University to the market place and to foster economic development." Inside this university apparatus and apart from the humanizing agenda of the main campus, knowledge acquires value only to the extent that it serves business needs. The research park, says its Web site, is "the place where collaboration between the University and private sector companies can grow. Penn State has a long history of working with industry, and speaks the language of business. Of an annual research budget of $440 million, $75 million was in industry-sponsored research." The other research dollars, of course, come from individuals, nonprofit foundations, and the government. Although the role of the government is continually downplayed in these relationships, it serves the critical roles of both funding research and encouraging relationships between the university and industry.

One of the most significant technologies in this relationship is the structure of the U.S. public research university itself. Aided by advice from the OECD and money from the World Bank, the educational model constructed from the U.S. public research university functions as a technology. In 1998, for instance, the World Bank approved a $150 million loan to Hungary to solve its national economic crisis—a loan equivalent to an annual budget at a low-end U.S. public research university. The World Bank explains that "to be eligible for support, all institutions will be required to adopt the policy reforms for higher education, including the introduction of a credit system, reduction in compulsory lecture

hours, imposition of tuition fees, and implementation of student financial aid" ("World Bank to Support Higher Education in Hungary"). These
reforms, derived directly from the U.S. model of higher education, form
the institutional infrastructure that allows for post-professionalization,
corporate interactions, and the eventual development and transfer of future technologies. A credit system standardizes courses for easy transfer
and credentialization; reduction in compulsory hours usually signals fewer
liberal arts requirements and more flexibility in practical professional
courses; tuition and financial aid often go hand in hand—once the government stops funding education, banks can provide student aid in the
form of interest-bearing loans. Collectively, these reforms constitute the
new educational technology of the intellectual-financial complex.

According to World Bank reports, countries in the Eastern bloc region
like Hungary are rapidly adopting this U.S. model of education. They
characterize the transformation of educational structures in political economic terms as a move "from a Soviet-type education system to a more
international (Western) system" ("An Assessment"). As a consequence of
this change, "business administration is developing at a rapid pace, with
more students, better business schools, and higher tuition fees. . . . Light,
applied business courses are often preferred to more serious, theoretical
economics courses" ("An Assessment"). Along with this new curriculum,
institutions rely increasingly on private financing as federal funding continues to drop. The World Bank further suggests that "many universities
need to be rebuilt from the bottom up to eliminate the strong vested interests of insiders" ("An Assessment"). Given the geopolitical history of
Eastern Europe and its position as a bridge to Asia, the vested interests
of insiders, in this regard, are individuals wedded to an anticapitalist political economic agenda. Attempting to unravel this historic animosity toward capitalism, the World Bank demands that "leading higher education
institutions must be open to international influences" (*Lessons of Experience* 68). The bank's emphasis on internationalism, globalization, and cooperation softens and democratizes the doctrine of capitalist production
and helps pry open yet another regional market for technological development. But the international treaties and World Bank Structural Adjustment Program that both regulate services are anything but democratic.

Making educational restructuring a contingency for national economic relief seems more like a high-stakes move in the game of economic imperialism than a collaborative decision based on democratic deliberation.

The Eastern bloc nations have received the attention and resources of many business-minded organizations since the collapse of the Soviet Union, but other nations—such as those in Africa—require even more attention, and unfortunately receive less. For instance, the World Bank provided Mozambique with a $60 million credit, part of which supported its ten-year strategic plan for higher education. With an annual average of only $6 million, this loan represents a mere fraction of any U.S. public research university's fiscal-year budget. The credit, however, will enable institutional reform in both public and private universities, create scholarships for eligible students, institute a bachelor-degree-type program that includes "degrees better targeted to the job market," and, most important, fund the development of a distance learning network ("Supporting Mozambique's Growing Needs"). As corporations move production overseas in search of cheap labor pools, they acquire the task of training and managing these distant workers. If international production requires international post-professionals, then such needs will be fulfilled by the U.S. research university system: the U.S. university structure has become a global standard for higher education, distance learning has transported U.S. curriculum overseas, and corporations have created a professionally educated pool of cheap labor. It is becoming just as easy to create technologies that transfer the post-professionalizing apparatus into nation-states with low production costs—including cheap building maintenance, low faculty salaries, few regulations, and frequent tax breaks—as it is to transfer low-skilled jobs to factories overseas in search of cheap labor. Ultimately, this creates post-professionals in cheap overseas locations so that professional work can be outsourced along with factory work.

One of the ways the model of education developed by the U.S. public research university complex moves throughout the world is through the legislative activities of international agreements like NAFTA. NAFTA paves the way for distance education, international satellite campuses, and the worldwide adoption of the U.S. technology of higher education. Chapter 12 of NAFTA focuses on cross-border trade in services, defining education as a service and specifying that a service provider does not have "to establish or maintain a representative office or any form of enterprise, or to be resident, in its territory as a condition of the cross-border provision of a service." NAFTA Article 1210 states that nothing shall "require the Party to accord such recognition to education, experience, licenses or certifications obtained in the territory of another Party." But, states the text, opportunities to prove equivalency must be accorded. While this clause offers a rhetorical loophole to avoid appearing as though NAFTA were requiring specific kinds of professionalization, the treaty does, in fact, give U.S. universities a monopoly over high-technology knowledges. Certification models, accreditation organizations, and distance learning apparatuses are all located within or derived from the U.S. research university model. Such monitoring practices are particularly significant to post-professional services—lawyers, accountants, and financial consultants. These services, because they are "professionalized," require "postsecondary education, or equivalent training and experience," according to Article 1213. An annex to Article 1210, however, suggests that "the Parties shall encourage the relevant bodies in their respective territories to develop mutually acceptable standards and criteria for licensing and certification of professional service providers." These standards apply to education, examinations, and "professional development and recertification—continuing education and ongoing requirements to maintain professional certification." NAFTA legislates that post-professionals constantly return to universities or their accreditation organizations to be acclimated into current post-professional trends. This creates a guaranteed market for higher education and technological development at the same time it standardizes knowledge according to U.S.-derived practices of inquiry.

The OECD reemphasizes NAFTA's discussion of constant recertification, lifelong learning, and accreditation because, says Joel Spring, "they are tools for managing the labor market in the interests of the business community" (*Education and the Rise of the Global Economy* 176). In its own words, the OECD claims that the "overriding concern is to sustain the dynamic evolution of the system, on the strength of past achievements, as a major factor in the cultural, scientific, and technological development of highly industrialized societies and the welfare of their citizens" (*Poli-*

cies in the 1980s 13). The OECD strives to sustain the economic privileges of this educational system and its contributions to advanced technology by advising the World Bank and others involved in funding higher education. Persuaded by this discourse, the World Bank encourages "close linkages with industry in advanced training courses, cooperative research programs, consultancies, continuing education programs, science parks, and such benefits for industry as incubation centers, tax advantages, and state-sponsored research vouchers" (*Lessons of Experience* 75). Because this university structure enables technological development, an international infrastructure has emerged to ensure its growth and progress. According to a July 7, 2004, article in *The Times of India,* some U.S.-based high-tech employees take it upon themselves to outsource their jobs in an effort to reap higher profits and reduce long work hours. The article cites one ambitious employee who hired a program developer in India to do his job. The U.S. employee earns $67,000 for the job he outsources to an Indian worker for $12,000. Repeating this process and working from home, the programmer is able to take on jobs with three or four companies, hire his own overseas workers, and spend little more than an hour a day per job to manage the work of his outsourced employees. In this way, the U.S.-based employee makes well over $200,000 by working for four companies and outsourcing each of his jobs to an Indian employee who makes just over $10,000 ("Outsource"). Professional training within the corporate university seems to have led not only to sovereign corporations colonizing faceless individuals overseas but to individual professionals repeating this process on their own and in what appears to be an entirely unregulated production process.

The university functions as the critical technology for perpetuating dominant ideologies, enhancing financial arrangements, developing high technology, and producing post-professional subjects. Universities produce ideas, create surplus value, and develop research, but they also produce a class of individuals that many educational theorists have reduced to the title of "human capital." While the OECD and the World Bank might be "the two agencies primarily responsible for spreading human capital analysis of education to developed and developing countries," the discourse on human capital theory surfaces in nearly all discussions of education within the global economy (Spring, *Education and the Rise of the*

Global Economy 159). In the next section, I explore how human capital theory functions as a technology of the self—determining and delimiting how individuals understand themselves and their role in the world. This technology, I argue, significantly reconstructs global ethnoscapes as well as the worldwide service industry.

Human Capital Theory, Ethnoscapes, and Multiculturalism in the Global University

According to the general arguments about human capital theory, poor countries should specialize according to their comparative advantage, which lies in the abundance and low price of their labor. However, the global economy requires a skilled, post-professionalized labor force just as it needs an unskilled, cheap labor force. In the era of globalization, comparative advantage depends on raising the quality and productivity of human capital, professionalized or not. Therefore, human capital theory studies, predicts, and advises corporations as well as universities about the "capabilities that can be acquired by individuals through education and training" (Guthrie and Pierce 185). Because of the productive shift to include digital technologies and the information industries, "human capital is becoming a critical economic resource, rather than being a dispensable factor of production" (182). As chapter 3 discussed, corporations are always working to improve productivity in order to extract more surplus value from labor and reap greater potential profitability. Although technological change increases productivity, "human capital acts as the conduit that enables technological changes to be translated into added productivity" (186). An increasingly flexible, highly specialized post-professional class contributes to this drive for productivity. The OECD and other organizations promote a version of higher education, labeled the "human resource model," that must constantly demonstrate how it trains students who serve the market economy (D. Smith 13). This model evaluates education according to the kind of workers it can produce—manual, obedient workers as well as highly specialized, flexible, post-professional workers.

Characteristics of this post-professional class abound throughout descriptions of the faculty, students, and curriculum of U.S. research universities. For instance, research faculty are often described as both knowledgeable of the increasingly multicultural world and internationally connected to that world. Illustrating this phenomenon, the mission statement of Nebraska's International Affairs Department claims that "many of UNL's faculty have national and international reputations and have formed strong linkages with scholars and institutions around the world." According to its university mission statement, these faculty members "interact with colleagues around the world and are part of the network of knowledge and information that so influences our society." While some of its faculty members are displaced from their country of origin, most are simply frequent international travelers. These instructors are particularly valuable because they help disseminate world knowledge to their university students. The international affairs unit believes these faculty members help prepare students for "life and work in a rapidly changing and increasingly interdependent world." The University of Nebraska "brings international and multicultural dimensions to its programs through the involvement of its faculty in international activities." A post-professional class requires an internationalized subjectivity in order to conduct business fluidly both at home and abroad; therefore, Nebraska relies on these faculty members to disseminate international and multicultural knowledge to students.

Representing a slightly different method for instilling this multicultural subjectivity, the University of Washington possesses an interdisciplinary program called Global Trade, Transportation, and Logistics Studies. Because "the efficient movement of goods and materials around the world takes place through an increasingly high tech, sophisticated multi-modal process," explains this program's mission, "the University of Washington has undertaken an initiative to prepare students for careers in international trade and transportation systems." Through its emphasis on trade and transportation, the program clearly embeds this international subjectivity with current trends in international business. Of course, not all students wish to be business majors. Consequently, the University of Michigan has developed a Global Summer Business Institute specifically designed for undergraduate liberal arts students. The institute is created for nonbusiness students who have developed a "strong interest in international studies through study abroad, language study, or other coursework." Michigan advertises this program to students who "want [their] liberal arts degree to be more marketable" and to students who want to work abroad. These students are encouraged to study language, art, and culture but are reminded that their future success is inevitably connected to the needs of the business world. Post-professionals, whether in the sciences or in the humanities, must seek employment in the current global climate; thus, the program argues that students need to develop an ability to maneuver within the business world.

This business world connects the international to the local, encouraging universities to develop community outreach and expanded access programs. Pennsylvania State University, for instance, stresses connections with local communities through distance learning opportunities. Penn State's World Campus aims to provide "global online access to a Penn State education." Its motto—"Wherever you want to go, the World campus can help you get there!"—emphasizes the ease of accessing higher education and claims to create a stronger, more mobile workforce. As a main selling point, it stresses that "corporate and organizational decision makers can take advantage of professional development opportunities for their employees that don't require time out of the office." Because the World Campus allows students to "access an international, on-line learning community" without ever leaving one's office chair, it illustrates that some post-professionals become highly mobile while others become ever more stagnant. The World Campus collects knowledge and people from around the world and virtually contains them within its on-line learning community, replaying the standard colonial gesture: the people, cultures, and materials of the world exist for the gaze and control of the strongest and wealthiest imperialist centers.

Post-professionals with specific, marketable skills are multiculturally trained and circulate freely while nonprofessionals with different skills are often relatively immobile.[13] Maintaining the correct equilibrium of the global workforce, universities utilize broad access in conjunction with strict accountability mechanisms that delimit the number of students within research university programs. Although community colleges and a tiered higher education model are often justified by arguments that junior colleges provide a springboard to universities for underprepared students, the movement of students from community colleges into universities has been slim. In fact, "it was noted at the end of the 1970s that the net flow was not from the community colleges to the University of California but in the opposite direction" (OECD, *Higher Education in California* 73). Rather than seeing this as a failure, the OECD notes that "supply and demand for skilled professional people is not regarded as a problem in California, partly for the reasons of flexible short-cycle education and training" (79). The OECD commends the university for including many nonprofessionals in its structural plan as "one part of an expanded industrial growth strategy to increase the skills of the 'reserve employment pool,' or the vulnerable and underemployed labor force, available in the global market" (Hyslop-Margison 207). In other words, it is better to include nonprofessional students into the university system on an as-needed basis than to produce too many professionalized workers and saturate the market. Further representative of the circulation of people in search of education and occupation, many post-professionals leave their country of origin in search of competitive wages as a result of pay scales that can be as much as seventy times lower than the U.S. rate. Whether these post-professionals move or remain in their country of origin, corporations often recruit them for significantly less money than they do for U.S.-trained workers.

In order to present themselves as valuable human capital, students need to be trained in assessing and marketing their skills. Technologies of the self require constant self-assessments that go hand in hand with the professionalizing practice of self-presentation. Forms of this technology in higher education—the résumé, portfolio, or curriculum vitae—require individuals to catalogue their skills, credentials, and accomplishments. Although these mechanisms allow for creativity on the part of individuals who can add or subtract items from an infinite number of individual assets, the push toward a more reductive skills card used in conjunction with higher education restricts this technology to items of immediate interest to the global marketplace. In Europe as well as Canada, for example, the Employability Skills Profile exists as a preformulated "document outlining the set of generic skills that employers supposedly require in the students they hire" (Hyslop-Margison 209). Consequently, educational institutions teach according to this list and students acquire marketable skills rather than strategies for questioning such skills. This personal skills card approximates a checklist of credentialized skills. The more skills a potential employee can offer, the more marketable he or she will appear.[14] Functioning as a form of human accounting, these cards supposedly provide an "accurate accreditation of embodied knowledge" and give businesses "clear information by which to make wise market decisions" (Spring, *Education and the Rise of the Global Economy* 170). The accreditation of embodied skills revises the notion of professional from one who is broadly knowledgeable about a collected area of study to one who can prove knowledge of multiple and transferable skills regardless of indepth professional expertise.

Like other mechanisms of global education, technologies of the self operate at the microlevel of journaling, chronicling, and constant self-scrutiny as well as at the macrolevel of international organizational accountability. While personal skills cards function at the level of the individual, organizations like the United Nations Educational, Science, and Cultural Organization (UNESCO) work internationally to facilitate credentialization of individual university skills. With nearly two hundred member nations, UNESCO articulates its mission "to contribute to peace and security in the world by promoting collaboration among nations through education, science, culture and communication in order to further universal respect for justice, for the rule of law and for the human rights and fundamental freedoms." Among its five principal functions is to establish international standards through "the preparation and adoption of international instruments and statutory recommendations." According to its *World Guide to Higher Education,* one of its specific goals is "the international recognition and validation of studies and degrees and diplomas" (ix). Precipitating this standardization scheme, UNESCO argues, is the need for "increased mobility of students, teachers, and research workers" (vii). UNESCO has worked with a number of nation-states throughout this project to help draw up regional agreements on the recognition of studies, diplomas, and degrees in higher education. These regional agreements vary, but the documents mostly assume that "education must be closely linked to plans for economic and social development" (344). Like personal skills cards, the standardization of credentials transforms individuals into interchangeable components of the global machinery.

The movement of individuals and the exchange of ideas functions as a multicultural phenomenon that both increases cultural appreciation

and advances the exploitation of people worldwide. While the globalization of U.S. higher education virtually mandates this multiculturalism by encouraging international collaboration, participating in global
technological development, and demanding conformity for easy movement among differing countries and people, Verna St. Denis argues that
a "national policy of multiculturalism reduces cultural groups to a common denominator of participating in activities involving food, dance, and
song in annual folkfests whose form becomes decontextualized from political claims" (44). The problem, once again, stems from the disjunctures among cultural appreciation, political agency, and economic profitability. By way of conclusion, the next section argues that the discourse
of global education derived from the U.S. public research university simultaneously creates a multiculturally savvy post-professional class and
subjugates cultural diversity to the economic agendas of globalization. It
does all of this through the regulatory practices of the political sphere—
state and national legislation, international treaties, and global standardization. This political regulation, interacting with economic production
processes and cultural consumption practices, constructs a boundary of
rhetoricality that functions to contain globalization within its neocolonial agenda.

The Discourse on Global Education as a Neocolonial Project

The rhetoric of globalization—whether found in university discourse,
international treaties, or recommendations from global organizations—
focuses on the connectivity of individuals worldwide, creating greater
awareness of one's relationship to distant people and distant places. As
diverse as this language often is, I suggest that it can be divided into two
rough categories: the rhetoric of multiculturalism and the rhetoric of
economic liberalization, both equally regulated through supranational organizations. On the one hand, the rhetoric of cultural globalization claims
that national and ethnic differences are being transgressed via the recent
surge in world travel and the accelerated circulation of both print and
electronic media. On the other hand, the rhetoric of economic globalization claims that international trade, monetary regulation, capital flows,
national employment rates, and living standards are now economically
linked around the globe. These two rhetorics function dialectically such

that the circulation of multicultural texts—including people, literatures, and images—contains and requires the structures of economic globalization. This contradictory logic creates a situation in which nation-states and universities toggle uncomfortably back and forth between the dual forces of economic cooperation and commercial competition. Universities merge these competing rhetorics by commodifying multiculturalism within the larger goal of capital accumulation. Area studies and anthropology, the two social science departments primarily dedicated to studying cultural differences, are often funded by the same federal and corporate agencies that fund economic globalization. Whether purposefully or by accident, this arrangement, to name only one of many, produces multicultural knowledge that conforms to the structural needs of corporate capitalism. The rhetoric of globalization, as it manifests within U.S. public research universities, often neutralizes the political charge challenging dominant sociohistorical narratives because multiplicity sells universities—cultural difference attracts a wider student body, alternative coursework fills seats, and cultural programs bring in grant money. Cultural difference is integral to university work, but it most frequently functions as a depoliticized form of multiculturalism compatible with the agenda of economic globalization. The political possibilities of more radicalized brands of multiculturalism no doubt exist—they are present in published research, in classroom pedagogies, and in student activism—and must be constantly managed by, among other things, David Horowitz's academic bill of rights and the neoconservative alarmism that has been running its course through national and state legislative bodies.[15]

As long as the unradicalized rhetoric of cultural globalization dominates university campuses, its inclusive discourse, which makes the repositioning of nation-states within the global economic hierarchy appear natural and fair, will prevent other forms of knowledge from being adequately deliberated. Therefore, management of university work takes place not only with Horowitz and his pet legislation but with international groups as well. Recall that the OECD valorized the University of California system for its internal structure and its international collaborations with Pacific Rim countries. It makes this argument along with the unapologetic and unequivocal claims that knowledge as well as economic stability originated in the West and have been benevolently passed on to the rest of the world. According to its seminal document, *Higher Education in California,* "the Pacific Rim countries have, for the most part, been passive beneficiaries of western, including the United States, influence in economics and in education and research" (66). Representing the Pacific Rim as passive not only erases major struggles and rebellions. It sets up this relationship using all the classic dichotomies of traditional colonialism: master/slave, center/periphery, civilized/uncivilized, advanced/backward, aggressive/passive, masculine/feminine, and entrance/reception. At the heart of this neocolonial relationship, the university dictates cultural assimilation because, as these authors contend, "the unassimilated minority is nonetheless a threat" (72). With half of its foreign research centers located in the Pacific Rim, it is not surprising that California universities specialize in the Pacific Rim area studies (65–66). These universities also encourage various Asian studies programs and support Asian student organizations. A student knowledgeable in Asian culture and history benefits contemporary economic structures only to the extent that he or she has become integrated into those economic structures; these programs, therefore, are often linked with business and scientific programs.

Private corporations and the federal government cooperate to fund this form of neocolonialism in the United States; internationally, institutions like the World Bank and the IMF underwrite this structure. The sophisticated international apparatuses linking funding agencies to educational reform approach what Pannu calls "market colonialism." In this colonizing structure, the "World Bank, which is also controlled by the major capitalist states, uses its enormous financial power, delicately fused with technocratically anointed and bureaucratically produced knowledge, to 'persuade' in myriad ways developing country ruling elites to follow policies that are consistent with and rooted in economic liberalism" (Pannu 93). Similarly, Chossudovsky suggests that "this new form of economic and political domination—a form of 'market colonialism'—subordinates people and governments through the impersonal interplay (and deliberate manipulation) of market forces" (2527). The shift from the colonial era of high modernity to the so-called postcolonial era of postmodernity has, according to many theorists, simply shifted colonialism from direct occupation to American cultural and economic hegemony. According to this argument, the United States maintains global hegemony by encouraging cultural difference and broad access to U.S. or U.S.-inspired higher education at the same time that the purse strings supporting such education are tied to specific, monolithic structures and curricula. Individuals are not forced into this education by a police state but are lured into it by a sense of belonging and a desire to succeed in an ever-changing world. The close connection between this education and the possibility of individual economic success is even more persuasive than a feeling of community belonging. Without the post-professionalizing knowledge taught in the university, many individuals and groups of individuals would find it difficult to maintain an adequate material existence. This rhetoric of democracy and social mobility recalls the language used in the mid-nineteenth century to convince politicians, professors, and students of the value of a public university education. What has changed is that the audience has become global and the institutionalizing boundaries have been redrawn according to the ever-fluctuating needs of capitalism.

In an especially direct assessment, David Geoffrey Smith argues that the form of globalization engendered by the OECD and World Bank is simply "the natural extension of the Euro-American tradition of capital development organized around the processes of production and consumption, inspired especially by the industrial revolution of the 19th century" (10). The late nineteenth century not only witnessed the height of colonialism—Edward Said's *Orientalism* claims that during this century "European direct colonial dominion expanded from about 35 percent of the earth's surface to about 85 percent of it" (41). The late nineteenth century also saw the birth of the U.S. public research university system. As traditional colonialism quickly derailed, the U.S. research university continued to grow and extend its influence across national borders. This transfer of power has been discussed widely. Said, one of the most prolific and important postcolonial theorists, argues that "the American Oriental position since World War II has fit—[he] think[s] quite self-consciously—in the places excavated by the two earlier European powers" of England and France (17).[16] After World War II, the United States was at the forefront of redevelopment and integral to the founding principles of the World Bank, the IMF, and GATT. U.S. higher education, promoted and regulated by these supranational organizations, has emerged as a viable colonial mechanism (while direct territorial occupation rapidly collapsed) because educational colonialism relies primarily on practices of technologies and "scapes" rather than force or coercion. In other words, this new model of colonialism functions primarily through rhetoric rather than through violence.

Perhaps one of the most important hegemonic tools, language invites access at the same time that it delimits how that linguistic, and consequently cultural, assimilation will evolve. International organizations police the discourse of globalization just as earlier legislation policed the culture and language of educational instruction. Citing such historical linkage, Spring suggests that "the current structure and language of the global economy is, in part, a result of past variations in colonial education policies" (*Education and the Rise of the Global Economy* 7). For instance, the U.S. "government used federal boarding schools to change Native-American languages and cultures" (20). This policy was not limited to Native Americans but also occurred in the Southwest with Mexican Americans and in overseas territories such as Puerto Rico and the Philippines. It is easy to forget that the current English-only movement has not erupted from increased immigration and racial tensions as much as it has repeatedly emerged throughout the many political struggles of our national history. As early as 1855, the California Bureau of Instruction mandated that all schools be conducted in English. Given this long history of assimilating cultural others through the use of English in schools, it should not be surprising that the vast majority of scholars worldwide publish their research in English—ranging from nearly 70 percent to 90 percent depending on the specific disciplinary focus (Crystal 102). Similarly, around 80 percent of all texts published on the Internet—the supposed conduit for global democracy—are written in English (Crystal 105). Using digital technologies and high-speed transportation systems to circulate these texts, neocolonialism simply places a high-tech twist on an old technique of policing language, limiting cultural expression, and regulating the interests of private property in conjunction with these linguistic and cultural boundaries.

I offer this analysis not to suggest that economic globalization is hopelessly totalizing but to emphasize the need for theorizing how to exercise agentive shifts and to dissuade us from misplacing our hope in global higher education as it currently exists. Many scholars take a rather pessimistic view that university campuses will empty multiculturalism of its ability to be politically disruptive in order to remake it as yet another economic input. Suggesting a less hopeless view, the World Bank readily admits, "reform implementation has been opposed by various interest groups and has touched off student-rioting in many countries" (*Lessons of Experience* 83). Because neocolonialism works by hegemony, its power is always precariously balanced and vulnerable to counterhegemonic movements. Students, faculty, and citizens in countries all over the world have come to see structural adjustment programs and their intervention into higher education as dangerous. The World Bank cannot have any major meeting, whether in a wealthy or poor county, without being confronted by protesters. If, as the bank suggests, successful reform requires "decision-makers to build a consensus among the various constituents of higher education," then we must follow the lead of these protesters and encourage disagreement (*Lessons of Experience* 84). We must make multiculturalism disruptive; we must make critical thinking challenging, painful, and transformative.[17] Dedicated to such an agenda, the next chapter proposes the working-class professional in opposition to the post-professional and offers examples for such transformative work.

III

5

Working-Class Professionalism
Toward an Historical Materialist Pedagogy

I am speaking of a *ruthless criticism of everything existing,* ruthless in two senses: The criticism must not be afraid of its own conclusions, nor of conflict with the powers that be. . . . Our motto must therefore be: Reform of consciousness not through dogmas, but through analyzing the mystical consciousness which is unclear to itself.

> —Karl Marx, letter to Arnold Ruge, 1844

A critique is not a matter of saying that things are not right as they are. It is a matter of pointing out on what kinds of assumptions, what kinds of familiar, unchallenged, unconsidered modes of thought the practices that we accept rest. . . . The work of deep transformation can only be carried out in a free atmosphere, one constantly agitated by a permanent criticism.

> —Michel Foucault, "Practicing Criticism"

Like Karl Marx and Michel Foucault, I believe that constant and rigorous critique enables the possibility of transformation. Although critique will not create such transformation without significant interventionist practices, a new and more ethical world simply will not emerge without repeated accompanying critique. The work of this ruthless and permanent criticism ought to be the primary focus of working-class professionals as opposed to the corporatized task of reproducing capitalism that currently characterizes post-professionalism, both on the surface of its practices and deeper within its inherent assumptions. I have proposed elsewhere that those in the university who oppose the constrictions placed on us by the era of global capitalism direct our classroom practices toward an anti-capitalist critique of the university and its role in globalization ("Identity, Postmodernity, and an Ethics of Activism"). In this final chapter, I want to extend that proposal to include classroom pedagogies that investigate other institutions critical to the rhetorical shifts of global capitalism, exemplifying an historical materialist pedagogy that pays equal attention to the cultural, political, and economic spheres that collectively constitute the boundaries of our global moment. Exploring rhetorical processes from an historical materialist perspective changes the alliances, responsibilities, and work of professionals as it calls into question the reproductive activities that lie at the heart of taken-for-granted notions of the university as well as its relationship to the state and its citizenry.

Educational theorist Paula Allman devotes her continuing education courses to just such a pedagogy, what she calls a revolutionary critical education. Although she does not identify her methodology as rhetorical, she uses all the practices necessary for rhetorical action—researching, interpreting, speaking, and deliberating in order to arrive at the best course of action in uncertain contexts. Heavily informed by the theories of Karl Marx and Paulo Freire, Allman reminds her readers that "Marx's explanation of capitalism is not just an explanation of people's economic relations and behavior. It is equally and importantly about why people tend to think about their material conditions and activities in a certain way" (16). She emphasizes that a Marxian analysis of capitalism, such as my critique of the U.S. public research university in the era of globalization, needs to account for material relationships as well as the psychic consequences of the social apparatuses legitimating those relationships.

If this dual critique and its accompanying transformative vision have not existed in a comprehensive or unified form, they have emerged at times within fragmented and often diverse responses to the capitalist political economy and its multiple regimes of power. For instance, post-colonial cultural theorist Chela Sandoval believes that popular agents of historical change have been in constant dialogue with academicians, quietly influencing Western theory throughout the last century. In her analysis of critical theories, *Methodology of the Oppressed,* Sandoval asserts that "the primary impulses and strains of critical theory and interdisciplinary thought that emerged in the twentieth century are the result of transformative effects of oppressed speech upon dominant forms of perception" (7). Contrary to the often-rehearsed criticism that critical theory consists of an elitist discourse imposed upon oppressed individuals, Sandoval contends that this theory emerges from the dialogic interaction of alternative speech practices and dominant ways of understanding. Reminiscent of V. N. Vološinov's notion that language always contains class struggle, critical theory—a necessary tool for working-class agency—belongs to neither an elite intellectual cadre nor grassroots activist groups. These theories represent instead the historical culmination of a dynamic relationship between oppressor and oppressed, colonizer and colonized, capitalist and laborer, professional and nonprofessional, professor and student, as well as dominant and alternative modes of thought. Because critical theory has been rhetorically produced through dialectic engagement, the working-class professional can employ critical theory to revive this dynamic and put it to new uses.

By tracing the history of these antagonisms, Sandoval identifies a mode of emancipation she believes will stand up against the neocolonizing conditions of the contemporary global moment. This methodology consists of five intellectual practices: radical semiotics; deconstruction; meta-ideologizing; differential perception; and democratics (2). For her, this broad methodology functions "as a *symptom* of transnational capitalism in its neocolonizing postmodern form . . . as well as a *remedy* for neocolonizing postmodernism both in spite and because of its similarities in structure to power's postmodern configuration" (179–80). It is this double-edged quality that likewise enables the post-professional space to be the juncture where traditional as well as oppositional opportunities arise. The post-professional class has emerged and evolved in order to define and delimit the acceptable boundaries of various capitalist stages, but its internal fissures also create the possibility of working-class professionalism dedicated to social change. If the professional classes rhetorically construct the truth-effects of any historical materialist moment—what Sandoval calls the dominant forms of perception—through their valuations and exchanges within the cultural, political, and economic spheres, then certainly this positionality has the agentive power to shift those boundaries. This shift must be done, as Sandoval tells us, in conjunction with the culturally, politically, and economically oppressed of the world. In rhetorical dialogue with others, working-class professionals can exert considerable historical power. I believe that this dialogic pedagogy will flourish if coupled with an historical materialist methodology.

In the introduction, I explained the rhetorical hermeneutic of valuation that I call historical materialism through the interlocking cultural, political, and economic spheres. I argued that tracing the complex and varied interactions among these spheres illuminates the rhetorical boundaries that such activity constitutes. In social epistemic fashion, figure 2 suggests that language creates reality, but it leaves the larger boundary of performance, persuasion, and possibility perforated to underscore that there is nothing solid, permanent, impenetrable, or final about this reality. That such reality can be torn apart, like the dotted lines on a sheet of a paper, has been a key assumption throughout this book. Yet we cannot tear apart lines we do not know exist, so the rhetorical hermeneutic work of the preceding chapters has been a necessary precondition to the performative work advocated by this chapter. Through a slightly different visualization of the valuation processes constituting the rhetorical hermeneutic of historical materialism, figure 3 shows how the key aspects of each sphere are parallel and collaborative, enabling new practices when conjoined. These new practices revaluate the discursivity constituting the rhetorical effect that bounds performance in order to encourage new performances through a pedagogy of historical materialism. The discrete work of cultural studies, policy studies, and political economy can be replaced with *transdisciplinary practices;* the circulation of commodities through consumption, regulation, and production can be rewritten within a *local-global identity* that refuses to separate consumption from production and sees regulation as a question of ethical engagement with others rather than as fair business practices; instead of defining myth, hegemony, and ideology as separate cognitive activities, we can rethink them as practices of perception that operate together and require us to perform a constant *critique of consciousness.* Taken as a group, the revision made possible by individual and collective agency as well as the permeable historical materialist boundaries of institutionalization create a

Rhetoric of Historical Materialism   **Pedagogy of Historical Materialism**

Cultural	Political	Economic		Alliance building
cultural studies	policy studies	political economy	→	transdisciplinary practices
consumption	regulation	production	→	local-global identity
Myth	hegemony	ideology	→	critique of consciousness

Figure 3: Historical materialist rhetoric: a pedagogical methodology.

rhetorical practice of transformation that falls under the title of *alliance building.*

The practices encompassed within this pedagogy of historical materialism, which are more like foundational beliefs than rigid behaviors, actively reconstruct the institutional boundaries of rhetoric for a given subject and enable us to move within that space differently. The pedagogy of historical materialism writes back to the constituent components—the cultural, the political, and the economic—that institutionalize our landscape on behalf of one agenda and destabilizes that constructive work within the continuous dialectic Sandoval emphasizes, allowing us to question old practices and develop new ones. This is not a revolutionary pedagogy but a rhetorical pedagogy that enables new possibilities, different performances, and alternative meanings to take place. One can hope, as I do, that this rhetorical pedagogy will hasten change within what Deirdre McCloskey upholds as the bourgeois values that sanction capitalist institutions, but revolutionary change seems more likely positioned within the *longue durée* of history favored by world systems analyses and other Marxists who take the need for radical historicizing seriously. An historical materialist pedagogy is absolutely necessary to facilitating changes in the university, but like all dialectical processes it does not operate in any directly causal way. Nonetheless, I am confident that a pedagogy of historical materialism can be used on behalf of such social transformation, and thus I use this concluding chapter as a proposal to intervene in the production of the post-professional class.

Rather than acquiesce to the university as a place to train self-sustaining university professors and capitalist post-professionals, university educators can refocus the historical materialist agenda in order to engage the public more productively as working-class intellectuals. This requires that they teach students to be working-class professionals and not simply professional cogs or passive citizens in the machinations of global capitalism. In this chapter, I clarify how a working-class professional differs from the post-professional that has been the focus of much of this study; further, I explain why pedagogies that focus on citizenship cannot address the complex exigencies of global capitalism and must be replaced with historical materialist pedagogies. These new pedagogies allow instructors and students to combine cultural and economic analyses and examine political effects through close attention to historical specificities. As figure 3 suggests, I offer three necessary preconditions for this pedagogy: transdisciplinary praxis; local-global identity; and repeated critique of consciousness. Together, these three preconditions create the possibility for a fourth practice: alliance building. These four foundations adapt Sandoval's general methodology—the five-prong process constituting a differential mode of oppositional politics—within the specific site of the U.S. public research university and allow for institutional remapping within and without the university. First, however, I begin with an explanation of the responsibilities of working-class professionals.

Positioning Working-Class Professionalism within an Intellectual Landscape

The differentiated educational structure discussed in the preceding chapters matches a similarly diversified workforce—one that includes multiple modes of production from industrial to postindustrial. In this framework, the workers at the bottom of the labor structure create the conditions for the possibility of workers at the top. If industrial laborers did not assemble computer parts and build a worldwide technological infrastructure, the post-professional class that produces commodified units of information simply could not exist. Even in popular periodicals like the *Atlantic Monthly,* one can find cautions against too easily universalizing the economic benefits available to these post-professionals. For instance, Charles R. Morris's review of economic globalization, "The Coming Boom," ends with the acknowledgment that "global competition, while opening unprecedented opportunities for educated manipulators of symbols, like lawyers, investment bankers, design engineers, and marketing experts, will impose iron limits on the wages of ordinary workers" (64). Just like earlier stages of capitalism, the global political economy creates a divided workforce: those who take the place of the professional-managerial workforce—the post-professional—will have many opportunities while the nonprofessional—the industrial and low-end service workers—will have as few or fewer opportunities as ever. Globalization has shifted the way capitalism takes place and consequently the way the university operates, but it has not fundamentally changed the dialectical and classed nature of capitalist society. Post-professionals naturalize and make virtuous the structure from which they benefit while working-class professionals, conscious of ongoing dialectical struggles, call it into question even at the risk of their own professional status.

As the working classes labor to produce the means of production, the professional classes, in their various configurations, labor to reproduce the polyvalent consciousness that accompanies the means of production. According to Karl Marx and Frederick Engels, from the moment this divided labor structure appears, "the first form of ideologists, priests, is concurrent" (*German Ideology* 51). As soon as material labor becomes severed from intellectual labor, a professional class emerges whose job requires the production of specific ideologies that naturalize and facilitate this division of labor. In modern capitalism, as Louis Althusser and Antonio Gramsci have illustrated, professional educators replace priests as the primary form of ideologists ("Ideological State Apparatuses" 152; "Problems of History and Culture" 18). These ideologists can either reproduce or challenge the historical materialist enclosure in which they find themselves. For instance, Gramsci argues that traditional intellectuals reproduce the world as it is while organic intellectuals imagine alternative sociopolitical spaces. Acknowledging a subject position similar to the organic intellectual, Althusser asserts that some intellectuals "in dreadful conditions, attempt to turn the few weapons they can find in the history and learning they 'teach' against the ideology, the system and the practices in which they are trapped. They are a kind of hero. But they are rare" (157). Another critical theorist supporting such counterintellectualism, Foucault defends the specific intellectuals who "intervene in contemporary political struggles in the name of a 'local' scientific truth" ("Truth and Power" 129). For each of these theorists as well as for Sandoval, the professional class offers hope, but only if it is willing to exit the reproductive treadmill and engage in political struggle against a status quo that enables its own existence, and only if it engages its dialectical positionality as well as its object of study with critical self-reflexivity and a commitment to action.

Various oppositional knowledges have been created in the professional disciplines, but no sustained critique has emerged with enough strength to institutionally redirect the project of the university. James W. Guthrie and Lawrence C. Pierce conclude that although critiques of higher education proliferate, "there is little reform which fundamentally challenges the current diverse structure of America's higher education system" (200). In fact, amid crisis and criticism, this university model and its postprofessional class have endured and moved increasingly around the world over the last twenty-five years of burgeoning globalization. The unique goal of the working-class professional, then, must be to oppose the capitalist reproductive mode of the U.S. public research university and its overseas adaptations. Both sweeping and ambitious, the goal is double: to reinstitutionalize the university vis-à-vis the revaluation of the critical terms circulating among its constituent spheres and to seize *kairotic* moments opened up through this new spatial and institutional construction. In other words, as we open up our teaching and research agendas to new kinds of inquiries, we create the possibility of structural change within the various institutions under investigation as well as the institutional structure of the university that supports such inquiries.

Conscious of the tremendous hurdle such commitments attempt to transverse, critical theory tends to paint a bleak picture of current academic practices, suggesting that the corporatized university has purged higher education of possibilities for transformative action. The political sphere has become mediated by the entertainment industries, compromising traditional notions of open dialogue. The cultural sphere has become commodified and emptied of much of its sacred powers. The economic sphere uses persuasion for branding products more than for discussion of the public good. Because this historical materialist terrain exists both within and without the university, alternative intellectual philosophies such as Marxist and postcolonial theories are watered down even within academic spaces, becoming nearly inseparable from other theories and professional ideas. As a testament to its role in the capitalist political economy, the U.S. public research university has always been more interested in policing its own obedience to the ethic of professional business sense than in working for the sociopolitical good. If we wish to use this university structure as a place for working-class professionalism, we must, as critical theorist Jim Merod suggests, create "an enlarged political ethos" for academicians across the disciplines, allowing them to move beyond rigid borders of traditional professionalism (13). According to this new ethos, intellectuals would have "a responsibility to instruct public consciousness in order to promote unpopular views otherwise shut out of political debate" (166). Specifically, Merod proposes that "oppositional critics of various sorts create a collective strategy, a genuinely shared pedagogical and theoretical activity that puts them in contact with one another in more restlessly experimental, more strategically decisive formats than intellectual work now possesses" (194). His proposal, with its emphasis on interdisciplinarity, alliance building, and collective problem solving, echoes the pedagogical structure of historical materialism. Indeed, the pedagogy of historical materialism may be characterized as a restlessly experimental approach to professional knowledge making and collectivity.

The need for such oppositional professionals is further articulated by Edward Said in the collection of his 1993 Reith Lectures. In this important text, he characterizes what I am calling the working-class professional as anyone with the ability to represent, embody, or articulate a message about the sociopolitical, cultural, and economic structures to the general public. "Neither a pacifier nor a consensus-builder," this intellectual must be "someone whose whole being is staked on a critical sense, a sense of being unwilling to accept easy formulas, or ready-made clichés, or the smooth, ever-so-accommodating confirmations of what the powerful or conventional have to say" (*Representations of the Intellectual* 23). Said unequivocally states that a critical intellectual's defining responsibility is "to universalize the crisis, to give greater human scope to what a particular race or nation suffered, to associate that experience with the sufferings of others" (44). Such intellectuals must conscientiously name difference, engage the public, collaborate on unifying agendas that do not impinge upon the variations among communities, and ultimately create social change. They must do all this while constantly subjecting themselves, other organizations, and their political agendas to thorough critique. In this way, these intellectuals and their work will continue to evolve with and adapt to fluctuating historical conditions. Unfortunately, most intellectuals eschew this responsibility for safe professional paths.

The safer, traditional professionalism of university faculty not only differs from but significantly endangers the possibility of these public, politicized, and activist intellectuals. The real threat to responsible, public intellectualism, insists Said, is "an attitude that [he] will call professionalism" (73–74). He contends that this professionalism can be countered by "amateurism" or "the desire to be moved not by profit or reward but by love for and unquenchable interest in the larger picture, in making connections across lines and barriers, in refusing to be tied down to a specialty, in caring for ideas and values despite the restrictions of a profession" (76). Said believes that intellectuals can make a conscious choice not to function according to the rhetorically constructed rules of professionalism. Though I applaud Said's attempt to contest the pressures of post-professionalism, I do not share his belief in the possibility of successful amateurism. University-trained intellectuals cannot make a nostalgic return to a moment before such professional training; instead, I suggest we move forward, reappropriate this training, and inaugurate the working-class professional. Calling on the spirit of an amateurism that asks academics to choose "the risks and uncertain results of the public sphere . . . over the insider space controlled by experts and professionals," working-class professionals organize themselves in loose collaborations to engage students as well as the public in transformative agendas (87). I recommend, that is, a collective of working-class professionals dedicated to building a global community of intellectuals through pedagogical and scholarly interrogations of the university and of the larger historical materialist boundaries of capitalism, transcending disciplinary, cultural, and national limits as they do. These intellectuals would seize the discourses available to them—cultural, political, and economic critical theories—in order to revalue their dominant logics through an attitude of working-class professionalism. They would exploit the double-edged quality of the "professional" to create the conditions for social change rather than conditions for more job placement or placid notions of citizenship.

Working-Class Professionalization: An Argument against Teaching for Citizenship

Like most categories, the notion of citizenship has contested origins. For some, the origins go back to forms of citizenship in Greece and medieval Europe. Others suggest that citizenship is essentially a modern concept that emerged out of the French Revolution and its aftermath (Kalberg; Seligman). According to this latter argument, citizenship requires a public sphere, a city culture, a nation-state, and ultimately a capitalist political economy. Citizenship, in this sense, emerged within a specific spatio-temporal moment and spread around the globe—however unevenly—with the extension of capitalism and its attendant democratic state apparatuses. Advocates of the capitalist political economic structure assume that "as countries develop and the public sphere expands as a consequence of industrialization, modern Western-style citizenship is an inevitable outcome" (Sassen, *Losing Control?* 34). This, of course, is the logic of such vexed projects as the Iraq war: if we oust the dictatorial regime of Saddam Hussein and replace it with capitalist figureheads, Iraqis will reap the benefits of citizenship and will be free. Those who follow this line of thinking believe that capitalism brings democracy and requires the globalization of citizenship. Yet most of the global population does not share the historical interests, cultural experiences, and political desires of the bourgeois class that first demanded citizenship rights. To the extent that this global population does act as appropriate citizen-subjects, then, it is acting contrary to its own historical materialist positionality. Once the global population is taken into account, the citizen-subject appears to function as a site of oppression rather than as a source of individual empowerment. To return to the Iraqi example, we can see how material contradictions are rhetorically managed by separating legitimate citizens from radical fundamentalists, insurgents, and terrorists. This rhetorical valuation, countered by other rhetorical explanation, has not acquired its hegemonic foothold in Iraq, allowing the political, material, and cultural fissures heightened visibility as they struggle to assert the boundaries of legitimate social practice. The universality supposedly inherent in citizenship simply cannot unify the many diverse players in the Iraqi political drama because citizenship is neither universal nor the pathway to democracy.

Nevertheless, the United States has ascended to a position of global leadership, in part, by cultivating this notion of citizen-subject through institutions of higher education. Public universities offer a claim similar to that of universal citizenship: create literate citizens and democracy will follow. T. H. Marshall's classic essay, "Citizenship and Social Class," helps frame this discussion. Marshall investigates the relationships among citizenship, education, and the capitalist class structure through an interrogation of conventional wisdom. Since the late nineteenth century, he contends, the general public has assumed that an expanding educational system along with the gradual reduction of heavy labor would provide the benefits of citizenship. Class differentiation would remain, but citizenship would flourish and ensure the civil, political, and social rights of all members of society. According to this theory, "the inequality of the social class system may be acceptable provided the equality of citizenship is recognized" (6). Indeed, the infrastructure of an evolving capitalist economy along with state-sponsored social services did guarantee many people the rights of citizenship. Writing in post–World War II England, Marshall was surrounded by a Keynesian economic plan that included national health care, large-scale housing programs, and mass education. But such a structure also contributed to the constant reproduction of a classed society. Though social programs like mass education promise equality through citizenship, Marshall emphasizes that its relationship to the capitalist political economy also enables education to operate as an instrument of class stratification (39).[1] He concludes that formal education serves the liberal-democratic state by shaping the subjectivities of its citizens in such a way as to restrict their socioeconomic mobility and maintain the national status quo, a goal quite contrary to the rhetoric of democracy, social mobility, and meritocracy so often associated with public education.

Although many theorists wrestle with this critique, it has yet to be resolved. Richard Ohmann, for instance, emphasizes that even while democratic citizenship functions through a contradictory and ideologically troubled political sphere, the main justification for universal education continues to be that "democracy can't work unless citizens are literate and informed" (1). Citizenship ensures rights under the law, the rights of private property, workplace rights, as well as freedoms in market exchange, and such rights require literate and knowledgeable citizens. Thus, Ohmann contends, "free labor and free capital needed a relationship like citizenship as their legal basis. So in effect, citizenship was the 'soil' in which capitalist inequality flourished" (3). J. Elspeth Stuckey goes so far as to argue that literacy is violent, deceptive, and specifically devoted to economic ends that perpetuate injustice. Regardless of the specificities of these different critiques, all agree that the universal category of citizenship exists as both an illusory ideal and a necessary foundation on which all claims to political, educational, and employment rights are based.[2] In order to universalize education in general and literacy in particular as forms that serve capitalism, there must be a group, such as the citizenry, to whom those privileges belong as well as others to whom those rights are denied. According to Ohmann, Stuckey, and others, citizenship exists as a rhetorical shell or an empty sign into which particular significations are deposited so that we can all act and participate from the classed positionality into which we are hailed. I want to suggest, then, that teaching for citizenship, however ill or well intentioned, often maintains the inequalities of the current cultural, political, and economic processes of capitalism.

Because the working-class professional opposes capitalist political economic and cultural reproduction, such an intellectual must also oppose teaching for citizenship. A working-class professional does not attempt to create bourgeois citizen-subjects as Sharon Crowley argues composition traditionally does; nor does a working-class professional attempt to create critical citizen-subjects as James Berlin so often advises ("Contemporary Rhetoric and Late Capitalism); nor does a working-class professional produce better informed citizen-subjects as William Keith and Rosa Eberly so carefully contend; nor does the working-class professional strive to produce the cosmopolitan citizen of the global era as John Tomlinson argues. The list, no doubt, could go on endlessly, so enamored with citizenship are thoughtful, ethically minded academicians. Against this prevailing trend, the task of a working-class professional consists of interrogating, intervening, and attempting to change the structures of society that link citizenship to a weak version of democracy in order to justify the exploitative historical materialist terrain of capitalism.

The rhetoric of historical materialism uses articulation theory to sever the deep ties between rhetoric and citizenship while it links rhetoric to institutionalization and class dialectics, but this does not dismiss the importance of much of the work that goes on under the name of citizenship. Rosa Eberly offers solid arguments on behalf of reenvisioning the classroom as what she calls a proto-public space. For her, "encouraging students to see themselves as actors in different and overlapping publics can help [students] realize the particular and situated nature of rhetoric and the need for effective writing to respond to particular publics at particular times" ("From *Writers*" 167). Like so many rhetoricians interested in citizenship, she wants to improve the way that students communicate within the public sphere—the site of potential political and personal change. Instead of teaching students to make ideal arguments for a teacher about a mock issue, Eberly asks students to make arguments about issues within real spaces. No doubt, this pedagogy encourages students to see themselves as agents capable of eliciting changes in the world and thus it certainly functions as a more practical rhetorical education than its book-centered, classroom-constrained antecedents. Constituting students as active public participants rests, however, on the notion of citizenship and the spaces open to citizens. In these rhetorically constructed boundaries, some identities cannot claim citizenship status as readily as others—ex-prisoners and those unfortunate enough to have names resembling them are one recent example. Others might find that citizenship rights do not extend to the issues most pressing to them—the many legal and economic benefits denied to same-sex partners, for instance. Still others might vote diligently without receiving the long-overdue increase in minimum wage necessary to their inflated living costs. The limits of citizenship suggested by these examples can be found through the rhetorical hermeneutic of historical materialism. These limits will not be superseded by proto-participation as long as that participation plays out within the traditional boundaries of our political economic terrain, but they might be altered by a pedagogy of historical materialism that maps and revises these boundaries.

To be fair, Eberly makes clear that she does not subscribe to the idealism of public deliberation. "Rhetoric and the Anti-Logos Doughball" clarifies her position on democratic deliberation: she wants to keep the baby and throw out the bathwater. For her, "the baby was the great promise of Habermas's insights into language use in political economies, into structures of legitimation, into social reproduction. The bathwater was his philosophical idealism" (288). I agree that babies generally should not be discarded, even if they are found sitting in tepid and filthy bathwater. For me, this baby is Marx's historical materialist analysis and the bathwater is the Eurocentric, phallocentric, and generally simplistic interpretations of the proletarian revolution that have come under the name of Marxism. Not knowing exactly how capitalism will fall nor exactly what will take its place should not prevent rhetoricians from actively critiquing and attempting to change its clearly oppressive practices and institutions. Like a pedagogy based on citizenship, I envision a classroom where students focus on an issue, analyze it from an historical materialist hermeneutic, deliberate about its valuation processes, propose alternative valuations, and engage others outside the university as they work through different rhetorical and material constructions of a given site.

Unlike an emphasis on citizenship, this pedagogy links the political, economic, and cultural problematics of contemporary society to the historical materialist foundations of capitalism. As I have said, Eberly's citizen-critics likely engage in many of the practices found in the classrooms of working-class professionals, but perhaps without specific attention to the classed nature of contemporary reality. Her pedagogy of citizen-critics in the proto-publics appears to consist of studying an issue, recognizing shared interests and citizenship rights that entitle them to shape future public decisions, deliberating about possible action, taking action, and disintegrating. In many ways, this parallels the kind of classroom for which I advocate, except that the classroom I envision does not focus on students as citizen-critics but on students as worker-critics. In other words, their ability to analyze issues, discover or create shared interests, deliberate about action, take action, and move forward in the world stems not from citizenship rights that are guaranteed but from the fact of our mutual classed subjugation and its interpenetration within the political and cultural spheres. For this kind of worker-critic to emerge and act, the rhetoric classroom has to refocus from citizenship onto issues of historical materialism.

An historical materialist investigation can emerge through political, economic, or cultural entry points, as it studies relationships among all these spheres. Students, for instance, can engage the political and material as they study the cultural. Again, like Eberly, I see the value of avoiding direct confrontation with political issues that often divide students along rather predictable lines: she believes that "whereas political questions often split the subject's interest over questions of property, discussions of literary and other cultural texts do not necessarily have to cause this split in subjectivity" ("Anti-Logos Doughball" 295). That students can be simultaneously aligned and divided is at the heart of an historical materialist pedagogy. Such a pedagogy attempts to engender not just proto-publics but dialectical publics—publics capable of seeing and engaging in the many dynamic contradictions of capitalism. Because the cultural is the space that attempts to resolve the contradictions of capitalism by creating a unified consciousness among diverse publics, it offers a wonderful place of entry into the question of rhetoric—particularly questions of how rhetoric circulates among the political, economic, and cultural realms in order to create institutions capable of imposing legitimate participation. The primary difference between this and citizenship education is that this rhetorical work requires students to study the cultural in relationship to the political and the economic. Rather than approaching the classroom from a rigid disciplinary angle, a working-class professional transcends disciplinarity through an historical materialist pedagogy that focuses on institutions and their relationship to people, communities, and language practices as well as to cultural, political, and economic infrastructures. Just as my rhetorical hermeneutic followed the cultural, political, and economic spheres to study the boundaries constructed from the valuations between and among these spheres, so too does this pedagogy require radically redefining disciplinarity. From such work, I believe, a self-reflexive working-class professionalism can emerge and assume agency for transformation inside and outside the university.

The Pedagogy of Historical Materialism: A Rhetorical Reinstitutionalization

Because much of the university curricula has become reified within a particular view of the global political economy, university post-professionals tend to follow a predictable route wherein knowledge exists as a thing-in-itself and not as a socially constructed artifact representative of larger historical, material, and cultural processes. Pedagogues invested in historical materialist critique stand out in this setting because they highlight what Mas'ud Zavarzadeh and Donald Morton call "the political economy of knowledge" (180). Such a pedagogy does not represent a particular reality nor does it validate any particular form of fixed existence; instead, the political economy of knowledge asks—in the Freirean tradition of problem posing—what cultural, political, and economic processes produced the text under investigation. It further inquires why that text was produced and in whose interests. It defamiliarizes the text under investigation and "intervenes in the reproduction of dominant cultural meanings that lend support to the continuation of existing social relations" (Zavarzadeh and Morton 54). Meaning, including university-produced disciplinarity, is created and re-created through historical materialist struggles that can be mapped onto a grid of intelligibility. The working-class professional privileges rhetorical inquiry into all aspects of meaning making and does not police disciplinary boundaries nor profess a disciplinary canon.

Historical materialist pedagogies combine the four spheres of knowledge making that I propose below in order to construct the ground on which working-class professionals can emerge. While these areas are crucial to the success of such pedagogies, they do not function as a practical guideline; rather, they represent theoretical foundations that need to be productively engaged and constantly refined. I avoid answering, too specifically, the question, "What are we to do?" as no such rubric has yet stood the test of history and many universal policy proclamations have contributed to serious material inequities. One of the problems I cite with both the U.S. public research university and with the transnational policymaking of globalization is, in fact, such standardized unilateral decisions. Against the clearly problematic move toward such propositions, I nonetheless believe that we need guiding agendas. Based on figure 3, I propose a loose, four-point initiative toward an historical materialist pedagogy: develop a transdisciplinary praxis; create a critical local-global identity; engage in repeated ideological critique; and forge alliances through a commitment to public intellectualism. What follows is a theoretical engagement with these foundational principles and a pedagogical example of how they might play out in a rhetoric classroom.

The theoretical engagement takes broad swipes at praxis while the pedagogical example discusses a specific course I taught on rhetoric and the institutionalization of reality TV. Meant to demonstrate the flexibility of this approach, the examples also emphasize how studying new rhetorical texts and studying them differently might in turn reconstruct the institutional space of the university.

A Transdisciplinary Praxis against Intellectual Divisions of Labor

According to Marx and Engels, the division of labor signifies one of the key characteristics of the capitalist mode of production. As part of this division, official intellectual labor severs its ties from physical labor. Consequently, they argue that these two activities "devolve on different individuals, and that the only possibility of their not coming into contradiction lies in the negation in its turn of the division of labour" (*German Ideology* 52). As I have already mentioned, this division means a particular class of workers emerges as the intellectuals or the ideologues of a capitalist society. But this is not where the division ends. Just as capitalism exponentially divides physical labor into an infinite number of isolated tasks, it similarly divides intellectual labor. Such departmentalizing, as Foucault's *Discipline and Punish* makes clear, creates docile bodies, easily surveyed and disciplined through divisions of time and space. The U.S. public research university system, for instance, divides an enormous range of professions into geographically distinct colleges, departments, and areas of specialty at the same time that it divides time into course hours, semesters, degrees, and tenure clocks. Methods of inquiry or knowledge production become equally divided and separated inside this highly compartmentalized teaching factory, to borrow a phrase from Marx. Even general methodologies like statistical analysis, ethnography, and discourse studies become actualized differently within different departments. As the trend toward particularization continues and "each partial operation acquires in the hands of the worker a suitable form peculiar to it, alterations become necessary in the tools which previously served more than one purpose" (*Capital* 460). This need for different tools occurs in the factory of knowledge in the form of slightly differentiated knowledge production. While the university administration "represents to the individual workers the unity and the will of the whole body of social labor," each individual professional functions almost as an isolated automaton who knows little about the work of others in the university (*Capital* 482). A university might, as one where I worked did, advertise its educational experience as a "culture of engagement," but individual faculty tend to succeed most when they plant their feet solidly on disciplinary ground and do not look up until they have met tenure requirements. For Marx, this system dehumanizes workers even though it quantitatively increases the number of products produced—grants received, research published, and patents filed.

This division of labor helps normalize knowledge in order to structurally reproduce the historical, materialist, and cultural building blocks of capitalist production. Explicitly revealing this corporatizing methodology, Charles William Eliot's 1869 inaugural address as president of Harvard College, argued that the people of the United States "do not apply to mental activities the principle of division of labor; and we have but a halting faith in the special training for high professional employments" (9). Believing that higher education had much to learn from corporations, Eliot proposed "the principle of divided and subordinate responsibilities, which rules in government bureaus, in manufactures, and all great companies, which makes a modern army a possibility, must be applied to the University" (26). While Eliot seems to be arguing for a new method of structuring higher education, the intellectual division of labor that he appealed to in this speech had, by 1869, already begun to characterize the U.S. public university system. Indeed, as chapter 1 suggested, the newly developing professional class and its accompanying curricula spearheaded and legitimated the adoption of such a division of labor. Nearly perfected within the U.S. public research university, this division enables the U.S. model of education to function adeptly within the evolving stages of capitalism. Just as capitalism continues to thrive in our contemporary moment, these divisions remain securely in place in the global university. In order to attain a job, a newly credentialized Ph.D. must market him- or herself within a specialized area of expertise. In order to publish one's work, that same individual must choose a respectable journal with an area of focus that matches this expertise. Once inside the university system, the professor must continue to publish in these particular areas and disseminate specialized knowledge to a highly selected and equally divided student body. The more professionalized we become, the more erudite our knowledge and the less accessible it is to the communicative processes determining the contour of our lived world. Accordingly, to care too much about the public at large or even the students in our classrooms is universally acknowledged as sacrificing professional goals and security for the much subjugated work of service and teaching.

Clearly one of the enduring strategies of capitalism has been to divide labor and laborers—both manual and intellectual. Peter McLaren's *Che Guevara, Paulo Freire, and the Pedagogy of Revolution* positions this divisiveness within the grid of global antagonisms centered in the United States. According to McLaren, Guevara "saw U.S. capitalism as a deceitful and mocking consciousness that has arrayed the rich against the masses; he characterized it as possessing an inveterate need to divide the world" (42). But capitalism does not simply divide the rich from the poor. Because it places the rich in competition with the rich and the masses in competition with the masses, capitalism divides the whole world; it divides each of us against those both like us and not like us. Collaboration in business as well as in academia is frowned upon through structures like noncompetitive clauses, protection of trade secrets, reduced credit for collaborative publications, and reduced pay for collaborative teaching. Anticapitalist strategies need to work against this kind of division. In the university, this translates into the creation of transdisciplinary, and not merely interdisciplinary, teaching and research.

The university and professional organizations, for some time now, have recognized the value of interdisciplinarity. Interdisciplinary work represents collaborations between multiple, though separate, disciplines in order to better produce and assess academic knowledge. This also creates a worker with multiple disciplinary skill sets—ideal for a global political economy in which people transfer jobs regularly. Structurally, however, interdisciplinarity reinforces and relies on disciplinary legitimacy. Like an international corporation located in one nation-state and utilizing other national labor and consumer markets, an interdisciplinary project is ultimately housed in one department while relying on the work of other departments. Interdisciplinarity simultaneously challenges the boundaries between disciplines and reinforces such divisions, creating a double consciousness that has been much lauded but generally produces reformist initiatives that have one foot in the university and one foot in the corporate world. I advocate, instead, transdisciplinary knowledge—knowledge that transcends disciplinary divisions by planting both feet on the ground of a working-class professionalism. Using the transnational corporation as its model, but placing the politics of the transnational corporation on its head, transdisciplinary praxis operates outside disciplines to enact its guerilla knowledge.[3]

While the guerrilla marketer maps the world according to geopolitically specific units to successfully sell a particular product to a diverse global audience, the guerrilla intellectual maps the specifics of each discipline to infiltrate its boundaries.[4] Guerrilla knowledge uses an historical materialist framework in order to critique disciplinary histories and practices. Reminiscent of Marx's infamous communist specters, guerrilla knowledge does not exist in any department but on the margins of every discipline, haunting them all. Structurally, guerrilla knowledge takes its cue from various nondisciplinary fields like rhetoric and cultural studies. These fields currently operate without disciplinary legitimacy in order to analyze a multiplicity of objects from literature and popular culture to new technologies and institutions. The guerrilla knowledge I seek would use historical materialism as a rhetorical hermeneutic of valuation to study institutionalized knowledges. The university, through its production of distinct disciplines and critical theories, makes such a structure possible. As Merod says, "critical awareness has achieved sufficient intellectual sophistication to undo its professional self-encasement by constructing both the conceptual and the institutional means for evaluating the way in which research of every kind gains legitimacy" (25). Maneuvering at the edges of legitimate professional work, guerrilla knowledge impacts more than the university. The university functions to reproduce the boundaries of production, consumption, and regulation that allow capitalism to thrive; therefore, guerrilla knowledge also affects society as a whole by creating opportunities to conceive of a world outside the historical materialist parameters of capitalism.

The need for transdisciplinary praxis takes us back to the discussion in the introduction about the uses and scope of rhetoric. Rhetoric, like cultural studies, functions better as a method of inquiry that provokes action than as a disciplinary practice that applies a specific formula in order to produce a predetermined product. Because of the natural alliance between rhetoric and transdisciplinary practices, I suggest that we expand rather than limit the uses of rhetoric. The University of Iowa's Project on the Rhetoric of Inquiry (POROI) offers one excellent example of how to begin thinking through the transdisciplinarity of rhetoric. From its inception as a reading group, the project has burgeoned to include seminars, symposia, lectures, conferences, a graduate certificate, an electronic journal, and a book series. Along the lines of this model, I advocate collaboration across disciplines, inclusion of rhetoric coursework and scholarship within every discipline, rhetorical programming within universities that interacts with local communities, and the implementation of rhetorical certificates for students. The structure for this work already exists within many university writing programs and can either be mirrored by or intertwined with rhetorical approaches. Taking on the practices and ethos of an undervalued field like writing would help this pedagogical intervention work under the university radar, enabling greater flexibility in its diverse practices at the same time that it authorizes these practices within the ongoing structures of the university.

This means course development that extends beyond traditional disciplinary mainstays, cross-lists with other departments, and reaches out to students other than those in our home departments. Many of my rhetoric courses, for instance, attract students from history, criminal justice, political science, literature, writing, anthropology, business, marketing, philosophy, information technology, and creative writing. When I appeal to students from such disparate disciplinary backgrounds, I do so with a commitment to approach course content from different angles. In a course I teach on the rhetoric of reality television, I define our parameters with a wide and rather unspecialized lens: rhetoric includes all symbolic acts that encourage ideas and behaviors in the world while reality television encompasses any program that uses unscripted accounts from amateur participants. These broad definitions of rhetoric and reality television as well as a sequence of readings that leads from popular reality television shows to more serious current issues encourage students to make connections between lived reality and televisual representations. It requires them to actively explore the rhetorical differences between a reputable news program's coverage of the war in Iraq and a tabloid television show that uses many of the same rhetorical strategies. The inclusiveness of this definition enables me to bring in reading material from a number of scholarly approaches—cultural studies, sociology, psychology, political science, law, criminal justice, communications, as well as television and film studies. Along with these, we read excerpts from writers, participants, viewers, labor and social activists, and corporate figureheads. We theorize, deliberate, and write about the effects of reality TV inside and outside class, simultaneously marking the current boundaries of its institutionalization and proposing alternatives. In particular, we focus on the legitimation of volunteer labor in the economic sphere, the naturalization of surveillance in the political sphere, and the individualization of consumption in the cultural sphere. The institution under analysis is reality-based television and the rhetorical approach is an interdisciplinary study of how it constitutes possibilities and subjectivities in ways that encourage viewers to shift attitudes and behaviors necessary to the machinations of global capitalism. What is significant is not its contents—not what we study—but the historical materialist approach and its foundations in transdisciplinary exploration.

Regardless of the specific institutional shape of the new rhetorical structure inside the university or of the specific institution under investigation in our classrooms, we must allow for transdisciplinary praxis to make connections across intellectual boundaries, develop courses, and create scholarship that studies the historical materialism of knowledge without owing allegiance to any one discipline. Collaborating through informal organizations, programs, or committees, transdisciplinary structures require no university legitimacy and course development simply necessitates that we extend our research skills beyond disciplinary databases.[5] The university has created the terrain from which the guerrilla intellectual emerges, armed to reassemble the university according to new and as yet unconceivable historical materialist structures. Like all guerrilla action, transdisciplinary praxis creates new options, but we must remember that none of these options will act as a panacea and that all of them will require sustained theoretical and practical critique. I believe that such sustained political engagement takes into account the need for positioning where one stands and how that positionality affects others worldwide. Transdisciplinary praxis requires a simultaneously local and global consciousness that is willing to take responsibility for one's role within the current era of global capitalism.

A Local-Global Consciousness against Generalizing Particulars

Many believe that Marx focused on historical relations rather than on individual consciousness. Even his infrequent discussions of individuals tended to focus on how people represent positions within historical relations—the greedy capitalist and the tireless worker. Consequently, radical theorists often sidestep the question of how to develop a revolutionary consciousness, citing the fact that Marx left no clear theory of the subject (Burniston and Weedon). Still fewer rhetoricians have thoroughly engaged the important question of how to pursue democratic discourse within and through a Marxist consciousness. A notable exception, James Arnt Aune's *Rhetoric and Marxism* offers a detailed study of how communication, consciousness, and rhetoric have been ignored throughout the works of Western Marxism, yet he manages to trace within these texts an implicit rhetorical theory that precariously balances romantic expressionism with a positivist ideal of perfect communication. Rather than privilege this class analysis and its troubled rhetorical approaches, he advocates cultural analyses, especially feminist ones, as the key to a more democratic sense of subjectivity. Other theorists, like Greg Dawes, seek a Marxist theory of subjectivity in V. N. Vološinov in order to argue that language dialectically constructs individuals; most, however, utilize Althusser for this task. In his seminal essay, "Ideology and Ideological State Apparatuses," Althusser demonstrates how various mechanisms— from education to the family to the media—transform individuals into subjects of capitalism. Althusser and other Marxists (Gramsci and Habermas, in particular) help explain how ideology shapes individual subjectivities, but they are less effective, as Aune notes, at suggesting ways of instilling individuals with an alternative revolutionary consciousness.

Working-class professionals must fill this gap by developing new theories of identity through a dual consciousness that translates between local and global phenomena. This dialectical understanding will move individuals into collectives even as it insists that universal analyses take account of local particularities. Without this consciousness, we will not be able to move beyond the narrow classed, raced, gendered, sexed, nationalized, and ethnic consciousness that prevents the transformation of global capitalism. I believe, in addition, that this new consciousness must be informed by postcolonial theory because globalization demands that the U.S. public research university operate worldwide and within an extremely uneven geography of cultural and productive developments. Aided by a local-global consciousness, working-class professionals will be able to translate their agendas as well as the agendas of others and initiate a more nuanced public discussion of globalization. This translation might include, for example, tracing one's cultural practice of frequenting a local coffee shop through the labor practices of poorly paid Ethiopian farmers as well as the regulatory practices of trade agreements and stock exchanges in order to arrive at new understandings of particularized experiences.[6]

The important task of translating cultural difference requires the working-class professional to occupy a liminal space between the self and the other as well as between the local and the global. McLaren argues that "as translators, critical educators must assume a transformative role by 'dialogizing the other' rather than trying to 'represent the other'" ("Liberatory Politics" 61). What better tool for dialogue than rhetoric? Rhetorical training can teach students and faculty to engage and identify with others from radically different situations. Postcolonial theorist Homi Bhabha defines this rhetorical translation as "imitating an original in such a way that the priority of the original is not reinforced precisely because it can be simulated, copied, transferred, transformed, made into a simulacrum and so on: the 'original' is never finished or complete in itself" (Bhabha and Rutherford, "The Third Space" 210). Translation does not require an original; it does not assume authenticity but attempts to transcribe the complexity of a given situation within the spirit of an anticolonial politics. Barbara A. Biesecker similarly avoids the originary as she redefines the rhetorical situation within a radical historical context "governed by a logic of articulation rather than influence" that obligates us "to read every 'fixed' identity as the provisional and practical outcome of a symbolic engagement between speaker and audience" (112). Both Bhabha and Biesecker rely on Derridian deconstruction to rethink identity as an act of articulating, translating, and rearticulating within particular rhetorical exigencies. A Marxist dialectics resembles this deconstructive act but differs importantly in its historical materialist grounding.

Historical materialism requires rhetorical translation to expose the degree to which the local is intertwined within and defined by other localities as well as by a larger global politics. A working-class professional will be in a position, then, to weed out localities that serve the interests of global capitalism from those localities that offer alternatives.[7] This local-global consciousness helps recognize and transform the contradictions that create asymmetries of power in the manufacturing of race, gender, class, sexuality, nationality, and ethnicity. More specifically, this oppositional consciousness understands that "local antagonisms evident both in the larger social community and in the educational arena are inextricably linked to the politics of neoliberalism driven by an expanding global capitalism" (McLaren and Gutierrez 196). Implicated in the larger totality, the local manifests as a site of resistance and independence as often as it latches onto the neoliberal politics of globalization. But a dual local-global consciousness provides the tools to better understand how power operates across different cultural terrains. Again, this is essentially a rhetorical task as rhetoric functions to massage political reality so that real-life contractions can be resolved through identification, imagination, and language.

Rhetorical practices that instill such a consciousness can be forged both in classrooms and in our professional lives. In much the same way that I traced the language of globalization within the U.S. public research university through international treaties and supranational organizations, we can ask our students to trace the rhetorical idioms present at various local sites through increasingly larger institutional relationships. In this work, students will be confronted with the question of why the same rhetoric functions within such obviously different venues as banks, political treaties, cultural artifacts, and educational institutions. We can also ask students to trace a particular cultural artifact across spatial and temporal boundaries, noting the changes that occur both as a result of the cultural boundaries of its new location and as a result of political policies. Such an assignment requires students to grapple with cultural appropriation as well as the economic bottom line. In addition to these research projects, we can put students in touch with students living in distant locations and require on-line deliberation between the two groups. To enhance this dialogue, we could require students to read news coverage from other national publications, many of which are readily available online. In this way, students will see the rhetorical situation of their dialogue in context with other rhetorically constructed dialogues worldwide, encouraging them to adopt a dialectical consciousness that translates between the local and the global. Given the international scope of the U.S. public research university as well as the digitalization of communication, there are more and more avenues available to challenge a unified, national consciousness.

My course on reality television, for instance, traced television shows and various programming themes back and forth within this local-global dynamic, attempting to think through television's relationship to the power structures of globalization. We examined *Big Brother,* a television format owned by a publicly traded company, listed on multiple stock exchanges, and sold to several dozen nationally based companies where it is adapted to its local audience before being broadcast. The universal applicability of *Big Brother* coupled with the uniqueness of each national version illustrates one of sociologist Roland Robertson's key characteristics of globalization: the twin forces of economic convergence and cultural divergence. This show, like the popular program *Survivor,* emerged from Western Europe, traveled to the United States, and continued to penetrate markets throughout the globe. Alternatively, shows like *COPS* and *America's Most Wanted* emerged in the United States and moved to Western Europe. Endurance programs that ask contestants to perform physically tasking stunts have their antecedents in Japan. The three regions central to economic globalization—the United States, Western Europe, and Japan—are also the three localities central to the production of current reality programming. It is important to note that there is no clear center and periphery among these regions. Each region originated some form of reality programming and each imported other forms, translating cultural and political subjectivities in the process.

Exploring the global circulation of identities within these shows, their valuation and revaluation within particular local sites, and the boundaries of reality they construct models the local-global sensibility I want students to adopt. *Big Brother,* among the most famous reality TV hits world-wide, served as an extended case study for developing this rhetorical standpoint. The first series of this show aired in the Netherlands in 1999 with an amazing 50 percent of the Dutch population tuning into the final episode. With this success under its belt, the production company Endemol went on to sell the *Big Brother* format to countries worldwide. Taking its title from George Orwell's *1984* wherein the characters eke out a life within a highly surveillanced society, *Big Brother* requires twelve contestants to live in a house under twenty-four-hour watch, without leaving and without outside contact. One contestant is voted out each week until the last one in the house is declared the winner. Australian critic Toni Johnson-Woods offers an excellent comparative analysis of different national adaptations of *Big Brother.* Together with an exploration of the Endemol Web site (http://www.endemol.com/), these readings introduce students to the dialectics of localization/globalization. Studying the political economy of communications, students learn that one production company, started by two Dutch businessmen, holds the copyright to the *Big Brother* television format, which is leased to television stations in countries around the world. From a policy perspective, students explore how international law unilaterally regulates the exchange and development of this program while cultural studies analyses remind them that its format is never imported without alterations. Each country changes the rules of the game—different cash prizes, different kinds of contestants, different activities, different houses with more or less comfort, different levels of surveillance, and different rules. No single show fully resembles another. Our investigation of the *Big Brother* phenomenon allows us to discuss national differences as rhetorical constructions embedded in cultural artifacts like this television program. We do this through a comparative analysis of *Big Brother*'s different national versions—asking stasis questions about what takes place, how we define certain acts, what special circumstances allow for alternative acts, and who has the authority to judge these acts.

These questions help us trace the circulation of textuality on television within the political, economic, and cultural spheres in order to explore rhetorical practices and possibilities. For instance, we discuss the quantity of financial investment necessary for South Africa to produce such a highly technologized television show within a decade of eliminating political policies that made such media illegal. And, reversing the focus, we conjecture about the practices of surveillance this show encourages in viewers who can purchase Webcam access and participate as the "Big Brother" who is always watching, acknowledging that technology in the cultural sphere inevitably impacts the economic sphere—research, production, sales, and maintenance of these technologies—as well as the political sphere where questions arise of civil liberty violations by televised search and seizures or by the so-called domestic spying program. Answers to these questions are difficult and not always clear, but students who practice rhetoric from within a local-global standpoint are well positioned to map out historical materialist boundaries of various institutions and their effects on our lived experiences. Such work is imperative, I believe, because it is only through a double consciousness that the local can finally emerge as the site for constant critique of capitalist consciousness and its current valorization of globalization.

Constant Critique of Consciousness against Hyperglobalism

"Writing from the Margins: Geographies of Identity, Pedagogy, and Power," coauthored by Peter McLaren and Henry A. Giroux, claims that educational scholarship has not theoretically addressed the foundations of education systems—whether transformative or traditional. In particular, it notes the absence of theories that can "legitimate the social practices necessary for defending a particular version of what schools might become" (20). Allman, in a more pointed assessment, asserts that educational theorists have failed to engage the key contradictions of capitalism. Without this theoretical work, she contends, education will never transgress the barriers initiated by the current global political economy. According to Allman, transformational education needs a theory that accounts for changes in the structural relationships between labor and capital; new forms of revolutionary consciousness that include the professional classes; an understanding that all productive labor (intellectual and physiological) produces surplus value; and the notion that transforming capitalism requires critically conscious effort (140–51). I believe that the rhetorical hermeneutic of historical materialism—a practice that identifies various movements and valuations within capitalist institutions as a first step toward changing the constructed nature of those institutions—offers the necessary intellectual apparatus to address the concerns of both Allman and McLaren and Giroux, within the university as well as other intuitions.

Historical materialism functions, first and foremost, by critique of consciousness in whatever form that takes—ideology, myth, or hegemony. Rigorous and continuous critique will enable intellectuals to better understand those areas that, according to McLaren and Giroux, have gone unanswered—"how subjectivities are schooled, how power organizes space, time, and the body, how language is used to both legitimate and marginalize different subject positions" (20). Further, an historical materialist framework for this critique will help theorists maneuver through the particular hurdles posed by contemporary capitalism that Allman believes are so crucial to the possibility of new educational futures. Such critique is not, as I have argued, as simple as reform, criticism, or even the teaching of critical skills—these have all existed comfortably within the university since its inception and have proven to be accommodating or irritating, but not disruptive. The point of critique (ideological, mythic, hegemonic, or otherwise) has always been to transform the world by pushing passed the boundaries of its current form. Marx famously expressed this sentiment in his Eleventh Thesis on Feuerbach: "the philosophers have only *interpreted* the world, in various ways; the point is to *change* it" (*German Ideology* 123). To change the world, one must first historically outline and theorize its present conditions, including its socioeconomic limitations and contradictions. This analysis builds the theoretical scaffolding around which new possible worlds can be constructed. If the rhetorical hermeneutic of historical materialism traces the lines of this constructed world, it does not require much adjustment to push students into thinking about how those lines are supported by the values embedded within the rhetorical lexicon that forged its boundaries.

Critique of consciousness adheres to the general principles of critique but focuses specifically on the forms of thinking that enable capitalist relations of production and consumption. Committed to an historical materialist framework, such critique investigates the way that cultural, political, and economic axes converge within a specific historical moment to construct a dominant—though necessarily incomplete—version of reality. Merod finds hope and possibility in such a methodology. Encouraging ideological critique, he contends that to "couple an investigation of the material, institutional, and economic grounds of our current historical situation with a critique of the reigning ideological and cultural structures is to engage (just possibly to invent) theoretical energies that promote the long-repressed analysis of *class struggle*" (14). Ideology, as the belief system that helps us understand the world and our place in it, encourages us to define reality in one particular way and not others. Myth allows us to justify practices according to belief systems that require us to accept truth based on faith not fact. And hegemony assures that the process of maintaining dominant ideologies, myths, and belief systems about the world constantly suppresses or absorbs any arguments that call this dominant consciousness into question. With so much psychic work performed to maintain dominant modes of thinking, we need to begin more stringently exploring and unraveling these processes.

Because the dominant mode of consciousness within capitalism works through a fast-paced and perpetually evolving process, our critique must be equally unceasing. Dominant thinking functions through many apparatuses but primarily through institutions responsible for representing and interpreting the world. Such institutions present a picture of reality that earns its legitimacy by appearing to resolve the many complexities, contradictions, and inequalities built into our lived experiences. The current age of hyperimaging makes this line between imaginary and real resolutions even more difficult to draw because the pervasiveness of the imaginary—books, magazines, films, television programs, Web sites, and other representations—often enables symbolic resolutions to acquire the status of real resolutions. When this happens, the predominant ways of making sense of the world prevail and alternative narratives become displaced onto the sociopolitical margins. To return again to the example of the Iraq war, note how the fabricated notion of weapons of mass destruction threatening our immediate safety became the reigning belief by virtue of its repetition, its connection to credible sources, and its play on the nation's raw fears over the September 11 attacks. More cautious arguments were stigmatized as those of a radical minority of truly unpatriotic individuals. This is not to say that a critique of consciousness posits a theory of false consciousness wherein those in power simply dupe the American public. On the contrary, this critique assumes that because all consciousness is contradictory, all meaning requires further analysis in order to justify the parameters of its truth-value.

Allman reinforces the notion that an historical materialist analysis need not subscribe to notions of false consciousness. Using Jorge Larraín's *Marxism and Ideology,* she defines dominant consciousness as negative ideology. In this conception, an ideological statement "reflects or refers to aspects of our reality that are real, and in that sense true, but which are only the partial truth, or fragments of something that we cannot fully comprehend unless we can grasp it in its entirety" (Allman 7). Not unlike Roland Barthes's classic notion of mythical speech, this definition of ideological statements emphasizes how an incomplete version of the world functions as though it were the entire picture. The power of ideology is not that it convinces its recipients of some false version of reality; its strength derives from its ability to transcend its own borders to construct universal truisms and erase its own rhetorical foundations. Beliefs become dominant when they become separated from their historically concrete situatedness and acquire meaning throughout all of society. At that point, historically situated value systems appear to be universally commonsensical. Textual, symbolic, or commonsensical resolutions of complex social issues must be continuously and carefully interrogated by critique because, as Merod intimates, they greatly aid the process by which social structures are legitimated and maintained. Critiques of consciousness ask how we came to believe what we do and require us to note the limitations of certain truth-values, thus beginning the process of delegitimation and change.

In order to understand the production and power of these statements, Allman contends that analysis of consciousness should focus on dialectical contradictions. In Marxist dialectics, a contradiction represents two opposite, but real, truths that together compose a full text. Such contradictions are neither illogical nor are they "healed" by attempting to reform reality in order to match discursive or ideological promises. Instead, a contradiction can only be resolved by transforming the reality in which we live. In our contemporary world, for instance, the notion of globalization operates through a dialectical contradiction between local, everyday cultural existence and the global image being propagated throughout the media and the political arenas. The dominant version of globalization—what David Held calls the "hyperglobalist view"—suggests that economic globalization brings about the best possible results for the majority of people in the world.[8] Indeed, this dominant belief not only heralds globalization as universally positive, it further equates globalization to progress and suggests that it represents the inevitable fifth act of the world drama. Globalization certainly benefits various individuals throughout the world, but this favorable aspect of globalization is not, of course, the whole truth. A critique of consciousness—informed by historical materialism—marks the arbitrariness of this particular concept of globalization standing in for reality by analyzing globalization in relationship to both its mode of production and its method of consumption. Globalization, the nomenclature for contemporary capitalism, functions according to its own internal dialectic, distinct from but related to earlier forms of capitalism. Working-class professionals can counter dominant globalization theories by inquiring into how innumerable contradictions within those theories are represented and resolved as well as by measuring that symbolic resolution against the historical and material conditions of lived experience.

To begin with, we can ask students to do rhetorical analyses into the cultural, political, and economic arguments for globalization and the modes of thinking they both enable and reproduce. Students might work within these different realms individually and then do comparative analyses. Such work will put students in the position of figuring out how rhetorical idioms patch together vastly different agendas under the same name. Returning to that same body of research, students might inquire more specifically into the situatedness of each apparently separate argument and begin tracing a series of relationships that were not otherwise clear to them during the initial investigation. Such a course might focus specifically on the rhetorics of globalization, but it might also focus more narrowly on the rhetorics of globalization within the university. For instance, students could study the many international partnerships within a university or they could look into globally focused curricula and statements of mission. With this information in hand, students could explore national and state political deliberation around the academic bill of rights, the PATRIOT Act, and the American Council of Trustees and Alumni (ACTA) publications, a complex dialogue that attempts to minimize "liberal" viewpoints on campus, suppress criticism of international politics, and stiffly regulate foreign students and faculty. An inquiry like this will require students to work through the contradiction between arguments about globalization and practices with regard to globalization, enabling them to evaluate and reevaluate individual and collective consciousness as well as the processes that create our dominant consciousness.

A critique of consciousness takes place throughout the entire reality TV course I teach but is especially evident in the section on television talk shows and their rhetorical structures for discussing controversial issues. A critical focus of the unit is how meaning is simultaneously and unevenly co-constructed by hosts/producers, guests/participants, and audience/ call-in viewers. Unlike docusoaps where the audience has twenty-four-hour access to the participants but cannot directly interact with nor offer their opinions to those participants, talk shows solicit direct viewer feedback. This co-construction manifests through power struggles and, therefore, builds itself on significantly uneven terrain. In an effort to study this dynamic on television talk shows from multiple angles, students read both Laura Grindstaff's "Producing Trash, Class, and the Money Shot"— a behind-the-scenes exposé of daytime talk shows—and excerpts from Patricia Joyner Priest's *Public Intimacies: Talk Show Participants and Tell-All TV*—a study of how talk show participants assess their television appearances after the final broadcast. Interestingly, Priest argues that although participants thought they were often cut off and unable to fully explain their positions, few of them felt exploited and most found the experience extremely positive. The value of the experience was attributed to an opportunity, however limited, to define their individuality and/or individual interests on television, an opportunity participants believe validates their sense of unique subjectivity. Viewing talk shows along with studies of their production and interviews with their participants gives students a glimpse into the variegated subjectivities assumed, constructed, and read off these shows, offering multiple entry points into our critique of consciousness.

Notions of subjectivity, individuality, and identification become the rhetorical tropes we explore in these shows. We study the struggle to define identity among the local audience, participants, hosts, and television viewers and how this struggle is rhetorically mediated not only by the available technologies—room placement, microphone access, and call-in questions—but also by policies about what, and therefore who, is appropriate televised material and by economies that help establish the parameters of content. We discuss the television talk show as an avenue for participation in rhetorical situations and try to assess that participation—how is it responding to and creating the rhetorical situation, how is that situation in flux and connected to other situations, how is the situation a conglomeration of rhetorical valuations exchanged among the political, economic, and cultural spheres? Why does one's sense of individuality hinge on this rhetorically constructed televisual process of self-disclosure and identification? More and more, television is being cut up into niche markets and the talk show is no exception; as a handful of networks give way to hundreds of cable and satellite stations, the audience tunes into ever more specific content programming. The television identities revealed, negotiated, and identified with provide glimpses into the multiple identities at play on the global landscape. As we think through these identification processes, we do so with a constant eye toward the circulation of subject positions within the political and economic realms. Cultural validation might deflate tensions in the political sphere where some identities are denied civil rights, or cultural validation might connect with marketers who are looking for new consumer spaces. Culture, however, does not operate outside these two spheres, so this kind of critique along with transdisciplinary practice and a local-global consciousness builds an intellectual path toward developing truly sustainable global alliances.

Building Alliances against the Containment of Professionalism

The role of the professional, both inside and outside the university, tends to be surrounded by professional boundaries—boundaries that it would be "unprofessional" to overstep. Such boundaries have contributed to the containment of knowledge and the isolation of one intellectual from another. According to Merod, these professional borders reinforce "an ideology of reading in which all things critical circulate through the classroom and stay there, unable to contend with society's bleak eloquence" (1). Merod is not the only critic to note the absence of political connectivity between the university and the rest of the world. McLaren also states his disappointment over education's failure "to develop a public philosophy that integrates the issues of power, politics, and possibility with respect to the role that schools might play as democratic public spheres" (*Pedagogy of Revolution* 19). Consequently, contemporary education has restricted the possible redefinition of faculty professionalism in both the classroom and as part of a wider movement for social change. In part this has been done through a careful right-wing movement to limit oppositional voices and realign university faculty with the economic and political status quo, but much has been accomplished simply through the strict requirements of disciplinary work. Against this normalizing trend, McLaren sees the need for university professionals to engage in alliances as critical to the success of future movements. He argues that unless educators are able to "forge such alliances with gay and lesbian peoples, workers movements, and the struggles of indigenous peoples, present and future generations face the prospect of becoming extensions of multinational corporations within the larger apparatus of capitalist expansion" (*Pedagogy of Revolution* 69). Merod's and McLaren's distress over the lack of political alliances between academics and others may be slightly overstated. Many such alliances do exist—one need only think about the role of service learning or interdisciplinary programs, or the role of academics within national and global protests. Nonetheless, their arguments do challenge academicians to more carefully theorize their role in the arena of coalition building. Social change requires that the theoretical and practical groundwork for alliance building be laid and I believe that Foucault's specific intellectual, with some adjustments, provides the foundations for such alliances.

Foucault's specific intellectual, like Gramsci's organic intellectual and Althusser's heroic intellectual, offers theoretical insight into the working-class professional's role within larger coalitional politics. Such intellectuals have certain expertise that enables them to develop alliances among groups both inside and outside the university. In order to avoid the inevitable limitations that working exclusively within the university and its disciplinary boundaries imposes, intellectuals have an obligation to engage with the public "at the precise points where their own conditions of life or work situate them (housing, the hospital, the asylum, the laboratory, the university, family and sexual relationships)" (Foucault, "Truth and Power" 126). Specific intellectuals enact guerilla knowledge within these local sites. Like Che Guevara, they create "revolutionary conditions rather than total victories, inspiring the popular forces" (McLaren, *Pedagogy of Revolution* 44). As with all coalitions, specific intellectuals will offer their talents to campaigns in other disciplines as well as to those firmly outside the university walls. In turn, the specific intellectual makes connections and builds confidence with other individuals and their organizations so that outside groups can be called upon to help with internal university issues or other situations in which specific intellectuals play a role. Such collaborations fundamentally change the way professionals understand and engage with community members at the same time that they alter community perception of the university.

Although Foucault seeks to expand the boundaries of intellectual projects and academic signification, he does not wish to eliminate the necessity of political work within the university. On the contrary, the university is subject to precisely the same rigorous intellectual investigation as sites outside the university. Not only is the specific intellectual specialized in a particular domain of knowledge, he or she also uses that expertise to help publicize different truth-values for groups of people who do not possess the same authority and power entitled to those who espouse the dominant discourse. In other words, the specific intellectual reappropriates the division of labor that has professionalized him or her in order to work against such divisions by building alliances within the general public. This specific intellectual privileges the clarity and configuration of an individual being-in-the-world rather than the nameless subject effaced within the universalizing doctrine of disciplinary projects. Such an intellectual allows for the possibility of rearticulating and integrating hitherto separate categories of knowledge and inquiry by transgressing historically bounded areas of study in order to most accurately respond to a particular question. One strategy for alliances, then, is to infiltrate the sites of knowledge production by calling on community experts to provide testimonies that challenge professional knowledge. Through guest lectures or panel discussions, community members could identify a local issue that needs investigation or they could illustrate how various problems within the global political economy manifest in the local community.[9]

While the university increasingly professionalizes students through outreach opportunities, the university's traditional role remains one of reproducing the status quo. Service learning, for instance, teaches post-professionals to engage in philanthropy but does not teach them to change the social structures that cause poverty, illiteracy, and crime. As specific intellectuals become increasingly important to all aspects of life, the study of how universities construct those intellectuals and under what conditions demands further attention. Computer experts in the age of the World Wide Web, pharmacologists in the age overmedication, medical professionals in the crisis of national health care, teachers in the crisis of education, and businesspersons in the so-called triumph of capitalism each determine in critical ways the social, political, and economic future of the country vis-à-vis their local positionality. Students seeking degrees in these fields become the specific intellectuals whose claims to truth are intimately connected to regimes of power in global capitalism. In other words, the multiplicity of centers, of particulars, in which students locate themselves as job-seeking individuals is precisely the location of power that distinguishes legitimate discourse from its imposters, separates the true from the false statements, and delimits material possibilities in the world. Because post-professionals are responsible for determining the politics of truth, working-class professionals need to be engaged in alliances that disrupt professionalizing projects like the university and its various credentializing units.

As part of the university's professionalizing mechanism, working-class professionals need to counter the rhetorics of university crisis, inefficiency, and demise with stronger, more specific statements about the university and its relationship to global capitalism. Foucault argues that "what is called the crisis of the universities should not be interpreted as a loss of power, but on the contrary as a multiplication and re-enforcement of their power-effects" ("Truth and Power" 127). Working-class professionals too often abandon the theoretical foundations needed to make these local power-effects intelligible to the public. Foucault foresaw the potential for such a problem when he cautioned against the inability "to develop these struggles for lack of a global strategy or outside support" (130). Building alliances that oppose traditional relationships between the university as a dominant cultural site and the multiple specific sites of its power-effects that simultaneously cooperate in the interests of global capital exemplifies one such strategy. There are justifiable reasons to be careful of the university as an institution, and there is also much to be gained from explorations of everyday practices outside the university. Nevertheless, it would be ultimately ineffectual to move into local sites without first using the university's theoretical and political powers as a point of connection. According to Foucault's theoretical foundations, the formation of professionals within specific and diverse geopolitical boundaries creates the necessity for bridging those boundaries by forging alliances among professionals and nonprofessionals. This requires establishing conferences, developing workshops, and collaborating on university-community programming. It also means becoming part of movements outside the university, attending other events, and participating in other dialogues. Ultimately, alliance building enhances the university community at the same time it intervenes in and helps change the local community, a first step toward changing the historical materialist landscape of global capitalism.

Taking a cue from Rosa Eberly, the students in my reality TV course began forging alliances and working as specific intellectuals by contacting the campus radio station. They approached the hosts of a local radio program focused on current affairs and proposed a format where they appeared as guests to discuss the role of reality TV in college life. Thus, the broadcast featured the regular hosts, students as guests, and students as call-in listeners. Not only did they enjoy this exercise and learn something firsthand about live production, they also finally understood what it meant to be a participant struggling to define the content, direction, and tone of a discussion. Students reported frustration at not being able to finish a comment or being inaccurately summarized by the official hosts. From this firsthand experience, we discussed the difficulties inherent in developing coalitions and working across different disciplines and mediums. Working with the radio station, students engaged in a proto-public space in order to argue about the rhetorical ramifications of reality television and found themselves squared off in bilateral positions that did not engage their knowledge and thus they experienced the frustrations of democratic participation. But in the process they learned how to create alliances to negotiate the difficult terrain of public deliberation. Students were able to follow up on certain calls and work toward new projects such as a campus forum on the role of television and student activism. The students planned this forum, invited speakers from across the university as well as speakers from local youth organizations, reserved space in the student union, and advertised and administered the seventy-five-minute program. In addition to these more visible projects, students participated in on-line discussions with fan groups from various television shows, interviewed a local bar owner who had just returned from his casting on *The RealWorld Paris,* and wrote proposals for more democratic-inspiring reality shows that they submitted to Endemol via their Web site solicitation process. Like publics, these alliances were not permanent but were developed around mutual concerns, responses to specific exigencies, and rhetorical practices.

These alliances, along with the other three components of this methodology, helped students explore reality television from the rhetorical hermeneutic of historical materialism—studying the valuations, exchanges, and revaluations of key discourses on these shows as well as how this process constructs a space that invites specific behaviors, ideas, and emotions. Figure 4 shows how this course constructed a dialectical sense of reality television's institutionalization process. While contestants generally enjoy their experiences on television and the use of unpaid labor often helps bring in greater corporate profits, this voluntary economy establishes precedent for consumers and individuals taking up the slack left by corporations and governments. We discuss how this voluntary aspect of television might equate to societies based on individual philanthropy and community aid rather than corporate or government responsibility. We also investigate how the naturalized surveillance on these shows and on the Internet has afforded opportunities for greater information gathering but has made it more acceptable for the government and corporations to watch individuals without their knowledge. Surveillance likewise seeps into cultural practices of individuals watching each other, engendering suspicion and division in society. Students tended to value how these shows create space for individuality and difference, but they were concerned about the imperative to disclose our differences, making some groups more vulnerable and encouraging others to align with normative groups. The study of institutional parameters mapped from the practices on reality television afforded students an opportunity to see rhetoric at

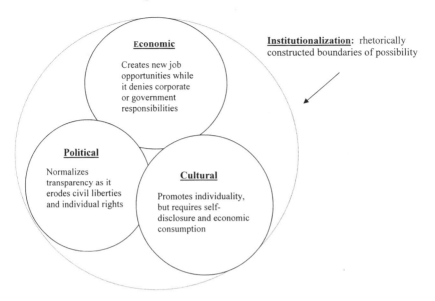

Figure 4: Reality TV's rhetoric of historical materialism.

work in their everyday, taken-for-granted lives, encouraged them to inquire into the dialectical nature of those processes, and left them with a sense of possibility and participation. By the end of the course, they were confident that they could think and act differently in the world, and felt agency—however limited—with regard to remapping this institutional space.

While this course focused on reality television and the rhetorical possibilities constructed by its institutionalization, I would like to think it simultaneously remapped rhetorical studies and possibly the university. We did not take rhetoric as a prescription for assessing and/or producing texts, we did not limit rhetorical participation to successful maneuvering of the political or legal spheres, and we did not professionalize one student for a career nor for citizenship. Instead, we used various rhetorical tools to explore the world, assess our experiences with that world, and discuss the spaces between what is and what could be. So conceived, the post-professional classroom gives way to a classroom committed to working-class professionalism and the university begins to be reinstitutionalized away from its position as a university-industry-government facilitated apparatus of global capitalism into a space for exploring alternative possibilities. I will end not with any specific pedagogy or methodology but with a call toward reinstitutionalizing that university.

A Manifesto against University-Industry-Government Facilitated Globalization

The World Bank's annual *World Development Report* provides an excellent case study for analyzing the cultural exigencies of economic globalization and an institutional foil against which to profess a manifesto of working-class professionalism. Each annual report characterizes worldwide economic development but often does so within a culturally sensitive rhetoric meant to appeal to the hopes, fears, and doubts associated with the most predominant cultural, political, and economic boundary reassessments of each subsequent year. For instance, the 1996 *World Development Report* begins by recounting the various communist revolutions of the first part of the twentieth century only to confirm that "this experiment in constructing an alternative economic system" has ultimately failed (1). As testament to this failure, the authors of the report feel comfortable citing Karl Marx and Frederick Engels' *Communist Manifesto.* Implicitly connecting the mid-nineteenth-century transformation into industrial capitalism with the late twentieth-century transition into global capitalism, they contend that "the *Communist Manifesto*'s portrayal of the turbulent arrival of capitalism in the nineteenth century seems a curiously apt depiction of today's transition landscape: Constant revolutionizing of production, uninterrupted disturbance of all social conditions, everlasting uncertainty and agitation. . . . All fixed, fast-frozen relations, with their train of ancient and venerable prejudices, and opinions, are swept away, all new-formed ones become antiquated before they can ossify. All that is solid melts into air" (1, ellipses in original). They continue by explaining how countries with various levels of development and different relationships to the capitalist market can productively integrate into the new post-Marxist, post-communist era of global capitalism. Globalization represents a transformative mechanism for initiating a new and inevitable political economic moment. Apparently, the World Bank believes that the earth has reached that mythical point of development when all past political economic and social systems concede to the forces of capitalism. History, as Francis Fukuyama says, has come to an end.

Unlike the original text of the *Communist Manifesto,* these authors deny the institutionalization of exploitation that produced this historic zenith. In the manifesto, Marx and Engels identify their political economic moment as the bourgeois epoch capable of establishing a "world market" that "chases the bourgeoisie over the whole surface of the globe. It must nestle everywhere, settle everywhere, establish conexions everywhere" (21). Although Marx and Engels foresee a worldwide capitalist political economy, they do not see this moment through the same rosy glasses as does the World Bank. Rather than representing the world market as the culmination of rational thought and inevitable progression, Marx and Engels indict global capitalism. In *The German Ideology,* for instance, they argue, "In history up to the present it is certainly an empirical fact that separate individuals have, with the broadening of their activity into world-historical activity, become more and more enslaved under a power alien to them (a pressure which they have conceived of as a dirty trick on the part of the so-called universal spirit, etc.), a power which has become more and more enormous and, in the last instance, turns out to be the *world market*" (55). This representation of the market's inevitable incorporation of individuals and communities around the globe lacks the World Bank's celebratory sentiment. Indeed, over one hundred fifty years after Marx and Engels' warnings and more than ten years after the World Bank declared its prophecy achieved all past epochs have not been swept under the inevitable force of history. Instead of abandoning the past in favor of global capitalism, therefore, the World Bank must persuade its readers of the transhistorical quality of the free trade structure. Perhaps hoping to forge an identification between non-Western values and the free market neoliberalism of Western-style globalization, the World Bank argues that capitalism represents the continuation and likely the culmination of previous cultural, political, and economic formations.

Emphasizing this historical progression, the 2002 *World Development Report* draws connections between indigenous societies in the less industrialized world and the inherent logic of free market capitalism. The report argues that poor countries in Latin America and Africa need to adopt the market policies that bring wealth to the industrialized nations of the world. It further suggests that this is not an adoption of foreign structures but the building of institutions that complement a long tradition of market-like practices. Characterizing the eleventh-century Maghribi traders of North Africa as a community defined by competitive production and free exchange, the report attempts to create identification between indigenous groups and Westerners by reconceiving indigenous trade practices within the rhetorical boundaries of contemporary globalization. It states that for Maghribi traders, "the rules of the organizations, although not written, were self-enforcing. Remaining in the coalition of traders best served each member's interests. Social ties cemented mutually beneficial business relationships, and cross-border trade flourished. Today, a millennium later, people everywhere face similar problems in striving to improve their well-being through market activity" (1). This political economic and cultural assessment constructs history according to an almost unbroken teleology from eleventh-century African tribes to the contemporary global political economy and contends that, inevitably, a new world simply awaits full global participation. As soon as all societies assume their rightful positions, this world will reveal its power by increasing the well-being of the market economy, with an implicit promise of increasing individual well-being as well. If economic incentive is not enough, then perhaps cultural heritage might help non-Western countries identify with the certain tides of globalization.

Contrary to this discourse of inevitability and supposed continuity as well as in alignment with Raymie E. McKerrow's insistence on the critique of both domination and freedom, working-class professionals deny the existence of any postrevolutionary world awaiting participation by a global citizenry with a new world consciousness. They know only the world that history has shaped, a world into which we are thrown and out of which we have the opportunity to make something better. It is our actions now that determine this future world and not some hoped-for epochal transformation. I am not arguing against revolution; I am arguing against waiting, against accepting something as better than nothing, against those who fear rocking the boat as well as those who steer the boat so poorly. I am arguing against a multiculturalism that understands difference as the possibility for profit rather than the condition for radical transformation. I am arguing against a neoliberal politics that lifts national boundaries and creates free spaces for corporations at the same time that it seals those boundaries against the movement of individuals and ideas that fundamentally deny such arbitrary borders. I am arguing against an economic globalization that invents new methods for creating surplus value, methods that accelerate the exploitation of both consumer and productive labor. I am arguing, most strongly, against the role that the U.S. public research university plays in this moment of global neo-colonialism and against the complacency of the post-professional who creates knowledge, trains future employees, and assumes its role within this complex historical materialist landscape without consideration for the systemic destruction that this positionality enacts in the world.

Alternatively, I argue in favor of the working-class professional who takes a stand against the professionalization of knowledge. Like many others, I believe this professionalization can only be opposed if we re-think class struggle in political, economic, and cultural terms. To rethink class means to intervene in the institutions that produce and reproduce class struggle. Although I seek to change the university as one such insti-tution, I am not in struggle against the post-professional subjects of that university. I will not be pitted against my colleagues, believing instead— as Karl Marx's Third Thesis on Feuerbach states—"it is essential to edu-cate the educator himself" (Marx and Engels, *German Ideology* 121). To educate the educator we must be in dialogue with those with whom we disagree. And we must be explicit about our goals: critique works against the processes that make capitalist systems palatable—there are many in-stitutions that numb the pain of capitalism, but the university need not be one. Such a pedagogy, like the four-point theory I advocate, disrupts the easy ebb and flow of university education and offers alternatives. Be-cause theoretical musings remain intellectual projects until they are prac-tically enacted, the working-class professional must emerge from univer-sity isolation and begin struggling with communities inside and outside our campuses. At heart, the working-class professional enacts what Marx calls a ruthless critique or what Foucault refers to as permanent criticism and follows this intellectual work with action. This process offers opportunities to create an oppositional edge within the traditional institution of the U.S. public research university—opportunities that are taken and not given.

What I have been trying to argue in this book is that a rhetorical hermeneutic can help us explore current historical materialist boundaries and then redefine those boundaries, and that such rhetorical work requires taking the opportunities available to us. Opportunities exist on a daily basis. They exist in the ongoing cultural debates that animate our campuses, they exist in the political disputes over higher education that litter our newspapers, and they exist in the economic documents that regulate much of university life. All of these represent rich rhetorical sites that can be understood through hermeneutic approaches as well as through other disciplinary angles. When we study, publish, teach, and practice these opportunities rhetorically, we take agency for the future of the university. Further opportunities exist in other capitalist institutions—prisons, corporations, and supranational organizations. Although these sites have been studied inside and out from humanistic and social science perspectives, they have not been thoroughly explored from the rhetorical hermeneutic lens of historical materialism. Such a lens will not attempt to understand the role, function, and effect of institutions as much as it will explore the truth-effects shaped by the practices rhetorically constructing these institutions. Doing this and noting the relationship between these truth-effects and the university's own rhetoricality opens up entirely new questions and allows us to transform opportunities into moments for redesigning the local worlds in which we all live.

When new fields emerge or old fields, like rhetoric, expand and begin taking on unorthodox practices, subjects, and methods, new knowledge gets created. Perhaps some of our fears about an expanding project of rhetoric are really not about policing disciplinary boundaries as much as they are about anxieties over this new knowledge. Perhaps some of this new knowledge calls old, comfortable positions into question. In addition to being the counterpart to dialectics, rhetoric also has a long tradition as the intimate partner of democracy and using a rhetorical hermeneutic disrupts this partnership as it highlights the rather suspect nature of democracy inside the historical materialist boundaries of capitalist institutions. But the disintegration of old allegiances need not be mourned if there are different connections to be celebrated and new ways to re-conceive old partnerships. At the same time I want to argue in favor of using a rhetorical hermeneutic to understand the U.S. public research university, I also want to argue in favor of new disciplinary practices and the new knowledges they construct. We need to muddy the waters of our well-crafted professional positions. We need to use disciplinary knowl-edges in radically different ways, we need to use our ability to interpret, analyze, and perform in ways that destabilize the solid foundations of the university, and we need to question seriously our role within the expand-ing global face of capitalism.

Notes

Introduction

1. Attempting to overcome this omission, McCloskey's most recent text, *The Bourgeois Virtues,* makes a grand apology for capitalism as virtuous and ethical as well as economically superior to other systems. This text is the first installment of what will be a three-part treatise on the virtues of capitalism.

Chapter 1

1. For good histories of the university, see Hofstadter and Smith's two-volume documentary history, Veysey's study of the emergence of the uniquely American university, Cohen's excellent synthesis and overview of U.S. higher education, Barrow's analysis of the relationship between U.S. universities and the capitalist state, and Graham and Diamond's study of the post–World War II struggle between private and public research universities.

2. Notice, for example, the plethora of new books that emerged in the 1990s detailing the failure of higher education to live up to its democratic professional ideal. Though these books may not specifically compare the current state of higher education to a mythical past, they do rely on a de facto mythology of U.S. higher education as a democratizing project. A quick glance at titles such as *Education Still under Siege* (1993), *The Academy in Crisis* (1995), *The University in Ruins* (1996), *What's Happened to the Humanities?* (1997), *Will Teach for Food* (1997), *Academic Capitalism* (1997), *Failing the Future* (1998), *Capitalizing Knowledge* (1998), and especially *The Knowledge Factory* (2000) reveals the implicit rhetoric of an earlier, more democratic university system. Notice, for instance, that words like "crisis" and "failing" point out our current educational misdirection. Also note the recurrence of phrases that link education to the marketplace: "capitalizing knowledge," "knowledge factory," and "academic capitalism." These texts make important and persuasive arguments about the present university context, yet they do so through a rhetoric of crisis that

infers higher education has in some way betrayed a more innocent, more democratic, and less corrupt past. It is this nostalgia I wish to combat.

3. Whately became the Drummond Professor of Political Economy at Oxford University in 1829, only a year after his famous rhetorical treatise *Elements of Style.* While his dual intellectual interests in rhetoric and political economy may seem odd to contemporary scholars, the study of politics, economics, and ethics were carefully combined within both Scottish and English Enlightenment thinking. Whately, along with other scholars of the Enlightenment, struggled to position the study of citizenship, commerce, and ethics within the influential empiricist movement. In some ways, this intellectual project graphed sociopolitical and economic interests of the colonized Scottish onto England's dominant intellectual threads. For instance, Ian McBride, in "The School of Virtue," argues that the absorption of Scotland into the United Kingdom in 1707 left the ruling class without access to their governing apparatuses. Politically subjugated, this class refocused its efforts around economic improvement and the development of a virtuous society. This historical context, I think, helps illustrate why it was so important for Whately to argue that political economy was a scientific endeavor even though it combined the cultural, political, and economic spheres.

4. The major exception to this claim, however, is the first book-length rhetorical investigation of Adam Smith. Stephen J. McKenna's *Adam Smith* places Smith's discussion of rhetoric within his entire body of critical work, exploring the relationships among history, ethics, and rhetorical discourse.

5. This narrative of U.S. internationalism has been complicated by scholars such as Walter LaFeber and Michael H. Hunt, who eloquently recite how the United States waged important international imperialist campaigns, based on racial hierarchies and a desire to control markets through intervention into external political struggles, well before the end of the nineteenth century. John Carlos Rowe further contends that as early as the late eighteenth century U.S. internationalism relied on the rhetorical and cultural tactics often associated with contemporary neoimperialism (11). The neoliberal processes so rigorously critiqued within the contemporary politics of global capitalism can be found, he suggests, within the literary traditions of an emerging U.S. nation-state.

6. In his important early analysis of frontier literature as myth, *Virgin Land,* Henry Nash Smith argues that "the master symbol of the garden embraced a cluster of metaphors expressing fecundity, growth, increase, and blissful labor in the earth, all centering about the heroic figure of the idealized frontier farmer armed with that supreme agrarian weapon, the sacred plow" (123). St. John de Crevecoeur, Thomas Jefferson, and John Filson are just a few of the many advocates of agrarian society

who influenced this literary myth (*Letters from an American Farmer; Notes on the State of Virginia; The Discovery, Settlement, and Present State of Kentucke*). Later authors such as Willa Cather and Hamlin Garland, in, for instance, *My Ántonia* and *A Son of the Middle Border,* respectively, clearly transpose this frontier mythology onto the ideal of education in general and university education in particular through imaginative and autobiographical romanticizations of university education as the way to escape the struggles of farm life. However, they both eventually become disillusioned with the development of higher education. This disillusionment can be traced through three of Cather's frontier novels: *O Pioneers!, My Ántonia,* and *The Professor's House.* See, for instance, Catherine Chaput, "Democracy, Capitalism, and the Ambivalence of Willa Cather's Frontier Rhetorics."

7. It is important to remember that "the West" was a nomenclature given to everything outside of New England and the old South. Consequently, the argument that the West provided the formative space for public higher education includes what we would currently call the Midwest. Such a claim might seem to ignore several large public research universities in the East—the University of Virginia and Pennsylvania State University, for instance. Although public, these universities were founded in the nineteenth century as secularized versions of elite private institutions. For this reason, they more closely follow the trajectory of private Eastern colleges than public research universities.

8. Abraham Flexner's *Universities, American, English, German* contains a copy of a full-page newspaper advertisement that Columbia University ran during the academic year 1928–29. This ad, which is for home study courses, states that Columbia University "urges you to use part of your time to increase by study your capacity to do better the things that lie before you in life" (136). This ad and others like it suggest that education will improve one's future lifestyle. To my knowledge, there are no full studies of such ads, but this kind of language is recorded in documents written by university administrators, professors, and legislators who deliberated about the formation of the university. See, for instance, Allan Nevins, *The Origins of the Land Grant Colleges and State Universities,* Edmund J. James's edited collection, *The Origin of the Land Grant Act of 1862,* and Coy F. Cross, *Justin Smith Morrill,* on the discussion of the Land-Grant Act. Or, for a more general discussion, see Richard Hofstadter and Wilson Smith, *American Higher Education.* Additionally, the various rhetorical strategies used to promote the early public universities were codified in 1942 by Stuart Harral. He offers a complete plan for promoting universities in his *Public Relations for Higher Education.*

9. For more detailed analyses of U.S. imperialism from the nineteenth century through globalization, see Harry Targ, "Imperialism in Transition," and Chronis

Polychroniou, "The Political Economy of U.S. Imperialism." Howard Zinn's *People's History of the United States* also has helpful documentation of U.S. imperialism and its centrality to the national political economy.

10. It is important to note, however, that as the West became more industrialized, it became a significant constituent in the national political drama. Consequently, Western politics often collapsed the space between local and national even while attempting to separate the two. For instance, the West's Populist Party, which demanded rights and protections for farmers, alternatively welcomed universities and criticized them. Clyde W. Barrow argues that these "populist groups repeatedly opposed the collegiate monopoly" (90). For populists, a collegiate monopoly consisted of universities that were connected by rigidly similar entrance requirements and course offerings. They believed that this standardization held flagship state universities together and more closely aligned them with elite university education than with other public educational institutions. Yet populists also lobbied for the incorporation of public universities. This contradictory logic can often be found in the history of public research universities.

11. According to Bender, regional elites mediated between the interests of local laborers and national investors. As managers and experts, these regional elites were able to promote universities as beneficial to local interests. Although this role was initially played out within regional areas, Bender argues that it quickly ossified into a national ideology associated with public universities themselves. For further discussion, see Bender's chapter titled "The Cultures of Intellectual Life."

12. The full text of the Land-Grant Act can be found at Higher Education Resource Hub Web site, http://www.higher-ed.org/resources/morrill1.htm. Information such as a list of the 1862 land-grant colleges and universities and their degree offerings can also be found on-line. See, for instance, the Food and Agricultural Education Information System Web site, http://faeis.ahnrit.vt.edu/.

13. While most people associate the 1862 federal Land-Grant Act with the formation and improvement of publicly funded state universities, not all land-grant universities were public. One notable exception is Cornell University, which received New York's land grant. The New York State Senate deliberated about dividing the grant among the People's College, the State Agricultural College, and the numerous sectarian colleges throughout the state. However, Andrew D. White, founder of Cornell University, argued that the grant would be better used for only one strong, central university. Thus, the land was granted for the founding of Cornell. Ezra Cornell, for whom the university was named, waited until property prices rose before selling it to achieve the largest possible endowment from the grant. See the Cornell discussions in Hofstadter and Smith. Other private institutions receiving federal grants were MIT and Brown University.

14. *After 100 Years* is an interesting documentation of the process by which the Land-Grant Act became historicized within a series of centennial events that began by "sifting through hundreds of pages of source material, [to compress] the vital facts into a single leaflet" (9). The report boasts that this simple leaflet "became the most widely quoted work on Morrill during the centennial year" (9–10). Among Vermont's celebratory events were the renaming of Vermont Route 132 "Justice Smith Morrill Highway," the production of national teaching materials, articles in Vermont newspapers as well as national publications, the production of a one-act play titled *The Merits of the Case* in the Vermont House of Representatives, and an international conference held at the University of Vermont under the rubric of an "orientation course on the meaning of education for all" (12). The rhetoric of these events, primarily generated from the single leaflet, universally valorized the Land-Grant Act for its innocent, democratizing efforts. Contemporary scholars of land-grant universities often use the same rhetoric. For instance, James T. Bonnen argues that "the land grant idea was above all a profoundly democratic movement" (2). Bonnen asserts that the Land-Grant Act was intended to provide broad access to higher education, to educate and train the professional cadres of an industrial, increasingly urban society, and to strengthen and defend American democracy by improving and assuring the welfare and social status of the largest, most disadvantaged groups in society (2). However, much like other contemporary authors, Bonnen believes that we have lost sight of this larger democratizing project because we have forgotten "the land grant system's obligation to serve its society" (6). See, for example, David D. Cooper's "Academic Professionalism and the Betrayal of the Land-Grant Tradition."

15. The idea of using higher education to increase profits for the elite classes did not originate in the late nineteenth century. Instead, such a sentiment can be found as early as the 1819 pamphlet published by Simeon De Witt, surveyor-general of the state of New York, titled *Considerations on the Necessity of Establishing an Agricultural College, and Having More of the Children of Wealthy Citizens Educated for the Profession of Farming* (Nevins 18). According to this pamphlet, higher education could provide a place to correctly train wealthy farmers and to increase national wealth rather than be a means for expanding democracy to the laboring class. In fact, in some places it was commonly believed from as early as the eighteenth century that colleges brought profit to towns and contributed to public wealth.

16. The relationship between the public university system and the Carnegie Foundation is one of the most critical in shaping U.S. higher education. Indeed, John Brubacher and Willis Rudy's *Higher Education in Transition* argues that "the most startling and epoch-making force for the improvement of professional education" was the creation of the Carnegie Foundation for the Advancement of Teaching (205).

They associate CFAT with the standardization of professional schools, especially medical schools. CFAT raised awareness over the many low-grade medical schools granting degrees and helped reduce this number by enforcing universal standards.

17. Because states could not afford pensions for university professors, most states eagerly adopted Carnegie's educational structure in order to gain entrance into this program. In fact, Nebraska was the only eligible state whose legislature defeated the CFAT resolution, largely "through the efforts of Mr. William Jennings Bryan" (CFAT, *Report* 84). The fact that Bryan, a leader of the Populist party and advocate for the impoverished position of farmers, opposed this resolution only reinforces the fact that the CFAT recommendations contributed to the reproduction of rigid class boundaries with the small farmer occupying a particularly low position. Others also opposed the Carnegie plan. James McKeen Cattell, for instance, criticized the Carnegie pension scheme as a method that ultimately controlled university professors. A series of Cattell's early articles, like the one opposing the Carnegie pension plan, were published along with several letters from leading private and public university presidents in a collection titled *University Control.* In this text, Cattell proposed, among other things, to open up university governance to "the widest possible participation" (26) and replace the university president with a committee of three (34–35). In his proposal he claimed that "a large corporation holding the university in trust for all the people is clearly a step in the direction of public ownership" (29). While Cattell's study suggests that as many as 85 percent of all university faculty are dissatisfied with their administration, most of the letters responding to his proposal take issue with all or part of Cattell's alternative proposal. Some letters critique Cattell's suggestion because it called for too large and too heterogeneous a governing body. Others were overwhelmed by Cattell's proposal to add university financial and educational administration to a growing list of professorial responsibilities. In addition to noting professors' already burdensome research, teaching, and service requirements, these letters viewed Cattell's suggestion as unrealistic. Like Cattell's proposal, the privately funded pensions for public university professors polarized individuals into camps of advocates and dissenters.

18. In the adoption of business schools as well as in many other characteristics, public research universities took the lead that private institutions—some as elite as Harvard University—followed. The assumption that elite private universities set the pace for higher education often fails to stand up to the test of history. Since the emergence of a system of U.S. public research universities, there has been a constant competition between private and public institutions with individual universities, rather than whole systems, taking the lead in academic production.

19. It should be noted, however, that CFAT solicited Morris L. Cooke, a leading figure in corporate management, to study the applicability of Pritchett's cor-

porate model to university administration. Surprisingly, Cooke found that the corporate analogy was overemphasized within universities. Universities, he decided, were governed by a much less clear hierarchical structure than was previously assumed. Such ambiguity made corporate management processes inappropriate, he concluded. See Cooke's *Academic and Industrial Efficiency*. Interestingly, this report did not seem to change either CFAT policy or public opinion.

20. Veblen's work on consumption is elaborated in *The Theory of the Leisure Class*. He argues that conspicuous consumption structures social difference. Veblen was among the first theorists to discuss the communicative quality of consumer habits. According to his theory, for instance, professional mannerisms, vocabulary, and titles communicate one's prestige and class more so than one's annual salary.

21. A preliminary search reveals that 106 university libraries throughout the country, representing a considerable percentage of schools at that time, purchased the 1915 edition of this reader. Such popularity, however, was short-lived. Only 69 libraries throughout the nation purchased the 1918 reprint. Though there are many reasons for a collection of essays to come in and out of favor, one factor might have been the transition into the monopoly era of capitalism.

Chapter 2

1. Henry Etzkowitz and Loet Leydesdorff's introduction to their edited collection titled *Universities and the Global Knowledge Economy* calls this relationship the triple helix of higher education, emphasizing that the university participates in strategic association with both the government and the corporate sector. Notably, they also argue these partnerships first became solidified in the later nineteenth century—the triple helix has been part of the public university structure since its emergence.

2. While Lenin's text offers a cornerstone for early theories of monopoly capitalism, other scholars had already investigated these new political economic trends. For instance, Thorstein Veblen's 1904 *Theory of Business Enterprise* charted new forms of marketing and corporate finance beginning to emerge in the twentieth century. Also preceding Lenin was Rudolf Hilferding's *Finance Capital,* first published in 1910. However, neither of these texts was as widely read as Lenin's *Imperialism.*

3. It is helpful to classify mergers, or the joining or two companies, according to their economic function. A horizontal merger combines direct competitors in the same product lines and the same markets. This kind of merger was typical of monopoly capitalism. Vertical mergers, on the other hand, combine a company that buys certain goods with a company that sells those goods. For example, if a company that produces cell phone parts from beryllium buys or takes over a company that mines beryllium, this is a vertical merger. This kind of merger is most typical in

the global stage of capitalism. There are other classifications for mergers, but these two are most critical to my distinction between the discrete stages of capitalism.

4. There is a rich and growing body of work on the community college movement. For a more detailed history of the movement, see Steven Brint and Jerome Karabel, *The Diverted Dream,* Arthur Cohen and Florence Brawer, *The American Community College,* and Kevin Dougherty, *The Contradictory College.*

5. The idea of American exceptionalism has been discussed by scholars such as Sacvan Bercovitch (*The American Jeremiad*) and Perry Miller (*Errand into the Wilderness*); for further discussion of the concept, see Deborah L. Madsen's *American Exceptionalism,* Siobhán McEvoy-Levy's *American Exceptionalism and U.S. Foreign Policy,* and Seymour Martin Lipset's *American Exceptionalism.* These authors trace the ideological evolution of exceptionalism through different historical periods, geographical locations, and international policies.

6. As new legislation and the job market combined to push individuals into higher education, more jobs began requiring a college degree. Although more stringent application requirements corresponded with an increasingly educated workforce more than the specific needs of employers, there was clearly a reciprocal relationship between educational opportunities and minimum employment requirements. Braverman states that "employers tended to raise their screening requirements for job applicants, not because of educational needs but simply because of the mass availability of high school graduates" (303). In a similar acknowledgment, Herbert Bienstock, the New York director of the Bureau of Labor Statistics, stated in 1969 that employers were "seeking people with higher levels of education even when job content is not necessarily becoming more complex or requiring higher levels of skills" (*Collective Bargaining Today* 334). Demonstrating a visible link among academics, politics, and economics, the range of options available in higher education and the rising requirements together funneled a large part of the expanding workforce into school and prevented a potential economic crisis.

7. For a thorough discussion of the relationship between universities and monopoly capitalism, see Sigmund Diamond, *Compromised Campus,* David Guston and Kenneth Keniston, *The Fragile Contract,* Jacob Neusner and Noam Neusner, *The Price of Excellence,* and Rebecca Lowen, *Creating the Cold War University.*

8. Neusner and Neusner are not the only scholars of higher education to argue that the role of the university is to promote national political and cultural good. Many authors, ranging from the conservative to the liberal, hold this belief. See, for instance, Neil Postman, *The End of Education,* Bill Readings, *The University in Ruins,* and Annette Kolodny, *Failing the Future.*

9. According to Daniel Starch's "Analysis of 1944 Stock Ownership," the largest corporations in the United States during this period included American Telephone

and Telegraph, General Motors, Packard Motor Car, Pennsylvania Railroad, United States Steel, Anaconda Copper Mining, General Electric, Standard Oil, and Pacific Gas and Electric. Though there was a nascent communications industry, most major corporations continued to rely on a highly industrialized mode of production. This trend repeats itself in Canada. See, for instance, William K. Carroll's "Corporations in the 'Top 100,' 1946–1976."

10. Scott Nearing was dismissed from his position as professor of economics from the University of Pennsylvania in 1915. He claimed that his dismissal resulted from the board of trustees' disapproval of his campaigns against child labor and the misuse of public utilities. This discharge was one of the first cases to be challenged as an offense against academic freedom. Controversy over this case is recorded in Lightner Witmer, *The Nearing Case.*

11. For an historical comparison between the wartime university of World War I and the wartime university under the War of Terror, see M. Karen Powers and Catherine Chaput's "'Anti-American Studies' in the Deep South."

12. Although prosecuted under the Espionage Act, Nearing was found not guilty by a jury of his peers. After using the witness stand to defend his right to study and write about antiwar and socialist views, he took his oratorical skills on the road. According to Robert Jensen's *Citizens of the Empire,* "Nearing remained a popular lecturer, filling halls as large as Madison Square Garden for solo lectures and debates" (58). Nearing was not allowed to disseminate his beliefs within the university, but he was able to find welcoming audiences for several years as an independent lecturer.

13. Sinclair's title intentionally invokes the strict military march where soldiers walk synchronized and in line to imply that the U.S. public education system is one of rigid indoctrination. Published shortly after the culmination of World War I, Sinclair contends that "what we did, when we thought we were banishing the Goose-step from the world, was to bring it to our land, and put ourselves under its sway— our thinking, and, more dreadful yet, the teaching of our younger generation" (18).

14. Hutchins is not the first theorist to call for this return to a study of metaphysics. Indeed, one of the earliest critiques of the university, Giambattista Vico's 1709 text *On the Study Methods of Our Time,* calls for such a return. Originally delivered as a speech in fulfillment of his obligation as professor of rhetoric at the University of Naples, Vico enlarged and revised the 1708 speech for print publication. He argues that the Greeks had use for a university because they devoted themselves to the study of philosophy—"the mother, midwife, and nursling of all sciences and art" (74). Alternatively, the Romans had no use for a university because "they thought wisdom consisted in the art and practice of law, and learned to master it in the everyday experience of political affairs" (75). But as the Roman republic trans-

formed into principates, their education system transformed as well. Along with the new political structure came the need for "academies." While academies worked as long as one person could master all necessary knowledge, the proliferation of print texts and the interaction between states in the early eighteenth century gave rise to the need for universities. The problem for Vico is that in the university all the different branches of learning are "unnaturally separated and disjointed" (76). He argues that "education is so warped and perverted as a consequence, that, although [students] may become extremely learned in some respects, their culture on the whole (and the whole is really the flower of wisdom) is incoherent" (77). Not surprisingly, Vico calls for a return to the system in which all studies fall under the umbrella of a unified philosophy. He states that we should "co-ordinate all disciplines into a single system so as to harmonize them with our religion and with the spirit of the political form under which we live" (77). While Vico correctly problematizes the division of knowledge in the Italian university, his nostalgia for an early philosophical tradition belies a naivete about the importance of the political economy to the production of knowledge.

15. There is a strong movement to standardize both a European education and a global education. See, for instance, the Bologna Magna Charta Universitatum of 1988, the Sorbonne declaration of 1998, the 1999 Joint Declaration of the European Ministers of Education, and the 2001 Message from the Salamanca Convention of European Higher Education Institutes. These texts are all part of the European Higher Education Area project. There are also many resources on the Global Education movement. See, for instance, Global Education Associates, http://www.globaleduc.org, the American Forum for Global Education, http://www.globaled.org, and the center for Global Education, http://www.augsburg.edu/global. For a broad overview of this movement, see Paul Haakenson's *Recent Trends in Global/International Education*. In addition, supranational organizations like the World Bank and the Organization for Economic Cooperation and Development (OECD) have been publishing recommendations for standardizing educational structures internationally. See, for instance, the World Bank's *Higher Education* or OECD's *Education and Working Life in Modern Society*.

16. Gary Rhoades and Sheila Slaughter complicate the common assumption that students have become consumers by reminding us that in the era of increased privatization, the university also sells the student body as a captive audience to a variety of companies looking to secure customer loyalty within one of the more profitable consumer markets. Perhaps in a too definitive tone, Rhoades and Slaughter argue that "students are neither 'customers' nor 'consumers.' They are the 'industry's' 'inputs' and 'products'" (14).

17. Although nearly half of all higher education faculty nationwide are unionized, research university faculty are overwhelmingly not unionized. Gary Rhoades's study argues that with the exception of the SUNY system, "research university faculty (who do the most writing about education) are not unionized" (9). See, for instance, *Managed Professionals.*

18. For an interesting examination of how the system of professionalism supports this complicity, see Slaughter's "Professional Values and the Allure of the Market." She argues that the university's professional system has incorporated the idea that money is intrinsically valuable to such an extent that it cannot extricate itself from commercial logic.

19. According to the World Bank's *Higher Education,* private loan programs cost the government significant amounts of money to administer and to subsidize the interest that accrues while individuals are enrolled as full-time students. In some cases, they argue, it would be less expensive to offer students grant money than to administer loan programs (46). Given this, it seems that the profits made by the banking industry remain the most significant factor in the shift from grants to loans.

20. See, for instance, Darin Payne's "English Studies in Levittown."

21. For an excellent illustration of this connection using NAFTA's impact on Mexican higher education as an example, see Heriberta Castaños-Lomnitz, Axel Didriksson, and Janice Newson's "Reshaping the Educational Agendas of Mexican Universities." Slaughter and Leslie also contend that such agreements reinforce the trend toward competitive and proprietary relationships surrounding academic knowledge. These agreements recognize corporate patents and enforce the ownership of such knowledge through stiff penalties.

Chapter 3

1. See, for instance, Vicki Ruiz and Susan Tiano's *Women on the U.S.-Mexican Border.* The collection contains essays that describe how globalized production processes produce new techniques for disciplining women into patriarchal structures. See also Altha Cravey's *Women and Work in Mexico's Maquiladoras,* Susan Tiano's *Export Processing, Women's Work, and the Employment Problem in Developing Countries,* and Human Rights Watch's "No Guarantees."

2. While Karl Marx and Frederick Engels both acknowledge that exploitation occurs outside of wage labor, they do not believe that such exploitation directly produces surplus value. For instance, the subjugation of women to men and the exploitation of women's work as well as slave labor are historicized in Engels's *The Origin of the Family, Private Property and the State.* While a patriarchal familial structure that often exploits women's work enables capitalism, according to Engels, this form of

exploitation does not directly produce surplus value. Alternatively, I extend production into the cultural sphere and argue that surplus value is produced through wage labor as well as non-wage labor.

3. Certainly the television or radio audience never passively consumes what media produces. For a discussion of the many different ways that audiences engage media productions, see Ien Ang, *Desperately Seeking the Audience,* James Hay, Lawrence Grossberg, and Ellen Wartella, *The Audience and Its Landscape,* Ingunn Hagen and Janet Wasko, *Consuming Audiences?,* James Lull, *Inside Family Viewing,* Pertti Alasuutari, *Rethinking the Media Audience,* Robert Wicks, *Understanding Audiences,* and Martin Allor, "Relocating the Site of the Audience."

4. The dates vary slightly, but most theorists agree that the 1970s represents the critical decade for transitioning into the era of globalization. Carl Boggs, a critic of contemporary social and political theory, cites the 1970s as the time when the U.S. public sphere progressively narrowed and yielded to corporate interests. William Tabb, an economist and political scientist, cites Richard Nixon's 1971 decision to eliminate the Bretton Woods currency system of fixed rates and the subsequent dismantling of trade restrictions as the turning point into globalization. Saskia Sassen, a sociologist with interests in urban planning and policy, argues that the 1970s mark the transition from nation-state as protector of individual citizen rights to the international regulation of human rights. Labor scholar Kim Moody distinguishes globalization as the "rise, from the late 1970s onward, of neoliberalism: the policy of dismantling much of the national regulation of economic life throughout the already existing capitalist world in favor of market governance, a process euphemistically referred to as 'reform' or 'liberalization'" (43). Similarly, cultural theorists, like Frederic Jameson, as well as critical geographers, like David Harvey, argue that the incorporation of the postmodern aesthetic in the early 1970s is linked to economic globalization. Collectively, these theorists strongly suggest that the numerous cultural, political, and economic changes taking place in the early 1970s mark the inchoate transition into globalization.

5. For a thorough explanation of the process of reification, see Georg Lukács, "The Phenomenon of Reification." This groundbreaking essay discusses how Marx's classic discussion of commodity fetishism—the way that relations between people in a capitalist society become dehumanized and take on the characteristics of things—leads to a lack of class consciousness. Lukács explains how the capitalist mode of production corresponds to both relationships between people and our understanding of those relationships.

6. See, for instance, Keith Morrison, "The Global Village of African American Art," David Nostbakken and Charles Morrow, *Cultural Expression in the Global Village,*

Jessie Carroll Grearson and Lauren B. Smith, *Love in a Global Village,* Michael Shuman, *Towards a Global Village,* and James Will, *The Universal God.*

7. Sivanandan and other scholars mentioned throughout this book make use of the terms "First World" and "Third World" to denote, respectively, wealthy nations associated with the center of capitalism and poor nations associated with the margins of capitalism. These terms have been seriously undermined as totalizing all nation-states within a binary narrative of Western progress and Eastern primitivism. Perhaps most notable among these critiques is Aijaz Ahmad's "Jameson's Rhetoric of Otherness and the 'National Allegory.'" In the spirit of Ahmad's insights, I have attempted to avoid this culturally problematic terminology at the same time that I have chosen to leave this language in quoted material in order to maintain the integrity of others' work.

8. Evidence of this event is collected and archived on a Web site for further exposure (http://www.punchdown.org/rvb/F15).

9. It is important to note that Appadurai argues for historicizing the local within the global as distinct from methodologies of global history. Historian Bruce Mazlish argues for a global history that starts "from our present position, where new factors building on the old have given a different intensity and synchronicity to the process of globalization" (1). Rather than studying individual historical figures or nation-states, Mazlish argues for a global history that is interdisciplinary and includes the study of topics such as investment, satellite communication, and computer language, in historical terms. Mazlish's global history is different from that of Appadurai in its attempts to draw connections between multiple localities across the globe without connecting them to a larger process of globalization as a totality.

10. For a detailed analysis of libertarian doctrine—in fiction, manifestos, and nonfiction—in conjunction with the rise of the contemporary free market, see James Arnt Aune's *Selling the Free Market.*

11. For an excellent and thought-provoking analysis of the limitations of Jameson's critique of the postmodern, see Chela Sandoval's *Methodology of the Oppressed.* Sandoval argues that Jameson is unable to detect that the new postmodern culture evolving along with globalization "makes accessible, to oppressor and oppressed alike, new forms of identity, ethics, citizenship, aesthetics, and resistance" (37). That is, Sandoval sees hope in postmodern theorists like Bhabha and Anzaldúa where Jameson finds only the prison house of postmodern discourse.

12. As always, Spivak explores parallels between Marxism and deconstructionism through her own Marxist, feminist, deconstructionist methodology. She focuses such exploration on value in her essay "Limits and Openings of Marx in Derrida." In this essay, Spivak shows the various aporias existing in Marx's work and argues

that the disavowal of these aporias accounts for the failure of socialism. In this way, deconstruction can supplement the "the rational kernel of Marx's writings in its own style of work, rather than attempt to settle scores with Marxism" (98). Merging these two theories of valuation, Spivak gives equal attention to both the production and the consumption of commodities and emphasizes the need to understand capital as a process rather than as discrete events.

13. Patricia Parker's essay "Metaphor and Catachresis" does an excellent job of contextualizing the debate between metaphor and catachresis within the rhetorical tradition, contending that both metaphor and catachresis work because signs operate separately from signifiers. This argument legitimately questions the difference between metaphor and catachresis as well as the ability of individuals to control language in the last instance. Nonetheless, I remain convinced that catachresis and metaphor differ because catachresis stresses difference while metaphor emphasizes similarity.

14. Although this section primarily focuses on the creation of digital technology and its implications for financial production, there are also significant implications for consumption. For instance, the digitalization of information and the proliferation of Internet access have rendered the sale of software on diskette fairly uncommon. Consumers increasingly download a file from the Internet and pay via credit card. Aided by computer technology, such consumers produce their own items by downloading these files. While this might be more convenient than going to a store, it signifies the loss of jobs and the growth of unpaid consumer labor.

15. For an analysis of the economic and cultural diversity within the global marketplace, see Salah S. Hassan and Erdener Kaynak's *Globalization of Consumer Markets*. This collection of essays argues that while production is becoming globalized and some products, such as electronics, clothing, and beverages, cut across national boundaries, the consumer is not similarly universalizable. These essays argue that success in the global marketplace requires appeals to local and cultural differences. Unfortunately, they also take an unproblematic view of the marketplace as the taken-for-granted terrain on which to continually expand capitalist production and consumption. Multiculturalism, for these authors, simply represents the most recent strategy to extend the capitalist market.

16. It is worth recalling Herbert Marcuse's essay, "The Struggle against Liberalism in the Totalitarian View of the State." Marcuse argues that liberalism is particularly dangerous because it operates through the same logic as totalitarianism and can transform easily into a state of totalitarianism. The neoliberal ideology I have been discussing inched closer toward a totalitarian presence in the months after the attacks. Our neoliberal policies quickly realigned themselves within a much more repressive political regime, illustrating the easy slippage between liberalism and to-

talitarianism. As a result of this slip, for instance, individuals and their politics are policed more carefully; for a time, it became almost impossible to publicly oppose the nationalistic response to these attacks without significant negative repercussions.

17. Another, less publicized, example of the university's shift into casualized labor can be seen in the university staff. Most universities no longer have any full-time staff to maintain its facilities. Instead, they contract out workers on a temporary and insecure basis. These contracts allow universities to add and to eliminate workers on an as-needed basis. Additionally, the university sheds its economic responsibility for these workers' benefits, and accrues further savings.

Chapter 4

1. In many ways this project mirrors Kenneth Burke's attempt to analyze the dialectic of constitutions. Burke examines constitutions and how the principles articulated therein shape the rhetoric of political promises. His analysis can be found in *A Grammar of Motives*.

2. It should be noted that the global discourse on higher education predominantly moves from west to east and from north to south. While Mexico, Japan, Korea and several Eastern bloc countries currently participate as members of the OECD, these countries were not part of the organization during its foundational moments or during the development of its educational policy. Instead, this policy was determined primarily by the United States and Western Europe, using the U.S educational system as its model.

3. This chapter focuses on Appadurai's flows—with the exception of mediascapes or the movement of image-based texts. Because a mediascape is defined by the flow of images and I will focus on print-based material, it is not a useful category for this chapter. Mediascapes, however, would be critical to most analyses of material rhetorics.

4. As of the 2000 edition of the Carnegie Foundation taxonomy, there were 102 public institutions classified as extensive research universities. This is an increase from 84 in 1994. Although not directly related to this study, I conjecture that this relatively large shift signifies a trend wherein institutions are either rising to research status or falling to the associate's level, leaving a void where the general liberal arts college once thrived. A list of the Carnegie research universities can be obtained from their Web site, http://www.carnegiefoundation.org/Search/SiteSearch.htm. A report on university research and development funds, titled *Academic Research and Development Expenditures,* which includes a list of federal funds to institutions, can also be found on-line at http://www.nsf.gov/sbe/srs/nsf02308/htmstart.htm.

5. This stratification takes place both within the public research university and across the various other institutions of higher education. For instance, Dorothea Furth, the OECD's director for scientific affairs, argues that although "the prototype of the multipurpose model of short-cycle education is the American Junior or Community College" (15), these institutions are characterized by a "fairly close link with university education" (16). Community colleges connect to universities by a credit system that allows individuals the hope of transfer and the aspiration of social mobility. The U.S. public research university models the multiversity ethos, but other institutions with clearly different missions are also necessary for the best possible national stratification.

6. The specialized intellectual or the post-professional should not be confused with Foucault's specific intellectual. The specific intellectual has an "immediate and concrete awareness of struggles" ("Truth and Power" 126). He or she participates in these struggles because he or she has the "same adversary as the proletariat, namely the multinational corporations, the judicial and police apparatuses, the property speculators, etc." (126). In other words, the specialized intellectual or the post-professional, for Foucault, produces the sociopolitical and economic constructs that subsequently warrant struggle with the specific intellectual. I will pick up on this need for oppositional or what I will call working-class professionals in chapter 5.

7. Each mission statement that I cite can be found on-line. As rather brief texts, I will not note the page numbers of these statements. The full citation, including the URL, can be found in the works cited with the university as the author.

8. This notion of service functions within a metaphysics that presupposes knowledge, aid, and agency for others whether they exist locally, nationally, or internationally. Martin Heidegger's "What Is Metaphysics?" suggests that "this position of service in research and theory evolves in such a way as to become the ground of the possibility of a proper though limited leadership in the whole of human existence" (95). This limited form of leadership, he argues, suppresses the unknown through its drive to name, categorize, and totalize all of existence. There is certainly reason, then, to suspect that the sign of service contains an imperializing gesture.

9. Along with these changes in the function of higher education, the administration of universities worldwide also mimics the U.S. public research university. According to the World Bank, for instance, national governments should loosen their reins over universities so that independent "agencies can formulate and monitor higher education policies, guide budgetary allocations, and evaluate and publicize institutions' performance" (*Lessons of Experience* 9). Universities should not be accountable to the nation-state but to independent agencies—like the Carnegie Commission in the United States—that better understand the corporate environment of current research. Higher education and its knowledge production are disciplined by increased market authority, naturalized in the form of signs and other systems.

10. Just as California and other U.S. public universities have begun educating students for the global political economy, James W. Guthrie and Lawrence C. Pierce argue that there exists "a common need to create an educational system that will provide each nation with the human resources required in a modern, competitive economy" (202). See, for instance, "The International Economy and National Education Reform."

11. In this way, monopoly capitalism can be thought to have absorbed many individual responsibilities for the social good in order to create new markets led by the government—education, retirement, health care—and global capitalism can be understood as shedding social responsibility for these programs in order to more properly position such categories within a capitalist market.

12. This policy has been incorporated into other national education systems worldwide. For instance, the World Bank reports that in India, education donations from industry or individuals are 150 percent tax deductible (*Lessons of Experience* 43).

13. Of course, many migrant workers travel along with changing seasonal work, moving back and forth across borders. Nevertheless, they are confined to a fairly limited, if international, region of the world. See, for instance Guy Standing's *Labour Circulation and the Labour Process* and B. Singh Bolaria and Rosemary Bolaria's *International Labour Migrations*.

14. Although this kind of accreditation is mandated even at the lower levels, some instructors are subverting its purpose. See, for example, Alison Taylor's "Employability Skills." She argues that although these cards delimit instruction in certain ways, they can also be used to teach students about corporate deskilling.

15. The Academic Bill of Rights (ABOR) is pending legislation in the U.S. House of Representatives that purports to protect conservative students from indoctrination or retribution by liberal or radical faculty. Supporters of the ABOR suspect that campuses are overrun with such professors who are uniform in their opposition to U.S. international policies and bent on propagandizing unsuspecting students with their unpatriotic and unbalanced worldviews. Conceived by conservative columnist David Horowitz, the ABOR has the potential to undermine rather than enforce academic freedom.

16. Edward Said uses the term "American Oriental position" to denote the way that the United States constructs an Orientalism or a discourse about non-Western people and places through "institutions, vocabulary, scholarship, imagery, doctrines, even colonial bureaucracies and colonial styles" (*Orientalism* 2). The university functions as a critical component of this discursive regime but never the only productive apparatus.

17. For a discussion of how to use multiculturalism subversively, see Peter McLaren's edited collection, *Revolutionary Multiculturalism,* or his single-authored text, *Che Guevara, Paulo Freire, and the Pedagogy of Revolution.* For a discussion on re-

claiming critical thinking, see Hyslop-Margison, "The Market Economy Discourse on Education." While Hyslop-Margison claims that "developing a critical approach to learning, then, currently assumes the same rhetorical value as concepts such as citizenship education, democracy, and natural learning," she offers new strategies for reappropriating critical thinking (211).

Chapter 5

1. Specifically, Marshall argues that because of a built-in tracking system, higher education is only available to a select few. This tracking system is, of course, a well-established component of the English model of education. However, we cannot forget that the United States has its own system of tracking—one so well naturalized that few even realize it exists. By assessing and segregating students into different curricula early on in their educations, the U.S. system tracks students just as well as the English system. See, for instance, Jean Anyon's "Social Class and the Hidden Curriculum of Work," Yossi Shavit and Walter Muller's "Vocational Secondary Education, Tracking, and Social Stratification," and Jeannie Oakes and Martin Lipton's "Tracking and Ability Grouping."

2. Citizenship, argues Arjun Appadurai, is the main Enlightenment term for spreading capitalist ideas across the globe. Significantly influencing current global ideoscapes, citizenship adapts according to various social, political, and historical constraints and takes whatever form best enables the capitalist political economy. For a more in-depth discussion, see Appadurai's *Modernity at Large*.

3. Guerrilla strategies of any sort are inevitably informed by Mao Tse-Tung's classic text, *On Guerrilla Warfare*. Mao argues that the basic strategy of guerrilla warfare "must be based primarily on alertness, mobility, and attack. It must be adjusted to the enemy situation, the terrain, the existing lines of communication, the relative strengths, the weather, and the situation of the people" (73). While Mao readily admitted that guerrilla strategy would never succeed on its own, such tactics were indispensable to revolutionary practices. Guerrilla strategy weakens the enemy and creates the possibility of revolutionary action.

4. For a discussion of guerrilla marketing, see Arif Dirlik, "The Global in the Local." Dirlik describes guerrilla marketing as a strategy in which "the corporation domesticates itself in various localities without forgetting its global aims and organization" (34). A guerrilla marketer utilizes the local terrain to further his or her agenda.

5. The University of Arizona's Committee on Lesbian, Gay, Bisexual and Transgender Studies provides an excellent example of a transdisciplinary praxis. In a little over ten years of existence, this organization has produced innumerable programs both inside and outside the university, developed strong collaborations with

community activists, constructed a free-floating first-year course on lesbian and gay studies, obtained a prestigious multiyear Rockefeller grant, and organized multiple international conferences. Because this organization has never obtained official status as a university-sanctioned committee, it has fewer constraints than other organizations. And because it obtains its funding from external grants, the committee is able to offer a wide variety of diverse and constantly changing intellectual opportunities.

6. For a particularly insightful documentary about the production, distribution, and consumption of coffee, see Nick Francis and Marc Francis's *Black Gold:Wake Up and Smell the Coffee* (Fulcrum Productions, 2006).

7. For an excellent discussion of this dialectical consciousness, see David Harvey's introductory chapter, "Militant Particularism and Global Ambition," in his *Justice, Nature, and the Geography of Difference.* Relying heavily on Raymond Williams, his chapter discusses how knowledge of a local site can be complicated by extending the distance of one's view globally.

8. For a more detailed discussion of hyperglobalization, see Held's essay, "The Timid Tendency," in the briefly resurrected special issue of *Marxism Today.* He argues that together the media and the political sphere construct an orthodox view of globalization as extremely beneficial for the majority of the world's population. According to this view, we need more—not less—globalization.

9. While these kinds of relationships can be forged individually, it is often helpful to have an organization that functions to put various community activists in contact with university activities. This database of information facilitates relationships and minimizes the initial preparation time needed for such projects.

Works Cited

Ackerman, Bruce. *We the People.* Cambridge, MA: Harvard University Press, 1991.

After 100 Years: A Report by the State of Vermont Centennial Land-Grant Committee. Montpelier, VT, 1962.

Ahmad, Aijaz. "Jameson's Rhetoric of Otherness and the 'National Allegory.'" In *In Theory: Classes, Nations, Literatures.* London: Verso, 1992. 95–122.

Alasuutari, Pertti. *Rethinking the Media Audience: The New Agenda.* London: Sage, 1999.

Allman, Paula. *Critical Education against Global Capitalism: Karl Marx and Revolutionary Critical Education.* Westport, CT: Bergin and Garvey, 2001.

Allor, Martin. "Relocating the Site of the Audience." *Critical Studies in Mass Communication* 5.3 (1988): 217–33.

Althusser, Louis. "Ideology and Ideological State Apparatuses." In *Lenin and Philosophy and Other Essays,* trans. Ben Brewster. New York: Monthly Review Press, 1971. 127–86.

American Association of University Professors. "Governance in the Public Interest: A Case Study of the University of North Carolina System." June 2005. http://www.goacta.org/publications/reports.html.

American Labor Sourcebook. Ed. Bernard Rifkin and Susan Rifkin. New York: McGraw-Hill, 1979.

Anderson, Benedict. *Imagined Communities: Reflections on the Origin and Spread of Nationalism.* London: Verso, 1983.

Andrejevic, Mark. *Reality TV: The Work of Being Watched.* Boulder, CO: Rowman and Littlefield, 2004.

Ang, Ien. *Desperately Seeking the Audience.* New York: Routledge, 1991.

Anyon, Jean. "Social Class and the Hidden Curriculum of Work." *Journal of Education* 162 (1980): 67–92.

Anzaldúa, Gloria. *Borderlands/La Frontera: The New Mestiza.* San Francisco: Aunt Lute, 1987.

Appadurai, Arjun. *Modernity at Large: Cultural Dimensions of Globalization.* Minneapolis: University of Minnesota Press, 1996.

Aronowitz, Stanley. *The Knowledge Factory: Dismantling the Corporate University and Creating True Higher Education.* Boston: Beacon Press, 2000.

Aronowitz, Stanley, and Henry Giroux. *Education Still under Siege.* Westport, CT: Bergin and Garvey, 1993.

Aune, James Arnt. *Selling the Free Market: The Rhetoric of Economic Correctness.* New York: Guilford Press, 2001.

———. *Rhetoric and Marxism.* Boulder, CO: Westview, 1994.

Austin, J. L. *How to Do Things with Words.* Cambridge, MA: Harvard University Press, 1975.

Bakhtin, M. M. "Discourse in the Novel." In *The Dialogic Imagination,* ed. Michael Holquist, trans. Caryl Emerson and Michael Holquist. Austin: University of Texas Press, 1981. 259–422.

Baran, Paul, and Paul Sweezy. *Monopoly Capital: An Essay on the American Economic and Social Order.* New York: Monthly Review Press, 1966.

Barrow, Clyde W. *Universities and the Capitalist State: Corporate Liberalism and the Reconstruction of American Higher Education, 1894–1928.* Madison: University of Wisconsin Press, 1990.

Barthes, Roland. *Mythologies.* New York: Hill and Wang, 1998.

Bell, Daniel. *The Coming Post-Industrial Society: A Venture in Social Forecasting.* New York: Basic Books, 1973.

Bender, John, and David Wellbery. "Rhetoricality: On the Modernist Return of Rhetoric." In *The Ends of Rhetoric: History, Theory, Practice,* ed. John Bender and David Wellbery. Stanford: Stanford University Press, 1990. 3–39.

Bender, Thomas. *Intellect and Public Life: Essays on the Social History of Academic Intellectuals in the United States.* Baltimore: Johns Hopkins University Press, 1993.

Bennett, Tony. "Putting Policy into Cultural Studies." In *Cultural Studies,* ed. Lawrence Grossberg, Cary Nelson, and Paula Treichler. New York: Routledge, 1992. 23–37.

Benston, Margaret. "The Political Economy of Women's Liberation." In *Materi-*

alist Feminism: A Reader in Class, Difference, and Women's Lives, ed. Rosemary Hennessy and Chrys Ingraham. New York: Routledge, 1997. 17–23.

Bercovitch, Sacvan. *The American Jeremiad.* Madison: University of Wisconsin Press, 1978.

———. "The Ends of American Puritan Rhetoric." In *The Ends of Rhetoric: History, Theory, Practice,* ed. John Bender and David Wellbery. Stanford: Stanford University Press, 1990. 171–90.

Berlin, James. "Contemporary Rhetoric and Late Capitalism: Culture as an Imperializing Force." In *Marxism Today: Essays on Capitalism, Socialism, and Strategies for Social Change,* ed. Chronis Polychroniou and Harry R. Targ. Westport, CT: Praeger, 1996. 193–204.

———. *Rhetorics, Poetics, and Cultures: Refiguring College English Studies.* Urbana, IL: NCTE, 1996.

Bernard, H. Russell. *Social Research Methods: Qualitative and Quantitative Approaches.* Thousand Oaks, CA: Sage, 2000.

Bhabha, Homi. "The Commitment to Theory." *The Location of Culture.* London: Routledge, 1994. 19–39.

———, ed. *Nation and Narration.* London: Routledge, 1990.

Bhabha, Homi, and John Rutherford. "The Third Space: Interview with Homi Bhabha." *Identity: Community, Culture, Difference,* ed. Johnathon Rutherford. London: Lawrence and Wishart, 1990. 207–21.

Biesecker, Barbara A. "Rethinking the Rhetorical Situation from within the Thematic of *Différence.*" *Philosophy and Rhetoric* 22.2 (1989): 110–30.

Bledstein, Burton J. *The Culture of Professionalism: The Middle Class and the Development of Higher Education in America.* New York: W. W. Norton, 1976.

Blumenstyk, Goldie. "Colleges Seek a Record Number of Patents." *Chronicle of Higher Education,* December 3, 2004, A27–29.

Blumin, Stuart. *The Emergence of the Middle Class: Social Experience in the American City, 1760–1900.* Cambridge: Cambridge University Press, 1989.

Boggs, Carl. *The End of Politics: Corporate Power and the Decline of the Public Sphere.* New York: Guilford Press, 2000.

Bok, Derek. *The Cost of Talent: How Executives and Professionals Are Paid and How It Affects America.* New York: The Free Press, 1993.

Bolaria, B. Singh, and Rosemary Bolaria. *International Labour Migrations.* New York: Oxford University Press, 1997.

Bonnen, James T. "Land Grants Are Changing." October 21, 1996. http://www.adec.edu/clemson/papers/bonnen1.htm.

Bourdieu, Pierre. *Outline of a Theory of Practice.* Cambridge: Cambridge University Press, 1977.

Bousquet, Marc. "Composition as Management Science: Toward a University without a WPA." *JAC: A Journal of Composition Theory* 22.3 (2002): 493–526.

Bowman, James Cloyd, Louis I. Bredvold, L. B. Greenfield, and Bruce Weirick. *Essays for College English.* New York: Heath, 1915.

Braun, M. J. "The Political Economy of Computers and Composition: 'Democracy Hope' in the Era of Globalization." *JAC: A Quarterly Journal for the Interdisciplinary Study of Rhetoric, Writing, Multiple Literacies, and Politics* 21 (2001): 129–162.

Braverman, Harry. *Labor and Monopoly Capital: The Degradation of Work in the Twentieth Century.* New York: Monthly Review Press, 1998.

Brereton, John. *The Origins of Composition Studies in the American College, 1875–1925: A Documentary History.* Pittsburgh: University of Pittsburgh Press, 1995.

Brint, Steven, and Jerome Karabel. *The Diverted Dream: Community Colleges and the Promise of Educational Opportunity in America, 1900–1985.* New York: Oxford University Press, 1989.

Broad, Dave. "Globalization versus Labor." *Monthly Review* 47.7 (1995): 20–31.

Brookings Institute. "America in the Age of Globalization." *Economic Studies,* July 2001. http://www.brookings.edu/globalization (accessed July 24, 2001).

Brown, Phillip, and Hugh Lauder. "Education, Globalization and Economic Development." *Journal of Educational Policy* 11 (1996): 1–25.

Brubacher, John, and Willis Rudy. *Higher Education in Transition: An American History, 1636–1956.* New York: Harper, 1958.

Buchbinder, Howard, and Pinayur Rajagopal. "Canadian Universities: The Impact of Free Trade and Globalization." *Higher Education* 31 (1996): 283–99.

Burke, Colin. *American Collegiate Populations: A Test of the Traditional View.* New York: New York University Press, 1982.

Burke, Kenneth. "The Dialectic of Constitutions." In *A Grammar of Motives.* Berkeley: University of California Press, 1969. 323–401.

———. *A Grammar of Motives.* Berkeley: University of California Press, 1969.

———. "Introduction: The Five Key Terms of Dramatism." In *A Grammar of Motives.* Berkeley: University of California Press, 1969. xv–xxiii.

Burniston, Steve, and Chris Weedon. "Ideology, Subjectivity, and the Artistic Text." In *On Ideology,* ed. Centre for Contemporary Cultural Studies. London: Hutchinson, 1978. 199–229.

Carnegie Foundation for the Advancement of Teaching. *Fourth Annual Report.* New York, 1909.

———. "The 2000 Carnegie Classification: Background and Description." http://www.carnegiefoundation.org/Classification/CIHE2000/background.htm.

Carroll, William K. "Corporations in the 'Top 100,' 1946–1976." In *Corporate Power and Canadian Capitalism.* Vancouver: University of British Columbia Press, 1986. 242–45.

Castaños-Lomnitz, Heriberta, Axel Didriksson, and Janice Newson. "Reshaping the Educational Agendas of Mexican Universities: The Impact of NAFTA." In *Universities and Globalization: Critical Perspectives,* ed. Jan Currie and Janice Newson. London: Sage, 1998. 275–93.

Cather, Willa. *My Ántonia.* Boston: Houghton Mifflin, 1988.

———. *O Pioneers!* New York: Penguin, 1989.

———. *The Professor's House.* New York: Vintage, 1990.

Cattell, James McKeen. *University Control.* New York: The Science Press, 1913.

Chaput, Catherine. "Democracy, Capitalism, and the Ambivalence of Willa Cather's Frontier Rhetorics: Uncertain Foundations of the U.S. Public University System." *College English* 66.3 (January 2004): 310–34.

———. "Identity, Postmodernity, and an Ethics of Activism." *JAC: A Journal of Composition Theory* 20.1 (2000): 43–72.

Chatterjee, Partha. *Nationalist Thought and the Colonial World: A Derivative Discourse.* London: Zed Books for United Nations University, 1986.

Cheney, George, and Dana L. Cloud. "Doing Democracy, Engaging the Material: Employee Participation and Labor Activity in an Age of Market Globalization." *Management Communication Quarterly* 19.4 (May 2006): 501–40.

Chossudovsky, Michel. "Global Poverty and New Economic Order." *Economic and Political Weekly* 26.44 (November 2, 1991): 2527–37.

Cintron, Ralph. *Angels' Town: Chero Ways, Gang Life, and Rhetorics of the Everyday.* Boston: Beacon Press, 1997.

Clark, Burton. "The 'Cooling-Out' Function in Higher Education." *American Journal of Sociology* 65 (1960): 569–76.

Clark, Gregory. *Rhetorical Landscapes in America: Variations on a Theme from Kenneth Burke.* Columbia: University of South Carolina Press, 2004.

Clark, Norman. "The Critical Servant: An Isocratean Contribution to Critical Rhetoric." *Quarterly Journal of Speech* 82.2 (May 1996): 111–24.

Cloud, Dana L. "Affirmative Masquerade." *American Communication Journal* 4.3 (Spring 2001): 1–12. http://acjournal.org/holdings/vol4/iss3/special/cloud.htm.

———. *Control and Consolation in American Culture and Politics: Rhetorics of Therapy.* Thousand Oaks, CA: Sage, 1998.

———. "The Materiality of Discourse as Oxymoron: A Challenge to Critical Rhetoric." *Western Journal of Communication* 58.3 (Summer 1994): 141–63.

Coats, A. W. "The Internationalization of Economic Policy Reform: Some Recent Literature." In *The Post-1945 Internationalization of Economics,* ed. A. W. Coats. Durham: Duke University Press, 1996. 337–54.

Cohen, Arthur. *The Shaping of American Higher Education: Emergence and Growth of the Contemporary System.* San Francisco: Jossey-Bass, 1998.

Cohen, Arthur, and Florence Brawer. *The American Community College.* San Francisco: Jossey-Bass, 1996.

Collective Bargaining Today. Washington, DC: Bureau of National Affairs, 1971.

Commons, John R. *History of Labour in the United States.* New York: Beard Books, 1918.

Connors, Robert J. *Composition-Rhetoric: Backgrounds, Theory, and Pedagogy.* Pittsburgh: University of Pittsburgh Press, 1997.

———. "Personal Writing Assignments." *College Composition and Communication* 38 (1987): 166–83.

Cooke, Morris L. *Academic and Industrial Efficiency: A Report.* Bulletin 2. Boston: Merrymount Press, 1910.

Cooper, David D. "Academic Professionalism and the Betrayal of the Land-Grant Tradition." *American Behavioral Scientist* 42 (February 1999): 776–85.

Cravey, Altha. *Women and Work in Mexico's Maquiladoras.* New York: Oxford University Press, 1998.

Crevecoeur, St. John de. *Letters from an American Farmer.* New York: Oxford University Press, 1997.

Cross, Coy F. *Justin Smith Morrill: Father of the Land Grant Colleges.* East Lansing: Michigan State University Press, 1999.

Crowley, Sharon. "The Bourgeois Subject and the Demise of Rhetorical Education." In *Composition and the University: Historical and Polemical Essays.* Pittsburgh: University of Pittsburgh Press, 1998. 30–45.

Crutsinger, Martin. "Greenspan Wary of Trade Protection." Associated Press,

April 4, 2001. http://news.excite.com/news/ap/010404/13/greenspan (accessed April 4, 2001).

Crystal, David. *English as a Global Language.* Cambridge: Cambridge University Press, 1997.

Cumings, Bruce. "Boundary Displacement: Area Studies and International Studies during and after the Cold War." In *Universities and Empire: Empire and Politics in the Social Sciences during the Cold War,* ed. Christopher Simpson. New York: The New Press, 1998. 159–88.

Currie, Jan. Introduction to *Universities and Globalization: Critical Perspectives,* ed. Jan Currie and Janice Newson. London: Sage, 1998. 1–13.

Dawes, Greg. "A Marxist Critique of Post-Structuralist Notions of the Subject." In *Post-ality: Marxism and Postmodernism,* ed. Mas'ud Zavarzadeh, Teresa Ebert, and Donald Morton. Washington, DC: Maisonneuve Press, 1995. 150–88.

de Certeau, Michel. *The Practice of Everyday Life.* Berkeley: University of California Press, 1984.

Derrida, Jacques. "Signature Event Context." In *Limited, Inc.* Evanston, IL: Northwestern University Press, 1972. 1–23.

Dey, Eric, Alexander Astin, and William Korn. *The American Freshman: Twenty-Five-Year Trends, 1966–1990.* Los Angeles: Higher Education Research Institute, 1991.

Diamond, Sigmund. *Compromised Campus: The Collaboration of Universities with the Intelligence Community, 1945–1955.* New York: Oxford University Press, 1992.

Dirlik, Arif. "The Global in the Local." In *Global/Local: Cultural Production and the Transnational Imaginary,* ed. Rob Wilson and Wimal Dissanayake. Durham: Duke University Press, 1996. 21–45.

Dougherty, Kevin. *The Contradictory College: The Conflicting Origins, Impacts, and Futures of the Community College.* Albany: State University of New York Press, 1994.

Eberly, Rosa. *Citizen Critics: Literary Public Spheres.* Urbana: University of Illinois Press, 2000.

———. "From *Writers, Audiences,* and *Communities* to Publics: Writing Classrooms as Protopublic Spaces." *Rhetoric Review* 18 (1999): 165–78.

———. "Rhetoric and the Anti-Logos Doughball: Teaching Deliberating Bodies the Practices of Participatory Democracy." *Rhetoric and Public Affairs* 5.2 (2002): 287–300.

Ehrenreich, Barbara, and John Ehrenreich. "The Professional-Managerial Class."

In *Between Labour and Capital,* ed. Pat Walker. Sussex: Harvester Press, 1979. 5–45.

Eliot, Charles William. "A Turning Point in Education." In *A Turning Point in Education: The Inaugural Address of Charles William Eliot as President of Harvard College, October 19, 1869,* ed. Nathan M. Pusey. Cambridge, MA: Harvard University Press, 1969.

Engels, Frederick. *The Origin of the Family, Private Property and the State.* New York: International Publishers, 1993.

Enloe, Cynthia. *Bananas, Beaches, and Bases: Making Feminist Sense of International Politics.* Berkeley: University of California Press, 1989.

———. "How Do They Militarize a Can of Soup?" Sex, Race, and Globalization Seminar Series, Tucson, AZ. April 2, 2001.

Etzkowitz, Henry, and Loet Leydesdorff. "Introduction: Universities in the Global Knowledge Economy." In *Universities and the Global Knowledge Economy: A Triple Helix of University-Industry-Government Relations,* ed. Henry Etzkowitz and Loet Leydesdorff. London: Wellington House, 1997. 1–8.

Etzkowitz, Henry, Andrew Webster, and Peter Healey. *Capitalizing Knowledge: New Intersections of Industry and Academia.* Albany: SUNY Press, 1998.

Filson, John. *The Discovery, Settlement, and Present State of Kentucke.* New York: Corinth Books, 1962.

Fish, Stanley. "Comments from Outside Economics." In *The Consequences of Economic Rhetoric,* ed. Arjo Klamer, Donald N. McCloskey, and Robert M. Solo. Cambridge: Cambridge University Press, 1988. 21–30.

Flexner, Abraham. *The American College.* New York: Century, 1908.

———. *Universities, American, English, German.* New York: Oxford University Press, 1930.

Folbre, Nancy, and Heidi Hartmann. "The Rhetoric of Self-Interest: Ideology of Gender in Economic Theory." In *The Consequences of Economic Rhetoric,* ed. Arjo Klamer, Donald N. McCloskey, and Robert M. Solo. Cambridge: Cambridge University Press, 1988. 184–203.

Forquer, George. "Extract from a Letter to the Voters of Sangamo County, Dated Springfield, June 23, 1832." In *The Origin of the Land Grant Act of 1862,* ed. Edmund J. James. Urbana-Champaign: University of Illinois Press, 1910. 39–43.

Foucault, Michel. *The Archaeology of Knowledge and the Discourse on Language.* Trans. A. M. Sheridan Smith. New York: Pantheon Books, 1972.

———. *Discipline and Punish: The Birth of the Prison.* Trans. Alan Sheridan. New York: Vintage, 1995.

———. *The History of Sexuality.* Trans. Robert Hurley. New York: Vintage, 1978.

———. "Practicing Criticism." In *Politics, Philosophy, Culture: Interviews and Other Writings, 1977–1984,* ed. Lawrence D. Kritzman. New York: Routledge, 1988. 152–56.

———. "Technologies of the Self." In *Technologies of the Self: A Seminar with Michel Foucault,* ed. Luther H. Martin, Huck Gutman, and Patrick H. Hutton. Amherst: University of Massachusetts Press, 1988. 16–49.

———. "Truth and Power." In *Power/Knowledge: Selected Interviews and Other Writings,* ed. Colin Gordon. New York: Pantheon Books, 1977. 109–33.

Friedman, Andrew. *Industry and Labour: Class Struggle at Work and Monopoly Capitalism.* London: Macmillan, 1977.

Friedman, Thomas L. *The Lexus and the Olive Tree.* New York: Farrar, Straus and Giroux, 2000.

Fukuyama, Francis. *The End of History and the Last Man.* New York: Harper, 1993.

Furth, Dorothea. "Short-Cycle Higher Education: Some Basic Considerations." In *Short-Cycle Higher Education.* Paris: OECD, 1973. 13–42.

Gadamer, Hans-Georg. *Truth and Method.* New York: Seabury Press, 1975.

Gans, Herbert J. *Popular Culture and High Culture: An Analysis and Evaluation of Taste.* New York: Basic Books, 1974.

Gaonkar, Dilip Parameshwar. "The Idea of Rhetoric in the Rhetoric of Science." In *Rhetorical Hermeneutics: Invention and Interpretation in the Age of Science,* ed. Alan G. Gross and William M. Keith. Albany: State University of New York Press, 1997. 25–85.

Garland, Hamlin. *A Son of the Middle Border.* New York: Grosset and Dunlap, 1917.

Gerstl, Joel, and Glenn Jacobs. Introduction to *Professions for the People: The Politics of Skill,* ed. Joel Gerstl and Glenn Jacobs. New York: Halsted Press, 1976. 1–23.

Gilmore, Ruth Wilson. "Globalisation and the U.S. Prison Growth: From Military Keynesianism to Pot-Keynesian Militarism." *Race and Class* 40 (1998/99): 171–88.

Glenn, Cheryl, Margaret M. Lyday, and Wendy B. Sharer. *Rhetorical Education in America.* Tuscaloosa: University of Alabama Press, 2004.

Goldin, Claudia, and Lawrence F. Katz. "The Shaping of Higher Education: The

Formative Years in the United States, 1890–1940." *Journal of Economic Perspectives* 13.1 (1999): 37–62.

Golding, Peter, and Graham Murdoch. "Culture, Communication, and Political Economy." In *Mass Media and Society,* ed. James Curran and Michael Gurevitch. London: Edward Arnold, 1991. 15–22.

Goodwin, Craufurd D. W. *The History of Political Economy.* Durham: Duke University Press, 2003.

Gouldner, Alvin. *The Future of Intellectuals and the Rise of the New Class.* New York: Continuum Books, 1979.

Graham, Hugh Davis, and Nancy Diamond. *The Rise of American Research Universities: Elites and Challengers in the Postwar Era.* Baltimore: Johns Hopkins University Press, 1997.

Gramsci, Antonio. "Problems of History and Culture." In *Selections from the Prison Notebooks.* Trans. Quintin Hoare and Geoffrey Nowell Smith. New York: International Publishers, 1991. 3–43.

Grearson, Jessie Carroll, and Lauren B. Smith. *Love in a Global Village: A Celebration of Intercultural Families in the Midwest.* Iowa City: University of Iowa Press, 2001.

Grindstaff, Laura. "Producing Trash, Class, and the Money Shot: A Behind the Scenes Account of Daytime TV Talk Shows." In *Media Scandals: Morality and Desire in the Popular Culture Marketplace,* ed. James Lull and Stephen Hinerman. New York: Columbia University Press, 1997. 164–202.

Gross, Ronald, and Paul Osterman. Introduction to *The New Professionals,* ed. Ronald Gross and Paul Osterman. New York: Simon and Schuster, 1972. 9–30.

Guston, David, and Kenneth Keniston. *The Fragile Contract: University Science and the Federal Government.* Cambridge, MA: MIT Press, 1994.

Guthrie, James W., and Lawrence C. Pierce. "The International Economy and National Education Reform: A Comparison of Education Reforms in the United States and Great Britain." *Oxford Review of Education* 16.2 (1990): 179–205.

Haakenson, Paul. *Recent Trends in Global/International Education.* Bloomington, IN: Eric Clearinghouse for Social Science Studies, 2000.

Habermas, Jürgen. *The Structural Transformation of the Public Sphere: An Inquiry into a Category of Bourgeois Society.* Trans. Thomas Burger. Cambridge, MA: MIT Press, 1989.

Habu, Toshie. "The Irony of Globalization: The Experience of Japanese Women in British Higher Education." *Higher Education* 39 (2000): 43–66.

Hagen, Ingunn, and Janet Wasko. *Consuming Audiences? Production and Reception in Media Research.* Cresskill, NJ: Hampton Press, 2000.

Hall, Stuart. "The Local and the Global: Globalization and Ethnicity." In *Culture, Globalization and the World-System: Contemporary Conditions for the Representation of Identity,* ed. Anthony D. King. Minneapolis: University of Minnesota Press, 1997. 19–39.

———. "The Rediscovery of 'Ideology.'" In *Culture, Society, and the Media.* London: Routledge, 1982. 56–90.

———. "Variants of Liberalism." In *Politics and Ideology: A Reader,* ed. James Donald and Stuart Hall. Philadelphia: Open University Press, 1986. 34–69.

Hall, Stuart, and Lawrence Grossberg. "On Postmodernism and Articulation: An Interview with Stuart Hall." In *Critical Dialogue in Cultural Studies,* ed. David Morley and Kuan-Hsing Chen. London: Routledge, 1996. 131–50.

Handbook of Labor Statistics. Ed. Maurice J. Tobin and Ewan Clague. Washington, DC: United States Department of Labor, 1950.

Haraway, Donna. *Simians, Cyborgs, and Women: The Reinvention of Nature.* London: Free Association, 1991.

Hardt, Michael, and Antonio Negri. *Empire.* Cambridge, MA: Harvard University Press, 2000.

Hariman, Robert. "Critical Rhetoric and Postmodern Theory." *Quarterly Journal of Speech* 77 (1991): 67–70.

Harral, Stuart. *Public Relations for Higher Education.* Norman: University of Oklahoma Press, 1942.

Harris, Jerry. "Globalisation and the Technological Transformation of Capitalism." *Race and Class* 40 (1998/99): 21–35.

Harvey, David. *The Condition of Postmodernity: An Enquiry into the Origins of Cultural Change.* Oxford: Blackwell, 1990.

———. *Justice, Nature, and the Geography of Difference.* Cambridge: Blackwell, 1996.

———. *The Limits to Capital.* Chicago: University of Chicago Press, 1982.

Hasian, Marouf, Jr., and Fernando Delgado. "The Trials and Tribulations of Racialized Critical Rhetorical Theory: Understanding the Rhetorical Ambiguities of Proposition 187." *Communication Theory* 8.3 (August 1998): 245–70.

Hassan, Salah S., and Erdener Kaynak. *Globalization of Consumer Markets: Structures and Strategies.* New York: International Business Press, 1994.

Hay, James, Lawrence Grossberg, and Ellen Wartella. *The Audience and Its Landscape.* Boulder, CO: Westview, 1996.

Hebdige, Dick. *Subculture: The Meaning of Style.* London: Routledge, 1979.

Heidegger, Martin. "What Is Metaphysics?" In *Basic Writings,* ed. David Farrell Krell. New York: Harper, 1993. 89–110.

Heilbroner, Robert L. "Rhetoric and Ideology." In *The Consequences of Economic Rhetoric,* ed. Arjo Klamer, Donald N. McCloskey, and Robert M. Solo. Cambridge: Cambridge University Press, 1988. 38–43.

Held, David. "The Timid Tendency." *Marxism Today* (November/December 1998): 24–27.

Hilferding, Rudolf. *Finance Capital: A Study of the Latest Phase of Capitalist Development.* 1910. Repr., London: Routledge, 1981.

Hirschkop, Ken. "Democracy and the New Technologies." In *Capitalism and the Information Age: The Political Economy of the Global Communication Revolution,* ed. Robert McChesney, Ellen Meiksins Wood, and John Bellamy Foster. New York: Monthly Review, 1998. 207–17.

Hofstadter, Richard, and Wilson Smith. *American Higher Education: A Documentary History.* 2 vols. Chicago: University of Chicago Press, 1961.

Hogan, J. Michael. "Historiography and Ethics in Adam Smith's Lectures on Rhetoric, 1762–1763." *Rhetorica* 2.1 (Spring 1984): 75–91.

Human Rights Watch. "No Guarantees: Sex Discrimination in Mexico's Maquiladora Sector." In *The Maquiladora Reader: Cross-Border Organizing since NAFTA,* ed. Rachael Kamel and Anya Hoffman. Philadelphia: American Friends Service Committee, 1999.

Hunt, Michael H. *Ideology and U.S. Foreign Policy.* New Haven: Yale University Press, 1987.

Hutchins, Robert. *Higher Learning in America.* New Haven: Yale University Press, 1936.

Hyslop-Margison, Emery. "The Market Economy Discourse on Education: Interpretation, Impact, and Resistance." *Alberta Journal of Educational Research* 46.3 (Fall 2000): 203–13.

Im, Hyug Baeg. "Globalisation and Democratisation: Boon Companions or Strange Bedfellows?" *Australian Journal of International Affairs* 50.3 (1996): 279–91.

James, Edmund J. *The Origin of the Land Grant Act of 1862.* Urbana-Champaign: University of Illinois Press, 1910.

Jameson, Frederic. "Notes on Globalization as a Philosophical Issue." In *The Cultures of Globalization,* ed. Frederic Jameson and Masao Miyoshi. Durham: Duke University Press, 1999. 54–77.

———. *Postmodernism: Or, The Cultural Logic of Late Capitalism.* Durham: Duke University Press, 1997.

Jefferson, Thomas. *Notes on the State of Virginia.* Chapel Hill: University of North Carolina Press, 1955.

Jensen, Robert. *Citizens of the Empire: The Struggle to Claim Our Humanity.* San Francisco: City Lights Books, 2004.

Johnson-Woods, Toni. *Big Bother: Why Did* That *Reality-TV Show Become Such a Phenomenon?* St Lucia: Queensland Press, 2002.

Kalberg, Stephen. "Cultural Foundations of Modern Citizenship." In *Citizenship and Social Theory,* ed. Bryan S. Turner. London: Sage, 1993. 91–114.

Karabel, Jerome. "Community Colleges and Social Stratification." *Harvard Educational Review* 42 (1972): 521–62.

Keith, William. "Identity, Rhetoric and Myth: A Response to Mailloux and Leff." *Rhetoric Society Quarterly* 30.4 (Fall 2000): 95–106.

Kennedy, George A. *Comparative Rhetoric: An Historical and Cross-cultural Introduction.* New York: Oxford University Press, 1998.

Kernan, Alvin. *What's Happened to the Humanities?* Princeton: Princeton University Press, 1997.

King, Anthony, ed. *Culture, Globalization and the World-System: Contemporary Conditions for the Representation of Identity.* Minneapolis: University of Minnesota Press, 1997.

———. "Introduction: Spaces of Culture, Spaces of Knowledge." In *Culture, Globalization and the World-System: Contemporary Conditions for the Representation of Identity,* ed. Anthony D. King. Minneapolis: University of Minnesota Press, 1997. 1–18.

Klamer, Arjo, and Donald N. McCloskey. "Economics in the Human Conversation." In *The Consequences of Economic Rhetoric,* ed. Arjo Klamer, Donald N. McCloskey, and Robert M. Solo. Cambridge: Cambridge University Press, 1988. 3–20.

Klamer, Arjo, Donald N. McCloskey, and Robert M. Solo, eds. *The Consequences of Economic Rhetoric.* Cambridge: Cambridge University Press, 1988.

Kolodny, Annette. *Failing the Future: A Dean Looks at Higher Education in the Twenty-First Century.* Durham: Duke University Press, 1998.

Kuhn, Thomas S. *The Structure of Scientific Revolutions.* Chicago: University of Chicago Press, 1962.

Kundnani, Arun. "Where Do You Want to Go Today? The Rise of Information Capital." *Race and Class* 40 (1998/99): 49–71.

Laclau, Ernesto, and Chantal Mouffe. *Hegemony and Socialist Strategy: Towards a Radical Democratic Politics.* London: Verso, 1985.

LaFeber, Walter. *The American Search for Opportunity, 1865–1913.* Cambridge History of American Foreign Relations, vol. 2. Cambridge: Cambridge University Press, 1995.

———. *The New Empire: An Interpretation of American Expansion, 1860–1898.* Ithaca: Cornell University Press, 1963.

Larraín, Jorge. *Marxism and Ideology.* London: Macmillan, 1983.

Leff, Michael. "Rhetorical Disciplines and Rhetorical Disciplinarity: A Response to Mailloux." *Rhetoric Society Quarterly* 30.4 (Fall 2000): 83–93.

Lenin, Vladimir I. *Imperialism: The Highest Stage of Capitalism.* New York: International Publishers, 1990.

Lipset, Seymour Martin. *American Exceptionalism: A Double-Edged Sword.* New York: Norton, 1996.

Lovell, Terry. "Cultural Production." In *Cultural Theory and Popular Culture: A Reader,* ed. John Storey. Hemel Hempstead: Prentice Hall, 1998. 476–82.

Lowen, Rebecca. *Creating the Cold War University: The Transformation of Stanford.* Berkeley: University of California Press, 1997.

Ludden, David. "Area Studies in the Age of Globalization." January 25, 1998. http://www.sas.upenn.edu/~dludden/areast2.htm.

Lukács, Georg. "The Phenomenon of Reification." In *History and Class Consciousness: Studies in Marxist Dialectics.* Cambridge, MA: MIT Press, 1971. 83–110.

Lull, James. *Inside Family Viewing: Ethnographic Research on Television's Audience.* New York: Routledge, 1990.

Lyotard, Jean-François. *The Postmodern Condition: A Report on Knowledge.* Trans. Geoff Bennington and Brain Massumi. Minneapolis: University of Minnesota Press, 1984.

Madsen, Deborah L. *American Exceptionalism.* Edinburgh: Edinburgh University Press, 1998.

Mailloux, Steven. "Disciplinary Identities: On the Rhetorical Paths Between English and Communication Studies." *Rhetoric Society Quarterly* 30.2 (Spring 2000): 5–29.

———. "Practices, Theories, and Traditions: Further Thoughts on the Disciplinary Identities of English and Communication Studies." *Rhetoric Society Quarterly* 33 (Winter 2003): 129–39.

Mao Tse-Tung. *On Guerrilla Warfare.* Trans. Samuel B. Griffith. Baltimore: Nautical and Aviation Publishing, 1992.

Marcus, George, and Michael Fischer. "Taking Account of the World Historical Political Economy: Knowable Communities in Larger Systems." In *Anthropology as Cultural Critique: An Experimental Moment in the Human Sciences.* Chicago: University of Chicago Press, 1986. 77–110.

Marcuse, Herbert. "The Struggle against Liberalism in the Totalitarian View of the State." In *Negations: Essays in Critical Theory.* Boston: Beacon Press, 1968. 3–42.

Marcuse, Peter. "The Language of Globalization." *Monthly Review* 52.3 (July/August 2000): 23–28.

Marshall, T. H. "Citizenship and Social Class." In *Citizenship and Social Class,* by T. H. Marshall and Tom Bottomore. Concord, MA: Pluto, 1992. 3–51.

Martin, Randy, ed. *Chalk Lines: The Politics of Work in the Managed University.* Durham: Duke University Press, 1998.

Marx, Karl. *Capital: Volume I.* Trans. Ben Fowkes. New York: Penguin, 1990.

———. *A Contribution to the Critique of Political Economy.* Trans. S. W. Ryazanskaya. New York: International Publishers, 1999.

———. *The Economic and Philosophic Manuscripts of 1844.* Ed. Dirk J. Struik. Trans. Martin Milligan. New York: International Publishers, 1964.

———. *Grundrisse.* Trans. Martin Nicolaus. New York: Penguin, 1973.

———. "Letter to Arnold Ruge." In *The Marx-Engels Reader,* ed. Robert C. Tucker. New York: W. W. Norton, 1978. 12–15.

Marx, Karl, and Frederick Engels. *The Communist Manifesto.* New York: Bantam, 1992.

———. *The German Ideology.* New York: International Publishers, 1995.

Mazlish, Bruce. "An Introduction to Global History." In *Conceptualizing Global History,* ed. Bruce Mazlish and Ralph Buultjens. Boulder, CO: Westview, 1993. 1–24.

McBride, Ian. "The School of Virtue: Francis Hutcheson, Irish Presbyterians and the Scottish Enlightenment." In *Political Thought in Ireland since the Seventeenth Century,* ed. D. George Boyce, Robert Eccleshall, and Vincent Geoghegan. London: Routledge, 1993. 73–99.

McCarthy, John C. "Near-Term Growth of Offshoring Accelerating: Resizing U.S. Service Jobs Going Offshore." Forrester Research, May 14, 2004. http://www.forrester.com/.

McCloskey, Deirdre N. *The Bourgeois Virtues: Ethics for an Age of Commerce.* Chicago: University of Chicago Press, 2006.

———. *The Rhetoric of Economics.* Madison: University of Wisconsin Press, 1998.

———. "Towards a Rhetoric of Economics." In *The Boundaries of Economics,* ed. Gordon C. Winston and Richard F. Teichgraeber. Cambridge: Cambridge University Press, 1988. 13–29.

McEvoy-Levy, Siobhán. *American Exceptionalism and U.S. Foreign Policy: Public Diplomacy at the End of the Cold War.* New York: Palgrave, 2001.

McGee, Michael Calvin. "A Materialist's Conception of Rhetoric." In *Explorations in Rhetoric Studies in Honor of Douglas Ehninger.* Glenview, IL: Scott, Foresman, 1982. 23–48.

———. "Text, Context, and the Fragmentation of Contemporary Culture." *Western Journal of Speech Communication* 54 (Summer 1990): 274–89.

McKenna, Stephen J. *Adam Smith: The Rhetoric of Propriety.* New York: State University of New York Press, 2006.

McKerrow, Raymie E. "Critical Rhetoric and the Possibility of the Subject." In *The Critical Turn: Rhetoric and Philosophy in Postmodern Discourse,* ed. Ion Angus and Lenore Langsdorf. Carbondale: Southern Illinois University Press, 1993. 51–67.

———. "Critical Rhetoric: Theory and Praxis." In *Contemporary Rhetorical Theory: A Reader.* New York: Guilford Press, 1999. 441–63.

McLaren, Peter. *Che Guevara, Paulo Freire, and the Pedagogy of Revolution.* Boulder, CO: Rowman and Littlefield, 2000.

———. "Liberatory Politics and Higher Education: A Freirean Perspective." *Revolutionary Multiculturalism: Pedagogies of Dissent for the New Millennium.* Boulder, CO: Westview, 1997. 42–75.

———. *Revolutionary Multiculturalism: Pedagogies of Dissent for the New Millennium.* Boulder, CO: Westview, 1997.

McLaren, Peter, and Henry A. Giroux. "Writing from the Margins: Geographies of Identity, Pedagogy, and Power." In *Revolutionary Multiculturalism: Pedagogies of Dissent for the New Millennium.* Boulder, CO: Westview, 1997. 16–41.

McLaren, Peter, and Kris Gutierrez. "Global Politics and Local Antagonisms: Research and Practice as Dissent and Possibility." In *Revolutionary Multiculturalism: Pedagogies of Dissent for the New Millennium.* Boulder, CO: Westview, 1997. 192–222.

McLuhan, Marshall. *Understanding Media: The Extensions of Man.* New York: McGraw-Hill, 1964.

McRobbie, Angela. "All the World's a Stage, Screen or Magazine: When Culture Is the Logic of Late Capitalism." *Media, Culture and Society* 18.3 (1996): 335–42.

Meiners, Robert. "The Evolution of American Higher Education." In *The Academy in Crisis: The Political Economy of Higher Education,* ed. John Sommer. New Brunswick, NJ: Transaction Publishers, 1995. 21–43.

Merod, Jim. *The Political Responsibility of the Critic.* Ithaca: Cornell University Press, 1987.

Miller, Perry. *Errand into the Wilderness.* Cambridge, MA: Harvard University Press, 1964.

Miller, Thomas P. *The Formation of College English: Rhetoric and Belles Lettres in the British Cultural Provinces.* Pittsburgh: University of Pittsburgh Press, 1997.

Millikan, Max, and Walt Rostow. "Notes on Foreign Economic Policy." In *Universities and Empire: Empire and Politics in the Social Sciences during the Cold War,* ed. Christopher Simpson. New York: The New Press, 1998. 39–55.

Mirowski, Philip. *Against Mechanism: Protecting Economics from Science.* Totowa, NJ: Rowman and Littlefield, 1988.

———. "Shall I Compare Thee to a Minkowski-Ricardo-Leontief-Metzler Matrix of the Mosak-Hicks Type? Or, Rhetoric, Mathematics, and the Nature of Neoclassical Economic Theory." In *The Consequences of Economic Rhetoric,* ed. Arjo Klamer, Donald N. McCloskey, and Robert M. Solo. Cambridge: Cambridge University Press, 1988. 117–45.

Miyoshi, Masao. "Ivory Tower in Escrow." *boundary 2* 27 (2000): 7–50.

———. "Sites of Resistance in the Global Economy." In *Cultural Readings of Imperialism: Edward Said and the Gravity of History,* ed. Keith Ansell Pearson, Benita Parry, and Judith Squires. New York: St. Martin's, 1997. 49–66.

Mok, Ka-ho. "Reflecting Globalization Effects on Local Policy: Higher Education Reform in Taiwan." *Journal of Education Policy* 15.6 (2000): 637–66.

Mok, Ka-ho, and Hiu-hong Lee. "Globalization or Re-colonization: Higher Education Reforms in Hong Kong." *Higher Education Policy* 13 (2000): 361–77.

Molina, Victor. "Notes on Marx and the Problem of Individuality." In *On Ideology.* London: Hutchinson, 1978. 230–58.

Moody, Kim. *Workers in a Lean World: Unions in the International Economy.* New York: Verso, 1997.

Morris, Charles R. "The Coming Boom." *Atlantic Monthly* 264.4 (October 1989): 51–64.

Morrison, Keith. "The Global Village of African American Art." In *African American Visual Aesthetics: A Postmodernist View*. Washington, DC: Smithsonian Institution Press, 1995. 17–43.

Nearing, Scott. "Educational Research and Statistics: Who's Who among College Trustees." *School and Society* 6.141 (September 1917): 297–99.

Nelson, Cary. *Will Teach for Food: Academic Labor in Crisis*. Minneapolis: University of Minnesota Press, 1997.

Nelson, Cary, and Stephen Watt. *Academic Keywords: A Devil's Dictionary for Higher Education*. New York: Routledge, 1999.

Neusner, Jacob, and Noam Neusner. *The Price of Excellence: Universities in Conflict during the Cold War Era*. New York: Continuum, 1995.

Nevins, Allan. *The Origins of the Land Grant Colleges and State Universities*. Washington, DC: Civil War Centennial Commission, 1962.

Newman, John Henry. *The Idea of a University*. 1852. New York: Longman, 1947.

1990 Census of Population: United States Social and Economic Characteristics. Washington, DC: GPO, 1990.

Nitzan, Jonathan. "Regimes of Differential Accumulation: Mergers, Stagflation and the Logic of Globalization." *Review of International Political Economy* 8.2 (Summer 2001): 226–74.

Noble, David. *America by Design: Science, Technology, and the Rise of Corporate Capitalism*. New York: Alfred A. Knopf, 1977.

———. "The Future of the Faculty in the Digital Diploma Mill." *Academe: Bulletin of the American Association of University Professors* 87.5 (September/October 2001): 27–32.

Noll, Roger. "The American Research University: An Introduction." In *Challenges to Research Universities*, ed. Roger Noll. Washington, DC: Brookings Institute, 1998. 1–30.

North American Free Trade Agreement (NAFTA). http://www.nafta-sec-alena.org/DefaultSite/index_e.aspx?DetailID=78.

Nostbakken, David, and Charles Morrow. *Cultural Expression in the Global Village*. Pengang: Southbound Press, 1993.

Oakes, Jeannie, and Martin Lipton. "Tracking and Ability Grouping: A Structural Barrier to Access and Achievement." In *Access to Knowledge: An Agenda for*

Our Nation's Schools, ed. John I. Goodlad and Pamela Keating. New York: College Entrance Examination Board, 1990. 43–58.

Ohio State University. "TechPartners." http://techpartners.osu.edu/tp_home.html (accessed May 14, 2002).

———. "The University Mission." *The University Context.* Revised 1992. http://www.apo.ohio-state.edu/mp/mpv1c1.html (accessed April 22, 2002).

Ohmann, Richard. "Citizenship and Literacy Work: Thoughts without a Conclusion." *Workplace: A Journal of Academic Labor* 4.1 (June 2001). http://www.cust.educ.ubc.ca/workplace/issue7/ohmann.html.

Ono, Kent A., and John M. Sloop. "Commitment to *Telos*—A Sustained Critical Rhetoric." *Communication Monographs* 59 (March 1992): 48–60.

Organization for Economic Cooperation and Development. *Alternatives to Universities.* Paris: OECD, 1991.

———. *Development of Higher Education, 1950–1967.* Paris: OECD, 1971.

———. *Education and Working Life in Modern Society.* Paris, OECD, 1975.

———. *Higher Education in California.* Paris: OECD, 1990.

———. *Policies for Higher Education.* Paris: OECD, 1973.

———. *Policies for Higher Education in the 1980s.* Paris: OECD, 1983.

"Outsource Your Job to Earn More!" *Times of India.* July 7, 2004. http://timesofindia.com/.

Pannu, R. S. "Neoliberal Project of Globalization: Prospects for Democratization of Education." *Alberta Journal of Educational Research* 42.2 (1996): 87–101.

Parker, Patricia. "Metaphor and Catachresis." In *The Ends of Rhetoric: History, Theory, Practice,* ed. John Bender and David Wellbery. Stanford: Stanford University Press, 1990. 60–73.

Payne, Darin. "English Studies in Levittown: Rhetorics of Space and Technology in Course-Management Software." *College English* 67 (2005): 483–507.

Payne, William Morton, ed. *English in American Universities.* Boston: D.C. Heath, 1895.

Pennsylvania State University. "Innovation Park at Penn State." http://www.innovationpark.psu.edu/.

———. "Penn State's Mission and Public Character." Revised 2002. http://www.psu.edu/ur/about/mission.html.

Perelman, Chaïm, and Lucie Olbrechts-Tyteca. *The New Rhetoric: A Treatise on Argumentation.* South Bend, IN: University of Notre Dame Press, 1969.

Pinto, Ambrose. "Globalization and the Changing Ideology of Indian Higher Education." *Social Action* 50.4 (2000): 333–47.

Polychroniou, Chronis. "The Political Economy of U.S. Imperialism: From Hegemony to Crisis." In *Marxism Today: Essays on Capitalism, Socialism, and Strategies for Social Change,* ed. Chronis Polychroniou and Harry R. Targ. Westport, CT: Praeger, 1996. 39–70.

Porter, James E., et al. "Institutional Critique: A Rhetorical Methodology for Change." *College Composition and Communication* 51.4 (2000): 610–42.

Postman, Neil. *The End of Education: Redefining the Value of School.* New York: Knopf, 1995.

Powers, M. Karen, and Catherine Chaput. "'Anti-American Studies' in the Deep South: Dissenting Rhetorics, the Practice of Democracy, and Academic Freedom in Wartime Universities." *College, Composition, and Communication* 58.4 (June 2007): 648–81.

Priest, Patricia Joyner. *Public Intimacies: Talk Show Participants and Tell-All TV.* Cresskill, NJ: Hampton Press, 1995.

Pritchett, Henry. "Shall the University Become a Business Corporation?" *Atlantic Monthly* 96 (September 1905): 289–99.

Readings, Bill. *The University in Ruins.* Cambridge, MA: Harvard University Press, 1996.

Rhoades, Gary. *Managed Professionals: Unionized Faculty and Restructuring Academic Labor.* Albany: SUNY Press, 1998.

Rhoades, Gary, and Sheila Slaughter. "Academic Capitalism, Managed Professionals, and Supply-Side Higher Education." *Social Text* 51.2 (Summer 1997): 9–38.

Roberts-Miller, Patricia. *Deliberate Conflict: Argument, Political Theory and Composition Classes.* Carbondale: Southern Illinois University Press, 2004.

Robertson, Roland. *Globalization: Social Theory and Global Culture.* London: Sage, 1996.

Rosteck, Thomas. *At the Intersection: Cultural Studies and Rhetorical Studies.* New York: Guilford Press, 1999.

———. "Cultural Studies and Rhetorical Studies." *Quarterly Journal of Speech* 81 (1995): 386–403.

———. "Form and Cultural Context in Rhetorical Criticism: Re-Reading Wrage." *Quarterly Journal of Speech* 84 (1998): 471–90.

Rowe, John Carlos. *Literary Culture and U.S. Imperialism: From the Revolution to World War II.* Oxford: Oxford University Press, 2000.

Ruiz, Vicki, and Susan Tiano. *Women on the U.S.-Mexican Border.* Boston: Allen and Unwin, 1987.

Said, Edward. *Culture and Imperialism.* New York: Alfred A. Knopf, 1993.

——. *Orientalism.* New York: Vintage Books, 1979.

——. *Representations of the Intellectual.* New York: Vintage, 1994.

Sandoval, Chela. *Methodology of the Oppressed.* Minneapolis: University of Minnesota Press, 2000.

Sassen, Saskia. *Cities in a World Economy.* Thousand Oaks, CA: Pine Forge Press, 2000.

——. *Globalization and Its Discontents: Essays on the Mobility of People and Money.* New York: The New Press, 1998.

——. *Losing Control? Sovereignty in the Age of Globalization.* New York: Columbia University Press, 1996.

Schiappa, Edward. "Second Thoughts on the Critique of Big Rhetoric." *Philosophy and Rhetoric* 34.3 (2001): 260–74.

Schiller, Dan. *Digital Capitalism: Networking the Global Market System.* Cambridge, MA: MIT Press, 2000.

Scott, Joan. "The Rhetoric of Crisis in Higher Education." In *Education under Fire,* ed. Cary Nelson and Michael Bérubé. New York: Routledge, 1995. 293–303.

Scott, Robert L. "On Not Defining 'Rhetoric.'" *Philosophy and Rhetoric* 6 (1972): 81–96.

Sebberson, David. "The Rhetoric of Inquiry or the Sophistry of the Status Quo? Exploring the Common Ground between Critical Rhetoric and Institutional Economics." *Journal of Economic Issues* 24.4 (December 1990): 1017–26.

Seligman, Adam B. "The Fragile Ethical Vision of Civil Society." In *Citizenship and Social Theory,* ed. Bryan S. Turner. London: Sage, 1993. 139–61.

Selzer, Jack, and Sharon Crowley, eds. *Rhetorical Bodies.* Madison: University of Wisconsin Press, 1999.

Shavit, Yossi, and Walter Muller. "Vocational Secondary Education, Tracking, and Social Stratification." In *Handbook of the Sociology of Education,* ed. Maureen T. Hallinan. New York: Kluwer Publishers, 2000. 437–52.

Shuman, Michael. *Towards a Global Village: International Community Development Initiatives.* Boulder, CO: Pluto Press, 1994.

Simons, Herbert W. "Rhetorical Hermeneutics and the Project of Globalization." *Quarterly Journal of Speech* 85 (1999): 86–109.

Simpson, Christopher. "Universities, Empire, and the Production of Knowledge: An Introduction." In *Universities and Empire: Empire and Politics in the So-*

cial Sciences during the Cold War, ed. Christopher Simpson. New York: The New Press, 1998. xi–xxxiv.

Sinclair, Upton. *The Goose-Step: A Study of American Education.* Pasadena, CA: Wholesale Distributors, 1922.

Sivanandan, A. "Globalism and the Left." *Race and Class* 40 (1998/99): 5–19.

Skidelsky, Robert. *John Maynard Keynes: Hopes Betrayed, 1883–1920.* New York: Viking Penguin, 1986.

Slaughter, Sheila. "Professional Values and the Allure of the Market." *Academe: Bulletin of the American Association of University Professors* 87.5 (September–October 2001): 22–26.

Slaughter, Sheila, and Larry L. Leslie. *Academic Capitalism: Politics, Policies, and the Entrepreneurial University.* Baltimore: Johns Hopkins University Press, 1997.

Sledd, James. "Disciplinarity and Exploitation: Compositionists as Good Professionals." *Workplace: A Journal of Academic Labor* 4.1 (June 2001). http://www.cust.educ.ubc.ca/workplace/issue7/sledd.html.

Smith, Adam. *Lectures on Rhetoric and Belles Lettres.* Ed. J. C. Bryce. Indianapolis: Liberty Fund, 1985.

———. *Wealth of Nations.* 1776. Amherst, NY: Prometheus Books, 1991.

Smith, David Geoffrey. "The Specific Challenges of Globalization for Teaching and Vice Versa." *Alberta Journal of Educational Research.* 46.1 (Spring 2000): 7–26.

Smith, Henry Nash. *Virgin Land: The American West as Symbol and Myth.* Cambridge, MA: Harvard University Press, 1978.

Smits, Hans. "Globalization and Education: Exploring Pedagogical and Curricular Issues and Implications." *Alberta Journal of Educational Research* 46.1 (Spring 2000): 1–6.

Solomon, Elinor Harris. *Virtual Money: Understanding the Power and Risks of Money's High-Speed Journey into Electronic Space.* New York: Oxford University Press, 1997.

Sommer, John W. *The Academy in Crisis: The Political Economy of Higher Education.* New Brunswick, NJ: Transaction Publishers, 1995.

Spivak, Gayatri. "Limits and Openings of Marx in Derrida." In *Outside the Teaching Machine.* London: Routledge, 1993. 97–140.

———. "The Making of Americans, the Teaching of English, and the Future of Culture Studies." *New Literary History* 21.4 (1990): 781–98.

———. *Outside in the Teaching Machine.* New York: Routledge, 1993.

———. "The Post-modern Condition: The Politics?" In *The Post-Colonial Critic: Interviews, Strategies, and Dialogues,* ed. Sarah Harasym. New York: Routledge, 1990. 17–54.

———. "Poststructuralism, Marginality, Postcoloniality, and Value." In *Literary Theory Today,* ed. Peter Collier and Helga Geyer-Ryan. Ithaca: Cornell University Press, 1990. 219–44.

———. "Scattered Speculations on the Question of Value." In *In Other Worlds: Essays in Cultural Politics.* London: Routledge, 1988. 154–75.

———. "Translator's Preface." In *Of Grammatology,* by Jacques Derrida. Trans. Gayatri Spivak. Baltimore: Johns Hopkins University Press, 1976. ix–lxxxvii.

Spring, Joel. *Education and the Rise of the Corporate State.* Boston: Beacon Press, 1972.

———. *Education and the Rise of the Global Economy.* Mahwah, NJ: Lawrence Erlbaum, 1998.

St. Denis, Verna. "Indigenous Peoples, Globalization, and Education: Making Connections." *Alberta Journal of Educational Research* 46.1 (Spring 2000): 36–48.

Standing, Guy. *Labour Circulation and the Labour Process.* London: Croom Helm, 1985.

Starch, Daniel. "Analysis of 1944 Stock Ownership." *Forbes* 56.4 (August 15, 1945): 14–16.

Stiglitz, Joseph E. *Globalization and Its Discontents.* New York: Norton, 2002.

Stuckey, J. Elspeth. *The Violence of Literacy.* Portsmouth, NH: Boynton/Cook, 1991.

Tabb, William K. *The Amoral Elephant: Globalization and the Struggle for Social Justice in the Twenty-First Century.* New York: Monthly Review, 2001.

Targ, Harry. "Imperialism in Transition: The Global Political Economy Moves toward the Twenty-First Century." In *Marxism Today: Essays on Capitalism, Socialism, and Strategies for Social Change,* ed. Chronis Polychroniou and Harry R. Targ. Westport, CT: Praeger, 1996. 71–85.

Taylor, Alison. "Employability Skills: From Corporate 'Wish List' to Government Policy." *Journal of Curriculum Studies* 30 (1998): 143–64.

Thompson, E. P. *The Making of the English Working Class.* New York: Vintage, 1963.

Tiano, Susan. *Export Processing, Women's Work, and the Employment Problem in Developing Countries: The Case of the Maquiladora Program in Northern Mexico.* El Paso: University of Texas Press, 1985.

Tomlinson, John. *Globalization and Culture*. Chicago: University of Chicago Press, 1999.

Torres, Carlos A., and Daniel Schugurensky. "The Political Economy of Higher Education in the Era of Neoliberal Globalization: Latin America in Comparative Perspective." *Higher Education* 43 (2002): 429–55.

Touraine, Alain. *The Academic System in American Society*. New York: McGraw-Hill, 1974.

Turner, Frederick Jackson. *The Significance of the Frontier in American History*. Ed. Harold P. Simonson. New York: Frederick Ungar Publishing, 1963.

Turner, J. B. "Industrial Universities for the People." In *The Origin of the Land Grant Act of 1862,* ed. Edmund J. James. Urbana-Champaign: University of Illinois Press, 1910. 48–111.

United Nations Educational, Scientific, and Cultural Organization UNESCO. *World Guide to Higher Education: A Comparative Survey of Systems, Degrees and Qualifications*. New York: Bowker Publishing, 1982.

The University of Arizona. "The Mission Statement." Revised 2001. http://www.arizona.edu/home/mission.html (accessed November 11, 2002).

The University of Michigan. "Global Summer Business Institute. http://www.umich.edu/~global/ (accessed May 14, 2002).

———. "Mission Statement." Revised 1992. http://www.umich.edu/pres/mission/ (accessed April 22, 2002).

The University of Nebraska. "International Affairs Mission Statement." http://www.unl.edu/iaffairs/mission.htm (accessed May 14, 2002).

———. "The Role and Mission Statement." Revised 1991. http://www.unl.edu/unlfacts/mission.html (accessed April 22, 2002).

The University of New Mexico. "Mission Statement." *The University of New Mexico Strategic Plan*. Revised 2001. http://www.unm.edu/~unmstrat.

———. "Strategic Direction on Preeminence." http://www.umn.edu/~unmstrat/Preeminence.htm (accessed November 11, 2002).

The University of North Carolina. "Mission Statement." Revised 1986. http://www.unc.edu/provost/mission1.html.

———. "North Carolina Global Center." http://www.unc.edu/depts./ncgc/home.htm (accessed May 14, 2002).

The University of South Carolina. "Global Track." http://mooreschool.sc.edu/p . . . ective_students/masters/imba/global.html (accessed April 22, 2002).

———. *Institutional Planning and Assessment 2000–01 Fact Book*. http://kudzu.ipr.sc.edu/01fact/perspect01.htm (accessed April 22, 2002).

———. "University of South Carolina Mission Statement." Revised 1997. http://kudzu.ipr.sc.edu/uscms99.htm (accessed April 22, 2002).

The University of Washington. "Global Studies Option." http://bothell.washington.edu/IAS/degrees/BLS/GST (accessed May 14, 2002).

———. "Global Trade, Transportation, and Logistic Studies." http://depts.washington.edu/gttl/.

———. "Role and Mission of the University." Revised 2001. http://www.washington.edu/faculty/facsenate/handbook/04–01–01.html (accessed April 22, 2002).

Urry, John. *Consuming Places.* New York: Routledge, 1995.

U.S. Census Bureau. "Labor Force Status and Employment Characteristics." 1990. http://www.census.gov/.

Veblen, Thorstein. *The Higher Learning in America: A Memorandum on the Conduct of Universities by Business Men.* 1918. New York: Viking, 1935.

———. *The Theory of Business Enterprise.* New York: Scribner's, 1904.

———. *The Theory of the Leisure Class.* New York: Viking, 1899.

Veysey, Laurence. *The Emergence of the American University.* Chicago: University of Chicago Press, 1965.

Vico, Giambattista. *On the Study Methods of Our Time.* Trans. Elio Gianturco. Ithaca: Cornell University Press, 1990.

Vološinov, V. N. *Marxism and the Philosophy of Language.* Cambridge, MA: Harvard University Press, 1986.

Waghid, Yusef. "Globalization and Higher Education Restructuring in South Africa: Is Democracy under Threat?" *Journal of Education Policy* 16.5 (2001): 455–64.

Waters, Malcolm. *Globalization.* Routledge: New York, 1995.

Wenger, Morton. "The Case of Academia: Demythologization in a Nonprofession." In *Professions for the People: The Politics of Skill,* ed. Joel Gerstl and Glenn Jacobs. New York: Halsted Press, 1976. 95–152.

Whately, Richard. *Introductory Lectures on Political Economy.* 1831. New York: Augustus M. Kelley, 1966.

White, Hayden. "Interpretation in History." In *Tropics in Discourse.* Baltimore: Johns Hopkins University Press, 1978. 51–80.

———. *Metahistory: The Historical Imagination in Nineteenth-Century Europe.* Baltimore: Johns Hopkins University Press, 1973.

Wicks, Robert. *Understanding Audiences: Learning to Use the Media Constructively.* Mahwah, NJ: Lawrence Erlbaum, 2001.

Will, James. *The Universal God: Justice, Love, and Peace in the Global Village.* Louisville: Westminister John Knox Press, 1994.

Williams, Raymond. *Culture and Society, 1780–1950.* New York: Columbia University Press, 1958.

———. *Keywords: A Vocabulary of Culture and Society.* New York: Oxford University Press, 1985.

———. *Marxism and Literature.* Oxford: Oxford University Press, 1977.

Williamson, John. *The Political Economy of Policy Reform.* Washington, DC: Institute for International Economics, 1994.

Witmer, Lightner. *The Nearing Case: The Limitation of Academic Freedom at the University of Pennsylvania by Act of the Board of Trustees, June 14, 1915.* New York: Da Capo Press, 1974.

World Bank. "An Assessment of Higher Education in Transition Economies." http://www.worldbank.org/transitionnewsletter/marapr99/pg6box.htm.

———. "Higher Education, Innovation and Market Response: The Singapore Experience." December 13, 1993. http://www.worldbank.org/html/extdr/hnp/hddflash/hcnote/hrn017.html.

———. *Higher Education: The Lessons of Experience.* Washington, DC: World Bank Publications, 1994.

———. "Supporting Mozambique's Growing Needs for Higher Education." March 7, 2002. http://www4.worldbank.org/sprojects/Project.asp?pid=P069824.

———. "World Bank to Support Higher Education in Hungary." February 26, 1998. http://www.worldbank.org/html/extdr/extme/1663.htm.

———. *World Development Report 1996: From Plan to Market.* Oxford: Oxford University Press, 1996.

———. *World Development Report 2002: Building Institutions for Markets.* Oxford: Oxford University Press, 2002.

Zavarzadeh, Mas'ud, and Donald Morton. *Theory as Resistance: Politics and Culture after (Post)structuralism.* New York: Guilford Press, 1994.

Zinn, Howard. *A People's History of the United States.* New York: Harper, 1990.

Žižek, Slavoj. *Mapping Ideology.* London: Verso, 1994.

———. "Multiculturalism, Or, the Cultural Logic of Multinational Capitalism." *New Left Review* 225 (September/October 1997): 28–51.

Zompetti, Joseph P. "Toward a Gramscian Critical Rhetoric." *Western Journal of Communication* 61.1 (Winter 1997): 66–86.

Index